...t, South Pacific island world, ...ote and secure under Queen ...e rule, has been touched by ...e past, and named the "Friendly Islands" by Captain Cook, but no man was ever more enchanted by its spell than a young Scotch doctor who saw it for the first time, right after the break of dawn, a few years ago. Staring at the green islands and the shimmering sea, he vowed that he would return one day to live there. That he kept his promise, and that a young American girl with a gift for storytelling was also drawn to visit the distant country, is our good fortune as well as his. For the girl is the author. The two met in Tonga, fell in love with the islands, the people, and with one another. Their love story, the stories of their Tongan neighbors, and the Tongan tales that have been passed down from generation to generation make for magic reading in ...

Tonga:

A Tale of the Friendly Islands

by PATRICIA LEDYARD

"Tell me a Tongan love story," Patricia Ledyard coaxed her friend Tu'ifua one day. "Love is the same in Tonga as anywhere else," Tu'ifua serenely replied. But Patricia Ledyard will tell you, there's not another

(Continued on back flap)

TONGA

A TALE OF
THE FRIENDLY ISLANDS

by

Patricia Ledyard

APPELTON-CENTURY-CROFTS, INC.

New York

Library of Congress Card Number: 55-12079

For my Important People

Here in Tonga—and Away

CONTENTS

TONGA

A Tale of the Friendly Islands

1 Two Came to Tonga

One day about a quarter of a century ago, the old *Tofua* rounded the rocky undercut little island of Kitu and slipped into the quiet waters of Vava'u. She carried a full load of passengers, most of whom, although it was just after dawn, were already up on deck; for their well-thumbed guidebooks had told them that the harbor they were entering—the northernmost stop in the kingdom of Tonga—was the most beautiful in the Pacific. For once the books did not exaggerate.

To the restless gray swells of the outer ocean, Vava'u's waters sparkling over jewel-colored reefs or darkening to black-blue depths presented an unforgettable contrast. It was, indeed, as if they were locked in enchantment by the many hilly green islands whose shores stretched out in golden sands or twisted and curved around dark and secret inlets.

As the *Tofua* steamed up the long island-bordered way, she sometimes passed so close to the land that her passengers could catch glimpses of villages of low reed houses with thick thatched roofs. Now and again, above the noise of the engines, they could hear the laughter and the shouts of the golden-skinned children who poured out of the houses and ran, leaping with excitement, to see the boat which was their only contact with a distant and mysterious world.

After a time, the engines slowed as the ship started to turn around a little cape which had shut off the view of the buildings and the wharf at Neiafu, the port where the ship would tie up for a few hours while she discharged her cargo. Most of the passengers pushed forward, betraying their eagerness to get into the town and run through the shops searching for picture postcards to send their friends back home. One among them, however, a young Scotch doctor, stood as if rooted to the deck and stared out at the cape. Above it there was a tiny village whose houses straggled haphazardly among the green hills. On the cape itself, just beyond the sands of the beach, was a house, a rambling old place with red iron roof and wide verandahs. The young doctor looked back down the harbor at the avenue of islands through which the ship had just passed; then he turned and caught a glimpse of curving water with the crowded roofs of the port above it. If I were sitting on that verandah, he thought, turning back to the house at the cape, I could see up the harbor and down the harbor. If I lived in that house, I could see dawn and sunset and— Abruptly he asked, "What place is that?" A ship's officer standing beside him replied, "That—it's a little village called 'Utulei and that house there, it was built a long time ago by some crazy white man."

"Well," said the doctor, "that's the place for me. I'll come back and live there."

The officer shrugged his shoulders and laughed. "Huh, lots of men say that, but they never come back."

The young doctor tossed his determined Scotch head. "Aye, but I'll come back," he said.

Six years ago in the cold and dreary library of a foreign university sat an American who was reading in anthropology. She shivered, cursed the wanderlust that had led her to such a dismal spot, and wearily opened a musty old book entitled *Mariner's Tonga*. Hours later, when she reluctantly shut the book, she was blind to her cheerless surroundings, for the pages of the book had filled her mind with the bright vision of a sunlit island country. In the days which followed, she returned to the library, but it never again contained her; for her errant thoughts kept carrying her off to the islands. For a time, prompted by the stern dictates of common sense, she resisted, reminding herself that Mariner, the young Londoner who had spent four years in Tonga and whose recorded impressions made such magic reading, had lived over a hundred years ago. Since his day, the country had become a British protectorate; it had been influenced by countless white men—good, bad, and indifferent. It had, in short, changed. All that she told herself, but none of it did any good; for she seemed convinced that the islands would still be as beautiful and the people as friendly as ever. At last she could resist no longer. "I must go to Tonga," she said to herself. "That is where I want to be."

The Scotch doctor did come back to Vava'u as he said he would, and the American came, too. I know because I am the American and the Scotch doctor is Farquhar who is my husband. We live today in the little village of 'Utulei in the house on the cape. From our wide verandahs we can see far down the harbor to rocky Kitu or around the corner up to the roofs of Neiafu. We see dawn and sunset and the life of Tonga which has become our life, too.

"Very nice," cry our old friends, "but where exactly are you? We can't find your 'Utulei on any map. We can't even find Vava'u, and Tonga's no more than a little line of dots straggling across the South Pacific ocean."

It's all quite true. 'Utulei isn't on the map. Even the whole Vava'u group is left out more often than it is included. Indeed, most people never heard of the kingdom of Tonga until our tall, smiling Queen Salote went to London to see Queen Elizabeth crowned and won the hearts of Britain and the world by her lavish display of that most characteristic of Tongan traits, friendliness.

Tonga, however, has been unconcerned by the world's neglect; for Tonga is, and has always been, a little world in itself. Today, to some 40,000 brown-skinned humans and a few fortunate white ones it is home. The brown people are old residents. They arrived in these islands so long ago that their coming is chronicled not by the pages of history, but by the distant legends of mythology. Part of the great Polynesian race, they set out with their relatives the Hawaiians, the Samoans, the Tahitians, and the Maoris from some original Asiatic homeland. Impelled, perhaps by war, perhaps by too rapidly growing a population, perhaps merely by a great surge of wanderlust, they spread over the vast Pacific, roving the sea lanes until one group after another found islands in which to make new homes.

Although the area that anthropologists call the Polynesian triangle stretches from New Zealand to Hawaii, from Hawaii to lonely Easter Island off the coast of Chile, and from Easter Island back across the South Pacific to New Zealand, the old-time Polynesians were not intimidated by so much ocean space. An undying love of adventure, an ever-constant gregariousness, and an amazing skill in navigation combined to keep them traveling from one group of islands to another in their famous seagoing canoes. As a result of constant visits with one another, the widespread Polynesians presented, when they were first discovered by Europeans, an amazing homogeneity. They all believed in the same gods, spoke essentially the same language, and followed the same customs. Today, in most parts of the Pacific, the old culture has disappeared; white men and white ideas dominate Hawaii, Samoa, Tahiti, and the Maori's home, New Zealand.

Unique among Polynesian places, Tonga still belongs to Polynesian peoples. True, it has been a British protectorate since the beginning of this century, but the sovereignty of the country is Tongan and the present ruler, Queen Salote Tupou, commands more power than that enjoyed by any other living monarch. No upstart ruler, she traces her descent from men and women who ruled in Tonga long before the Battle of Hastings had been fought. From those early times, too, have come down the customs which still regulate the daily lives of the Tongan people and make them, in effect, the only large group of Polynesians left in the world.

Tongans have remained Tongans, but that does not mean that they, too, have not been influenced by white men. In the beginning of the 17th century, the Dutchmen, Schouten and Lemaire, were the first Europeans to see the country, but like most of the other early explorers, including England's famous Captain Cook and France's La Pérouse, they merely stopped here on their way to other places. Actual white settlers date back less than two hundred years. Once there was a relatively large number of them, but today the population dwindles. The old-timers are dying and the government does not encourage new ones to come; for, to confess the truth at once, white influence has very often been bad influence. Even the tourist trade is not fostered; for it has been realized that a people which derives a big percentage of its income from that source loses its integrity and degenerates into a sort of side show (as the Maoris of Rotorua, the Mexicans of Taxco and the Indians of Taos have done). The Tongans are too proud and independent for that.

However, in Tonga, as in all parts of the modern world, isolationism is no longer a possible policy. The present is a time of mutual interdependence and Tonga knows that in her current state of cultural transition, she needs the knowledge and skills which some white men have. Consequently, there are in the country white government servants of various sorts—engineers, medical men, agricultural experts, teachers; white store people who hold most of the executive jobs in the big trading companies which have branches throughout all the Pacific; and white missionaries. It might seem that inasmuch as permission for white men to settle, or even travel here, is so grudgingly given, those of us who are here would have a shabby time of it. Nothing could be further from the truth; for Queen Salote treats her white people as honored guests and has commanded her subjects, likewise, to exercise all they know of old Polynesian courtesy and hospitality in their relations with their papalangi neighbors. ("Papalangi," the name given by the early Tongans to the first white comers, reflects their belief that the fair-skinned people came from heaven, "langi." Now, after almost two centuries of observation of behavior which is all too often quite the opposite of heavenly, no Tongan is so unsophisticated as to cling to the old idea, but the word remains. In Tongan mouths, it is much the same as the word "native" is in ours; at its best, it is simply a descriptive term; at its worst, it can reflect every possible shade of contempt.)

And what of Tonga itself? The kingdom is made up of some 150 islands whose total land space, approximately half that of the city of Los Angeles, lies spread out in the South Pacific over eight degrees of latitude and four of longitude. For neighbors, there is Fiji to the west and Samoa to the north. The country is divided into three main groups of islands which, from south to north, are Tongatapu, Ha'apai, and Vava'u.

On Tongatapu, the biggest single island in the country, is Nuku'alofa, the capital. It is the center of white population, and there anyone who cares to look can easily find the storybook characters of the South Seas—the gay young men who keep native mistresses and the sad old ones who sit all day over a bottle of gin; the black sheep of good families and a host of respectable dull clerks from families of respectable dull clerks; sanctimonious missionaries and rough, good-natured captains who know how to handle their liquor and their women. Tonga, of course, is not a British colony, but many of the white people of Nuku'alofa act as if it were one (some of them have even had the impudence to suggest it should become one!) and construct for themselves a typical colonial society with its endless stratifications, its endless snobberies, and its endless flurry of teas.

After Tongatapu, Ha'apai is, figuratively and literally, a breath of fresh air. It is made up of many small islands scattered over a comparatively large area of sea. Its men, fine navigators and fishermen, are noted for the philosophic calm which belongs to seamen around the world. Its women, equally industrious and equally calm, have made it famous for fine mats and baskets which they weave from the leaves of the pandanus tree. The monthly steamer does not call at Ha'apai, since its reefs are too tricky for larger vessels to navigate comfortably. Within the group, its own cutters keep up a constant flow of traffic, and occasionally the more daring of them will venture south as far as Tongatapu or north to Vava'u.

Generally speaking, however, contact with the rest of the country comes only at the irregular intervals when one or the other of the interisland motorboats, following its haphazard schedule, rolls into the main Ha'apai port, Lifuka, a sleepy, sun-drenched little village sprawled along a white sand beach. Busy with their own lives, Ha'apai's people are unconcerned about their isolation from the rest of the world.

In the past, history has touched there. It was at the island of Momuka, in southern Ha'apai, that Captain Bligh of the *Bounty* stopped to take on water just before his grumbling seamen mutinied and set him afloat in the tiny open boat in which he eventually made his way to the Dutch East Indies.

At Pangai, the main island of the group, Shirley Baker, the most colorful papalangi character in Tonga's history, retired to spend his last days. He began his career in the country in the latter half of the last century as a simple Wesleyan minister. At the height of his fame, he was Prime Minister—a place which, according to his friends, he gained in order to be of greater help to Tonga. His enemies, ascribing baser motives to his switch from spiritual to temporal power, accused him of a rapacious greedy wish to swindle an unsophisticated people. Whether friends or enemies were correct will never be truly known; for Great Britian, resenting the fact that one of her citizens had usurped so much power, sent a battleship down from Fiji and removed him from the country.

By the time he was allowed to return, the negotiations which led to Tonga's being made a British protectorate were well under way. Whatever his faults or his virtues, he must have been a fine, forceful man. One can know that by a glimpse of his statue, the biggest in the country, which stands in frock-coated, cast-iron majesty, over his grave in the Lifuka cemetery.

Of Tongatapu and of Ha'apai much could be said, for both are places full of charms and attractions; but we are provincial here, and Vava'u is part of the country. In it and through it, I have learned whatever I know of Tonga. I listen to its stories and live among its people. That is why all of what I write begins here and why most of it ends here, too.

2 And Thanks for Coming

When I wrote to tell my mother and father that, instead of coming home after my year of study in the southern hemisphere, I was going to Tonga to be headmistress of a mission-run girls' college in Vava'u, they deplored my decision. Their objections were based mainly on their desire to see me again and on the natural inability of parents to understand their offspring's desire to rove. Beyond that, my businessman father was anxious to see me "get on" in the world, and when I had explained to him what my work was to be and what salary I should receive in return for it, he could only write despairingly, *They've sold you a job no one else wants!*

It's quite true that when the mission people wrote me the details of the job I had accepted, the hours seemed long and the pay scandalously small, but neither of those facts seemed real objections to me. I'd never had a proper concern for money anyway and the job would enable me to see the land that, so suddenly and so undeniably, came alive for me on the day I read that dusty copy of *Mariner's Tonga* in the dreary library. I welcomed a job which would give

11

me long hours with the people whose hospitality and kindness had led Captain Cook to call their land "The Friendly Islands." I looked forward, too, to working with the mission. I told myself that, although the missionaries might be narrow in matters of dogma, they would be guided by the highest ideals and their daily lives would be simple demonstrations of the brotherhood of man. Alas for my illusions!

But on the day I boarded the Union Steamship Company's *Matua* at Auckland, those illusions were undimmed by the knowledge that was to come later. With the lightest of hearts, then, I waved to the friends who had come to say good-by. No nostalgic thoughts for the shores I was leaving, or for my native California, clouded my mind. I was bound for the islands of my dreams. I was off to Tonga.

Unfortunately, the high spirits with which I set out were not due to last long. Quite literally, they were shaken out of me on the very first day of the journey. Less than ten hours after the last of New Zealand's hills faded on the horizon, we ran into the fringe of a hurricane and the *Matua,* for all that she is a well-built modern motor vessel of 2,000 tons, was hurled about mercilessly by a sea whose wall-like waves seemed to be made not of water, but of some furiously mobile granite.

One by one the passengers with whom I had anticipated enjoying the easy intense comradeship that springs up so readily on board ship disappeared into the misery of their cabins. Soon there was only a handful of them left, and with them I enjoyed no fellowship. It was all we could do to exchange a brief

"Good day" when we collided with one another as we crept cautiously along the madly tilting passageways. Sometimes two or three of us made our way into the lounge and braced ourselves in the heavy leather chairs. When the anchoring chains snapped and sent us sliding with terrifying speed from one side of the room to the other, we clung desperately to the arms of the chairs and managed grim smiles of mock bravery as we swept past each other. And that was all the contact we had.

I was thankful when each long day was over, when bruised from many falls and unutterably weary, I fell into bed holding to the small victory of being "a good sailor." There I lay awake hour after endless hour listening to the tumult of the night that was a wild mixture of howling winds, crashing waves, banging doors, ringing bells, and the brittle sound of destruction made by smashing glass.

For four days the winds lashed us about. When on the fifth day they fell and the sea grew calmer, I felt too dispirited and tired to make overtures to any of the battered passengers who, pale and shaky, began to emerge from their cabins. Wrapped in my own isolation, I read my way through monotonous paper novels from the shelves in the lounge or stood glumly at the rail staring out at a world made of equal parts of dull gray sea and dull gray sky.

"Was this," I asked myself, as I stood there one day trying vainly to make out the horizon, "the way the far-famed South Seas looked?" Involuntarily, my thoughts went back to the long, sun-bright days in California. I remembered them with nostalgia, and

with a heart full of contrition I acknowledged that
my father had, perhaps, been right in thinking it was
a bit of madness that had sent me off to Tonga when
I might have been heading for the Golden Gate.

"Are you feeling sick, after all?" It was a solicitous
ship's officer who asked the question.

I managed a faint smile. "No, not sick," I said, "but
disappointed. I never expected the South Seas to
look like this."

His hearty laugh was reassuring. "You newcomers
are all the same," he said. "You read the books and
then you forget all about the hurricanes and the rain.
All you remember is the tales of moonlit nights and
coconut fronds rustling romantically in little breezes.
You forget that even in the South Seas there are
seasons, and that's too bad because you've come in the
rainy one."

"And how long will it last?" I asked.

He shrugged his shoulders. "Lord knows. The rainy
season used to begin in December and be pretty well
over by the end of March, but nowadays the weather
has gone crazy. It might end tomorrow or it might
go on all year."

"Oh," I said, and my spirits fell lower than ever at
the thought of a whole year of such heavy gray days.
I was wondering how I could ever endure them when
I felt a touch on my arm. I looked up to see the officer
pointing out to sea. "Look," he said, "there's Nuku-
'alofa."

"Nuku'alofa!" I exclaimed. The name sent a ripple
of excitement through me and the dismal day seemed
to brighten a bit. Nuku'alofa was the capital of Tonga

and it would be my first glimpse of the islands I had longed to see. There, too, I would meet the mission people for whom I should be working.

"Where?" I asked eagerly. "Where?" I stared as hard as I could in the direction to which he pointed, but I could see nothing that looked at all like land.

"There," he said, "just above the horizon."

I looked again. "You mean that line that looks like a dirty smudge on the sea?" I asked at last.

He nodded. "That's right," and moved away, leaving me alone to think what thoughts I would as I watched the line on the horizon grow darker and thicker as we came closer to it.

I was not destined on that first visit to see much of Nuku'alofa. As the *Matua* came near enough so that here and there a tree or a rooftop began to take shape, the heavy clouds which had been growing constantly darker burst and a thick sheet of rain poured obscurity over the world.

We had come alongside and tied up before the rain thinned at all. Then, although it still fell heavily, I could see through it to the wharf below. There, quite unconcerned with the weather, was a crowd of people whose upturned brown faces and gaily waving brown hands were completely taken up with welcoming the ship. As the engines stopped, I could hear their voices, too, full and rich and musical, calling greetings.

Suddenly the rain seemed unimportant. I leaned far over the rail and smiled and waved at the crowd, which responded immediately with a delighted roar of applause. I had come to the Friendly Islands and they were friendly. I waved again and the gaiety of the crowd rose up and covered me and I was part of it. I was leaning even farther over the rail, stretching to see as much of the crowd as I could, when I felt a touch on my shoulder and heard at my side a voice tinged with disapproval saying, "You are the new teacher, I believe."

Responding to the words, rather than the tone, I turned eagerly. "Yes," I exclaimed, "I'm the new teacher."

"And I, if I may complete the introduction, am the Reverend Branard Christopher Pauson."

Impressed by the pompous syllables, I could only stare at the undersized little man whose thin neck, sticking out of his clerical collar, looked so lonely and strangely naked.

After a minute, he said sedately, "Follow me, please. My car is on the wharf."

He turned and I went after him, across the deck and down the steep gangway onto the wharf where, suddenly losing sight of his black hat which bobbed on ahead, I found myself swallowed up by the crowd that a few short minutes before I had been watching from above.

"Malo e lelei, malo e folau," the people called to me. "Malo e lelei, malo e folau," and the words, incomprehensible though they were, had a warm and pleasant sound that was only intensified after a kindly old man, realizing that I was a stranger, leaned over and explained in halting English, "The people are saying, 'Good day. Good day and thanks for coming.'"

"Malo e lelei, malo e folau," the people called again and then the crowd fell back and the black hat reappeared and Mr. Pauson said, "I almost lost you in this crowd," but it was obvious from his tone that what he really meant was that I had lost him.

"I'm sorry," I murmured.

"Follow me closely, please," he said. I trotted obediently behind him while the rain, with renewed fury, beat down on us.

From the splashed windows of the car, I could see nothing of the town through which we rode, nor was I faced with the necessity of trying to make conversation with Mr. Pauson who, staring straight ahead, was completely occupied with driving. As I sat there, being bounced along over unknown roads, the weariness of the sea trip washed over me, leaving me in the vacant, rather dejected mood in which I arrived at the mission house.

There, in a dark living room permeated by a smell of mildew, I found the other white members of the mission and their wives. When the introductions had been made and we had been settled in chairs and provided with cups of tea, Mr. Pauson bent toward me, cleared his throat, and said, "We welcome you to this mission field and to the work we are doing here for Jesus Christ."

I smiled and mumbled thanks, but I could not rid myself of the uncomfortable idea that he was looking at my lipstick and that he disapproved of me.

Nor did I feel that any of the other people in the room were particularly friendly toward me. In spite of the fact that they all spoke a great deal of Christian fellowship, an air of faint hostility seemed to accompany their words. For one mournful moment, I let myself wonder why I had come. Then I remembered the gay crowd at the wharf and all the things I had read about Tonga, and everything else seemed unimportant.

"And how do you like Tonga?" one of them asked, trying to make conversation.

"I haven't had a chance to find out yet," I said honestly, and added, "But I already know I'll like the Tongans."

An indistinct gasp followed my words as a woman who sat close to me exclaimed, "Perhaps I'd better warn you that they make very poor servants. They're altogether too headstrong and independent."

I laughed outright. "On my salary, I'll scarcely be in a position to have servants."

"Of course you'll have servants on Vava'u. We all do here," she said loftily. "They work for us free because they love the church."

"And what do you do for them in return?" I blurted out. From the icy silence that filled the room as soon as the words had passed my lips, I realized that I should never have uttered them.

Slow ages passed before the Rev. Branard Christopher Pauson coughed and spoke. "My good lady," he said, "we bring them the gospel."

Thus rebuked, I said nothing, but pretending to be completely taken up with my cup of tea, listened while the talk in the room lapsed into what I was later to know as a standard island conversation, consisting of loud complaints about the difficulty of procuring European foodstuffs, grumbles against the government, and protests against the weather—all woven together with a liberal supply of gossip.

After a time, one of the wives suddenly remembered my presence and began to talk to me about Vava'u and the college.

"I am anxious to be there," I confessed to her, "so that I can see the school and get acquainted with the teachers before the semester begins."

Mr. Pauson, who seemed in a new and more affable mood, broke in to say, "If you'd like to see your head teacher, I can show her to you. She's been down here attending a teachers' meeting."

When I said that I should very much like to meet her, he asked one of the men to go off and send a message to the nearby house where she was staying and, while we waited, he inquired pleasantly enough into the details of my journey.

We had not talked long when we were interrupted by a firm knock on the door, followed by a low musical voice which announced, "I am Tu'ifua. You sent for me."

"Yes, come in," called Mr. Pauson. He nodded toward me. "It's your teacher."

The door opened and a freshening scent of sandalwood filled the room as a tall woman, moving quietly on bare feet, entered. She was clothed in a manner which I was soon to know as the usual Tongan one—a tuniclike dress worn over an ankle-length wraparound "vala," or skirt. Around her waist a small, soft mat was tied with a belt made of woven coconut fiber. Her dress and skirt were made of a thin voile-like stuff in a clear shade of lavender which, with her brownish-golden skin, gave her a bright air of coolness.

But I had only a glance for her clothes. My gaze was directed at once to her calm, serious face and, more especially, to her dark brown eyes which were the largest I had ever seen in a mortal being. I found myself wondering how they would look when they glittered with merriment and how when they misted over with sadness. I wondered it the more, perhaps, because, as she stood there, they reflected no emotion at all—unless, indeed, patience be an emotion. The patience that shone steadily from her eyes and was expressed in some undefinable way by every bit of her body was not the servile variety of slaves, but the proud sort for which the true name is dignity.

With dignity, then, she greeted the people in the room, repeating the name of each one and saying, "Good morning." When she had spoken to them all, she turned toward Mr. Pauson and waited for him to speak.

He let her stand there for a minute and then he brought her across the room and introduced her to me. There was a capable firmness about her handshake that I liked. I told her at once that I was glad we would be working together.

"Thank you," she answered simply, and she let her eyes rest on me for a minute of questioning appraisal before she said, "I shall be coming to Vava'u next week. I shall try to be a good help to you."

We were just beginning to talk about the college when suddenly Tu'ifua fell silent and I looked up to see that Mr. Pauson had moved over and stood between us.

"There will be time enough to discuss things with Tu'ifua when you're in Vava'u," he said to me, and, turning brusquely to her, "That'll be enough now, Tu'ifua. You may go."

Not a muscle moved in Tu'ifua's calm face. I thought then that perhaps she had not understood him, but she understood well enough; quietly bidding good-by to me and the others, she left the room, closing the door softly behind her.

"Well," said Mr. Pauson when she had gone. "That's your head teacher."

"She seems a charming person," I said.

He replied with a shrug of his shoulders, "She is quite intelligent and quite reliable . . . for a Tongan."

That afternoon Mr. Pauson discussed with me routine details of the college and I learned with what I suspect was very poorly disguised relief that I should be, as he termed it, "alone" in Vava'u—by which he meant, no other white member of the mission would be working in the group.

Just before dark, he drove me back through the rainy streets to the wharf. He shook my hand, and with what seemed to me a bit too much fervor prayed God to make me a worthy member of the mission. Then, admonishing me to write him often and fully about the college, he was off, and I turned and ran up the gangplank.

3 Her Majesty Queen Salote Tupou

I had no sooner stepped onto the deck than I realized that the *Matua* was not, that afternoon, the same ship I had left in the morning. Exactly what the difference was, I could not tell. Outwardly, everything seemed to be just as it had been before; the same collection of empty sun chairs sprawled across the gray decks, the lounge was still proper and stuffy with its heavy leather furniture, and the passageways were as dark as ever. Yet, some difference there certainly was, for the morning's dull, wind-tossed old vessel seemed full of a proud new spirit.

I was still pondering about the indefinable change when the officer with whom I had been talking just before we reached Nuku'alofa bustled by, resplendent in a freshly starched white uniform. Running a step to catch up with him, I asked, "What's come over this ship?"

He stopped. "Why, haven't you heard?" he asked unbelievingly and then, without waiting for an answer, said, "We are carrying the Queen tonight."

"The Queen? You mean Queen Salote?"

"Yes, Queen Salote. She's going up to New Zealand for a month's holiday and shopping."

Having imparted the information which so completely explained the *Matua's* altered character, he moved off with the air of a man who had important business. Before he disappeared into the officers' quarters, he called back, "You'd better stay up on deck. There'll be excitement. There always is when the Queen travels."

I knew at once that he was right. As I climbed to the top deck, I didn't have to look for excitement. It was inside me. Never in all my life before had I seen a queen, much less traveled on the same boat with one. Let the rational American side of my nature believe what it would about democracy being the highest possible form of government, that did not detract at all from my older knowledge, first gleaned from the books of childhood, that a queen was the most romantic of all figures. And Queen Salote! I had heard so much of her smiling charm and of the love she held for the people of her little kingdom that I could not help being eager to see her.

As I came out onto the deck, the rain was still falling, but its fury had abated until it had become a welcome, cooling mist. Far in the west, a gleam from the sinking sun broke through the clouds and with its Midas touch turned all the atmosphere to gold. Royal, golden showers—weather fit for a queen, I said to myself as I crossed over to the rail to watch the people below.

The crowd, a far larger one than that of the morning, was a crowd fit for a queen, too. It had the festive appearance that is the inevitable result when several thousand people, in holiday mood, deck themselves out in their best and brightest. Everywhere were colorful gay shirts and dresses. Around every waist a mat and . . .

"Why, the men wear skirts, too!" I exclaimed and did not realize that I had spoken aloud until a young Tongan woman who was standing beside me laughed.

"Yes, we all wear valas here, but women wear long ones that go to their ankles and men wear short ones that come just below their knees."

Then, as if she were helping me to adjust my mind to the idea of skirted males, she explained, "Valas are much cooler than trousers, you know."

"I suppose they are," I agreed. Since she seemed such a willing informant, I pointed to the mat she wore and asked, "But aren't those mats frightfully hot around your waist?"

"Certainly, yes," she replied emphatically, but added quickly, "Of course, we don't wear them when we are in our own homes. We only wear them when we're out in public or when we go to see the Queen or a chief or some other important person."

"And why do you wear them at all?" I pursued.

But the reason had been lost in the distant mists of time. She could only shake her head and say, "I don't know. It is our custom. It would be very rude for anyone to be without one when the Queen was coming."

There is no arguing about custom in Tonga or anywhere else, either; so Mele, for that was her name, and I talked of other things. After I told her that I was not just an ordinary tourist passing through, but was going to Vava'u to be in charge of the college there, she seemed very pleased and redoubled her efforts to explain things to me.

When I had first looked down at the wharf, it seemed that it was as full as it could possibly be, but with every passing minute, more and more people came pushing onto it. Some straggled in all alone and some came in laughing twos and threes. Now and then, the crowd parted and a group of children, neatly dressed in school uniforms, flowed through it to take up places close to the ship's side. Mele pointed out to me the different uniforms—the scarlet of the Seventh Day Adventists, the deep blue of the Wesleyans, the light blue of the convent girls, and the white of the government schools.

"And there," she cried excitedly, "is the band," and we saw the silver instruments come floating down the wharf over the mass of heads.

Closer by, directly below us, the gangway swayed and creaked under the weight of a never-ending stream of people who were pouring onto the boat. Some of them I recognized as the passengers who had been on board since we sailed from Auckland, but most of them were Tongans. There were men who bore on their shoulders heavy rolls of mats which, I was told, were sleeping mats, and others who staggered under loads of the massive five-foot-long yams which are a staple part of the native diet. Women, with babies riding on their hips or clinging to their backs, carried baskets of pineapples or bottles of scented oil or bunches of flowers. Everyone carried something and everyone hurried and everyone smiled.

"What a lot of things," I exclaimed to Mele, "and what a lot of people!"

"It is always the same," she explained. "It's that way whenever we Tongans travel, but when the Queen travels, it is—well, more the same."

We laughed together and watched the moving crowds again until, at last, the gangway hung empty below us and the people on the wharf began to stir restlessly and to keep turning about as if they were looking for someone.

"I think the Queen will come soon now," Mele whispered. The words had scarcely left her mouth before I saw, at the far end of the wharf, the crowd divide to make way for a long black car which drove slowly toward the ship. As it rolled past the people, their laughter and their talking died away until, by the time it came to a stop before the gangway, every voice in all that vast throng was stilled. Through the silence that hung like homage on the air, I heard the metallic click of the car door as it was pulled open by an attendant. In another minute, Queen Salote Tupou stepped onto the wharf and the band broke into the stirring strains of the Tongan national anthem.

Not one of all the queens of my imagination had been more truly regal than the one who stood down there in the midst of her people. Simply clad in a brown dress and vala with a soft mat about her waist and leather sandals over her bare feet, Queen Salote did not, by any lavish display of costume, flaunt her royalty. Yet it existed as some indefinable and inherent part of her. The newspapers, when they seek to describe the feeling of grandeur which she conveys, begin always by talking of her great height. It is true that she towers far above ordinary people and stands out even among her own tall Tongans, but it is not merely her imposing proportions that set her off from the crowd of common mortals. It is, rather, a certain force of character which is so striking that anyone has only to see her to feel it at once. Beyond that, there is the awe-inspiring aura of loneliness which surrounds her as it does all those whom Destiny has set above their fellows.

The last note of the anthem faded away and the echo of the Queen's footsteps filled the air as, the only moving person in all that crowd, she walked across to the gangway and climbed up to the ship. Once she had reached the deck and been welcomed aboard by the captain, the stillness broke. Cheers burst out, drums were pounded and the school children, piping shrill in careful rhythm, sang their little songs. And the cheers and the drums and the songs all spoke of the people's love for their queen and of the great pride they felt in her.

Fascinated, I still stood at the rail, watching first one group and then another, scarcely conscious that the deck about me had become almost as full of people as the wharf below.

"I must leave you now," a voice at my side was saying. I looked around to see Mele moving away.

"Good-by, then, and thank you for telling me so much," I called, and watched her as she wound her way through the crowded deck.

She had gone about fifteen feet from where I was
standing when she stopped to talk to someone. I saw
with a shock of surprise that it was Queen Salote who,
like any other passenger, had come up on deck to see
the farewelling crowd. For a minute, I wondered
what Mele was saying to the Queen and then, I must
confess, I stared at them harder and longer than I
should have. When they both turned and looked in
my direction, I remembered my manners and, lowering my eyes in confusion, stared out over the rail.

The gangway was coming up. The engines began
to throb as we started to pull away from the wharf.
There was a roar from the crowd before, once again,
it gave the Queen complete silence. Then, as the light
faded, and the ship drew well away, the band began
to play softly and everyone on the wharf sang with it.
The liquid Tongan words and the Polynesian phrasing of the music transformed into a composition of
plaintive beauty a familiar old street-corner hymn.
Listening to it, I knew that, although the mission
house might shelter nothing but rigid sectarianism,
there was in the Tongan people themselves a broad,
unshakable faith in a protecting God. The hymn
which they sang so earnestly to their departing sover-
eign was "God Be With You Till We Meet Again,"
but it was more than a hymn. It was a prayer so
deeply felt that when it was over, women sobbed into
their handkerchiefs and men stood unashamed with
tears coursing down their faces. I could not help
stealing a look at the Queen. She stood erect, her head
held proudly high, but there were tears in her eyes,
too.

Tongans, as I came to know, have none of the white man's fear of showing their emotions. They are sad and they are happy and sometimes one feeling follows another so quickly that they dry their tears with laughter. It happened so then. The hymn was just over when gaiety once more seized hold of the crowd. A small naked boy flung his shiny brown self off the wharf in the direction of the departing ship. He might well have been a signal. Before he ever touched the water, scores of people, young and old, most of them fully clothed with their mats still around their waists, plunged into the sea after him, screaming and shouting as if they offered themselves in some wild immolation to their beloved queen. Those who stayed on the wharf shouted, too, thundering out their wishes for a happy trip and a safe return and madly waving handkerchiefs and scarfs.

I peeped down the rail again. Once more the Queen was in perfect harmony with her people. Her face was wreathed in smiles. She waved happily toward the wharf which was growing ever smaller as we gathered speed and headed out to sea. The shouts faded and the evening grew still. A breeze sprang up. One by one the people about me went down to their cabins to look for wraps. I was going down, too, but when I saw that the Queen still stood at the rail, I stopped to watch her for a minute longer. As I stood there, she turned and smiled and came toward me.

I looked about quickly to see if there was someone behind me, but there was no one there. She must, indeed, be coming toward me! I had no time then to worry about the proper way to greet a queen or to

think about whether or not I should try to curtsy to
her. She came up beside me and stopped and, leaning
down at once, took my hand in hers and held it for a
minute in the friendliest way imaginable while she
said, "One of my girls—Mele—told me about you. I
am glad you've come to teach in Vava'u. I hope you'll
like it there."

What I managed to say in reply I cannot now remember, but soon I was talking away to the tall,
smiling woman as naturally as if she had been one of
the most ordinary of her subjects instead of queen of
them all. With the true charm of greatness, she set me
at ease at once and managed to make me feel a most
important person. I marveled, as I talked to her that
first time, at the great interest she showed in the
teaching job to which I was going. Now, I know that
she is no remote monarch who sits apart in her palace, but a very active ruler who has a genuine concern and a true share in everything that touches her
people.

"I don't suppose," the Queen said after a time,
"that you had an opportunity to see much of Tongatapu."

"No," I replied. "I was busy going over college
matters and"—I added ruefully—"there was too
much rain anyway."

She gave a rich, hearty laugh. "My people say it
always rains when I travel and it always rains when
the *Matua* comes; so you see, you couldn't escape a
downpour this time!"

"If it's your special weather," I replied, "I shan't
mind it so much."

"You'll find plenty of sunny days in Vava'u," she assured me, and with that she bid me a cheery good-by and disappeared into the ship, leaving me feeling that my "first queen" must surely be the most regal and the most gracious of them all.

I went to bed that night soon after dinner; we were due to enter Vava'u harbor at daybreak and I wanted to be up on deck in time to see it all. On the deep Pacific swell, the *Matua* rocked slowly, soothingly, but I found it hard to get to sleep. One after another all the events of the day kept crowding back into my thoughts. The rain and the mission staff and the stuffy parlor at the mission house I pushed to the back of my mind whenever they cropped up, but the tutor, Tu'ifua, and Queen Salote and all the wonderful happy crowds on the wharf I summoned up again and again. They came to me and we talked together and went spinning through wonderful adventures until, suddenly, they all disappeared as an impatient voice shouted into my ear.

"We're just passing the heads. Hurry up if you want to see the harbor."

I tried to turn back to my dreams, but the stewardess was a determined woman. She switched on the light above my face and commanded gruffly, "Get up or you'll be blaming me for not waking you."

So I tumbled out and by the time my feet touched the floor, I was glad to be awake. Hurriedly I got my clothes on, gulped down a steaming cup of tea which was waiting on the bedside table, and rushed up onto the deck.

I hear it said, often enough, that all Pacific islands are alike and that once you have seen one, you have seen them all, but I know that is not true. There is not another place in all the world like Vava'u. I have been certain of it since that first morning when I went up on deck and found that we were sailing down a long watery valley which was closed on either side by hilly little islands. I could not see the sun, but I knew it must be somewhere up there at the end of the harbor. Nothing else could account for the brightness in the sky or for the fact that every stray rain cloud that floated overhead was tinged with gold.

The islands themselves shone with a strange translucent greenness that sparkled from the varnished fronds of the coconuts and lay on the tangle of bush and vine at their feet. The whole world—land and sky and shimmering sea—was so fresh and new that I couldn't help thinking it must have been just so when, after the first Sixth Day, God looked at His creation and saw that "it was good."

A feeling of mingled awe and delight had taken hold of me by the time we neared the end of the long avenue of islands where the *Matua* swerved sharply around a little cape. On a hill, high above the cape, the palm-thatched roofs of native houses thrust themselves up among the world-covering green. As I watched, a group of laughing brown children came out from the settlement and ran swiftly down a rough footpath. Following them with my eyes, I saw for the first time the big old white house that lies at the foot of the hill in the middle of the grass above the beach. Then I heard some strangers who passed behind me on the deck saying, "That's the doctor's

house," but I had no time for a second look. At that
very moment my name was blasted over the loud-
speaker. "What's happened?" I asked myself as a
dozen disasters presented themselves to my mind,
but it was only a routine announcement. "Passenger
disembarking at Vava'u please report to the saloon
with passport and landing permit for inspection by
customs officials." I breathed a sigh of relief and
scurried down to my cabin. By the time I had found
the necessary papers, the ship had stopped and the
gangway had creaked down. I hurried off to the
saloon.

The big room was empty save for two men—a
Tongan and a European who were talking together as
I entered. The Tongan, who sat before a table filled
with papers, looked up. "Here's the passenger," he
remarked to his companion, who walked off to the
far side of the room, and to me he said, "Come and
sit down, please. I am the customs officer."

I took a seat opposite him and handed him my
papers. He thumbed through them for a minute
before he handed them back.

"All right," he said and he smiled at me out of a
face that was as round and merry as a fat Buddha's.

"Is that all?" I asked, not believing that it was
possible to go so quickly and so painlessly through
customs.

"That's all," he said, gathering up his papers and
going toward the door, "unless the doctor wants
you." As he went out, he called to the man across
the room.

I turned to face a big ruddy Scotsman who was
dressed in a pair of white shorts and an open-neck

white shirt. In his hand he held a rather battered
white sun helmet.

"Do you want to see me?" I asked.

He looked at me with a pair of serious gray eyes.
"I have seen you," he said gravely and added quickly,
"There's no need for an examination. I'm merely
here as a matter of form in case anyone who's getting
off is too sick to land, but as you're the only passenger
who's staying today and you're obviously very well, my
work for the morning is over."

I moved toward the door, but he was speaking
again. I stopped as he said, "I first knew a month ago
that you were coming. I hope you'll be very happy
here."

"Thank you. I know I shall be," I replied, and
added, "It's so beautiful."

He nodded agreement and I said, "I saw your
house as we were coming in. It looked a fine place."

"Ah," he said. "It is and you must come down and
see it when you're settled."

We talked together for a while longer and then
I said I must go and see about getting my baggage
ashore, but the doctor dismissed the whole subject
of baggage. "I'll ask one of the men here to see it
gets up to your house," he said, "and if you'd like
to go up and see your place, I'll walk along with you."

"That's very kind," I murmured.

But he replied in a gruff Scotch way, "No, not
kind. I go that way anyhow on my way to the
hospital."

And so it was, that with the doctor at my side, I
stepped off the boat and walked into the world of
Vava'u.

4 Vava'u and My Important People

Yes, Vava'u has become my world, but it might, by now, be no more than a distant memory had it not happened to contain two people who became important to me; for places—even the most interesting of them— have a way of growing into narrow prisons unless they are broadened by the presence of people who are significant to us. From the day I first sailed up the harbor, Vava'u has been my part of the country. Because I found Farquhar and Tu'ifua here, it has become also my world.

From my very first days on the island, I felt at home among the Tongans, and I did, of course, come to know a great many of them very quickly. There were almost a hundred girls in the college. Because Tonga is very much a "family country," my circle of acquaintances did not stop with my students, but included also their parents and their grandparents, their uncles and their aunts, their big cousins and their little cousins and all the host of more distant relatives whom they could only describe vaguely as "belonging to the family."

During my first few days in Neiafu, I was so busy

getting settled into my little house on the college grounds and getting the school program under way that I had time to think of nothing else, but when the house was in order and the college routine established, I discovered that, although I knew a great many people, I was not immune to loneliness. Every day I learned more of the Tongans and of their language and their customs, but I longed to have someone with whom I could discuss all the new things I was learning; for experience never seems really complete until it has been shared with a friend.

As time went on, my sense of being alone was heightened by the fact that, as I had realized ever since that day in the parlor in Nuku'alofa, I had nothing whatever in common with the other white members of the mission staff. Now and then, one or two of them came to Vava'u and stayed for a few days or a few weeks in the ramshackle old house across the street from the college; but, far from finding any companionship in their visits, I came to dread them as trying and unpleasant times.

It has always seemed to me that one's religious beliefs should be expressed more in living than in talking. The mission people who spoke constantly of God and Jesus (and, of course, of their own very strong connection with both) struck me as being nothing but spiritual exhibitionists. Yet I could have put up with their pious words had they not been accompanied by such a haughty spirit. It seemed to me that most of them scorned the idea of making friends with Tongans, but they showed a lively enough aptitude for converting them into house girls, yard boys, laundresses, and miscellaneous sorts of servants. Of my demands for adequate books, maps, and blackboards for the school they took a decidedly dim view. I soon discovered that their main idea in running a college was not to educate the girls, but to keep them from falling into the clutches of any of the rival sects. When it became clear to them that Tongans were my friends and not my servants, they set me down as hopelessly queer.

Because of my complete incompatability with the white missionaries and because the stress of duties at the college left me little time to seek other white company, I came to depend for society more and more on the Tongans with whom I worked. The dozen or so young men and women who were tutors in the college and teachers in the mission primary schools (which, in addition to my college work, I supervised) were a thoroughly likable group. Although they were themselves hampered by the limitations of a mission education, they were filled with professional zeal which made them anxious both to improve themselves and to aid the progress of their students. In spite of the fact that they were all teaching English, they did not themselves know it well enough to carry on an ordinary conversation or to read a book with ease. To try to clear away their linguistic confusion, I started a teachers' English class which met one night a week in my living room. In the beginning, it was a formal affair with the teachers sitting Tongan fashion on the floor and myself holding forth from the depths of the solitary easy chair. They brought their questions and I did my best to answer them. As time went on, the questions ceased to be purely grammatical ones. They asked about colloquial words and then they asked about customs and ways of life in America.

One night Koli, a tall, young primary school-teacher who had a flair for dramatics, stayed behind when the others had left.

"I wanted to ask you something," he explained, "but I was ashamed to ask it in front of the others."

"All right," I said, "what is it?"

"Well," he hedged, "it's not a word at all." And then he blurted out, "It's Hollywood. Have you ever been there? Could you tell me about it?"

So, to Koli I told about Hollywood and to the others I did my best to explain other phases of life in California, and they told me of their life, and before long we were interpreting for each other the different ways of Tongans and papalangis. The pleasant relationships formed in those days still continue and no visitors to the house at the cape in 'Utulei are more welcome than those young people.

It is not, however, of the many who delighted, but of the two who became truly important that I set out to write. The first of them came from the college. She was Tu'ifua, the head tutor, whom I had met first in Nuku'alofa. If the truth be told, she had a great deal more to do with running the college than I had. Besides teaching a full schedule of classes, she handled all the practical details of the girls' housing, eating, and routine recreational activities. In addition she had to interpret not only my speech, but also my ideas and my ways to the students. To me, she explained local conditions, Tongan customs, and

the established ways of the college. She was, in brief,
a sort of liaison officer between her culture and mine.
Long before my teaching year was over, she had
become more than that, too; she had become my
"pele" which, to use her own translation, means the
"one most important friend, the favorite, the one who
is really like your family."

To describe the growth of a friendship is never
easy. I only know that Tu'ifua and I had a distinctly
unpropitious beginning for ours, for it commenced
under the baleful shadow of my predecessor, the
former head mistress, with whom Tu'ifua had worked
for some years. In her presence, Tongans had stood
at respectful attention; around her house the unseemly
noise of song or laughter was seldom heard. In those
early days, supposing me to be another typical mission
white, Tu'ifua hid her true self behind a mask of
excessive politeness and an impassiveness so thick that
I used to despair of ever breaking through it.

She performed her duties at the college with an
admirable efficiency and each evening when she came
to my cottage to discuss the day's doings and the work
to be undertaken in the immediate future, she presented a report so clear and so well worked out in its
minutest detail that it was a pleasure to hear. So
long as we talked of the college, there was a delightful spontaneity and intelligence in her conversation,
but the minute our work was over, she would close her
notebook and rise to go.

"Sit down again," I would say and obediently she
would sit down, reopen her notebook and ask, "Have
I forgotten something?"

"No," I would say. "We've finished our work for tonight."

"Then I'll go now," she would say politely.

"Stay and talk," I would urge, and because she was accustomed to obeying commands from the missionaries, she would stay, but her talk consisted of no more than perfunctory answers to my questions with never a single question—no, nor the hint of one—from her.

How long our meetings continued in that manner I do not now remember, but I think we never really came to talk to each other until we started walking in the night. After a time, I no longer urged Tu'ifua to sit down again after our work was finished. Instead, we looked in at the study hall, checked with the duty tutor, shut the doors of my cottage, and walked out through the warm darkness of the mango-shaded town. Perhaps the motion of walking, perhaps the night which hid my white face, gave her courage to speak to me as one individual speaks to another. At any rate, the barriers of white superiority which had been so painstakingly erected were broken down and we became for each other two companions and, in time, two friends.

Most nights we went past the big white church down to the main street that runs along above the water's edge. Through the dark canyon made by the shadowy nighttime shapes of the two big store buildings, past the smaller stores, into the glaring light and the noisy crowd around the town's one movie house we walked, and beyond that into the darkness again to a place where the road lies on top of a steep cliff which plunges abruptly down to the harbor below.

There we sat one night, balancing on the fence rails, enjoying the breeze which swept up from the sea while we talked. Our conversation, I remember, touched on the travel plans which I had already begun to make for the time when my year at the college would be finished.

"But why do you want to go away?" Tu'ifua asked. "You say you like Tonga. Why not stay here? Why do you need to find someplace new all the time? You can't really live when you're always busy running around the world."

I tried to tell her of the restless wanderlust which had long ago taken possession of me. "When I was a little girl and lived in San Francisco," I said, "my mother and father used often to take me to the beach and let me wade in the chilly surf. And there was always a strange excitement about being there at the sea. When the waves frothed white about my feet, I'd dream of all the other girls—and of the boys and the men and women, too—who were at that very moment wading in the wide Pacific, and I'd vow that someday I would go to see them all, someday I would know all the distant places where they lived —South America, Australia, New Zealand, the Pacific islands, China, Japan—"

"Of course," broke in Tu'ifua. "All children have such dreams, but now you are grown."

She saw my frown and added quickly, "Anyway, you've been to Australia and New Zealand and lots of the islands and now you're in Tonga and you say you like it. It just doesn't make sense to go away."

"There are things to see and things to learn," I began, but my explanations were useless. She simply

couldn't understand them. Like most Tongans, she
was not only proud of her country, but was thoroughly
content to let it be for her all the world. So, at last,
I gave up trying to explain myself and weakly took
refuge in our differences. "Papalangis are like that,"
I said. "They just want to keep on going places all
the time."

There was a long silence between us then, tinged
as silences that cover a lack of understanding always
are, with sadness. Finally Tu'ifua spoke. "It is not
true," she said slowly. "Papalangis are not like that
—not all of them," and she turned her head and
stared out across the dark harbor waters to the cape
at 'Utulei where a small, steady light shone from the
lamp in the doctor's library. "The doctor is going to
stay here. He wants to live here always."

"Yes," I agreed, "but the doctor is different." And
I, too, stared through the darkness to his light, im-
agining as I did so how he would look reading away in
the book-cluttered room which I had lately come to
know, with Lassie, his fat brown puppy, asleep at his
feet. But my vision of him was driven away by
Tu'ifua's persistent "Why? Why is he different?"

"I don't know," I said. "Perhaps because he has
found what he wants and is content."

"Yes," agreed Tu'ifua emphatically, "and you, too,
if you'd only stay here and really live here, would be
content."

That night, out of my restlessness, I could find no
answer except a sigh, but in the weeks that followed,
the idea of leaving Tonga came to be less and less
attractive. True, there were still many places in the

world to be seen, but I began to suspect that Tu'ifua was right when she had said I couldn't really live when I was always running about. I found in myself an increasing desire to stay in a place and belong to it, and an increasing desire, too, to have that place be Tonga. City born and bred though I was, I had never had any love for the rush of traffic or for the endless daily machinery of our civilization which seemed, more often than not, to crush all humanity out of people. On the other hand, I had already come to feel at home in the slower tempo of island life which gives one plenty of time to know the sea and the sky and the land and the people one lives among. I was fast coming to feel that the doctor was perfectly right to be thoroughly content here. And there was not the slightest doubt about his contentment, which stretched beyond this world into the hypothetical regions of the next; for he used often to say that, if he had any choice in the matter, he'd be a Polynesian in his next life.

Yes, he used to say it often; for we often talked together. I have already said that my work at the college gave me little opportunity to know the Europeans. The doctor was the single exception. I had been with him when I first set foot on Vava'u, and from then on I saw a great deal of him. His visits, at first, were purely professional. A college full of girls—be they ever such healthy young animals—is always developing sniffles, or cuts, or sores, or pains in the middle, any of which might be serious and all of which are alarming. By dropping in each morning on his way up to the hospital, he kept a check on the college and relieved me of all worries about the health of my charges. While he looked at the day's collection of ailing girls, we talked, and sometimes we found the time all too short. Soon he fell into the habit of coming by on his way down from the hospital to share the cup of tea I used to have during morning recess. Later, he joined me in Tongan lessons which Tu'ifua gave us every afternoon, and we struggled together with the unending mysteries of Polynesian pronouns.

After a time, I wrote to a friend in California that he was all my white society and she replied that she suspected a romance. I scoffed at such an idea, but soon the doctor became for me simply Farquhar, and soon after that I was telling Tu'ifua that all my papalangi wanderlust was stilled and that I had decided to do as she suggested and really live in Vava'u.

5 Make Your Hearts Comfortable

"How exciting," wrote my friends in answer to my announcement that I had been married in Vava'u. "Tell us," they demanded, "all about your husband and all about your South Sea Island romance."

I replied, "Farquhar is Scotch and he is a doctor. He looks both. We are happy." To me, that always seemed a thoroughly satisfactory description of the person and the circumstances involved, but none of my friends thought it so. Their letters began to carry gentle reproaches to the effect that, really, I told them nothing.

I suppose I must plead guilty, but in self-defense I can say that anyone who tries to put a romance— especially his own—into words, is doomed to failure as certainly as one who tries to describe a rainbow. To be sure, it is simple enough to set down the details of the spectrum and to outline the arch and simple, too, to record where people went and what they said, but when you have finished, what do you have of the brilliance a rainbow sheds on the world or of the sparkle a romance throws over a life?

The best I can do for the friends who cry, "Tell us

45

all about it," is to set down a thing or two and to hope
that, out of the romances of their own lives, they can
put the story together and furnish it with the color
and the brightness which belongs to it.

The fact that it was in Farquhar's company that
I first set foot on Vava'u was a coincidence which only
later, in retrospect, became significant. Yet, on that
day of our meeting, by the time we had walked from
the ship to the gate of my house on the college
grounds, I felt he was someone to like and to respect.
The reason I came so quickly to that opinion was
that I found in him the attitude toward the Tongans
for which I had looked in vain in the missionaries.
He was obviously fascinated by their Polynesian
culture and he accepted them, individually, quite
simply as fellow human beings, thinking neither
more nor less of them because their color was
different from his own.

As time went on, we discovered that our common
point of view about the island people extended easily
and naturally into a common point of view about
people in general. We shared, too, a certain disregard
for most of the things that men struggle to possess,
thinking that, of them all, only books and friends
were really worth the trouble.

And so, having many points of agreement, we became good companions. That much is easily told. How
and when our friendship ripened into love is another
matter. I am a quiet sort of person myself and Farquhar is an outstanding example of Scotch inarticulate-
ness; so there are neither rapturous words to set down
nor a thrilling proposal to record.

Only I know that, after a time, I came to prefer fourth form English above all my other classes. There was, I hasten to confess, no sound academic reason for my choice. It arose simply because the class was held on the school verandah facing the main road, along which I could see, over the top of my reading book, the familiar form of Farquhar as he came down from the hospital and made his way to my little house. When, as occasionally happened, he didn't pass by and I found, after I had run home at recess, that he was not there waiting for our morning cup of tea, but had sent a note instead to tell me he was operating or had gone off to a village on an inspection tour, I drank my solitary cup with a painfully acute sense of loneliness.

I began, too, to look forward to Saturdays. Then, with one or two of the college girls, I usually went down to 'Utulei to the house at the cape. Farquhar provided us with tea and lunch, but he did not bother about entertaining us; for in 'Utulei, as I know so well now, the only possible guest is the one who can entertain himself. Sometimes I read with him, but sometimes I browsed alone in his library. Sometimes, sitting on the wide verandah and watching the little boats going up and down the harbor, we talked, but quite as often Farquhar left me to my own devices and the girls and I swam off the sandy beach or walked down to the reef below the village to gather shells. Those were good carefree days full of sun and sea and quiet joy. I think it not at all surprising that gradually 'Utulei came to seem as if it would be a good background for all my living.

There were other Saturdays, too, when we went off in launches down the harbor for picnics with the college or the hospital staff or some other local group. They, too, were good Saturdays. One I remember especially.

It began, really, on a Wednesday morning before school started. I was sitting alone in my house correcting papers when I heard a sharp knock at my front door. Jumping up, I discovered on the verandah a tall young man dressed in a fresh white shirt and vala with a neat little mat about his waist who, as I opened the door, drew himself up in a military way and saluted smartly. Then he bowed and handed me a letter.

It was addressed to me. I thanked him for bringing it, but instead of going away again, he stayed and urged, "Read it. Please read it now."

So I stood in the doorway and tore open the envelope and took out the letter.

Honored Head Mistress, it read. *The boys and girls of the Ovaka Primary School and their teacher ask you to come to a feast on Saturday. They show their schoolwork and dance and drill and please, you will judge their costumes.*

I hope you can come and may God make your heart comfortable.

    Signed, Tolani, Head Teacher Ovaka School.

"This is most kind," I said to the messenger, "but I don't know Tolani."

A smile broke over his face as he introduced himself. "Me. I am Tolani."

His tone grew so pleading when he added, "You'll

come? Please do come," that I promised at once and
thanked him for inviting me.

"I've had an invitation," I said to Farquhar when
he came by for a cup of tea later that morning.

"So have I," he replied, smilingly pulling out of
his pocket a letter from Tolani which was a duplicate
of mine, except that his was addressed to "Honored
Mr. Doctor."

"I couldn't resist that wish at the end," he said.

"Nor could I," I replied, and we laughed together.

On Saturday when the last of the college girls had
gone off to her village for the weekly home visit,
Tu'ifua, who had also been invited to Tolani's
picnic, and I locked up the school dormitories and
walked together down to the wharf. There we found
Farquhar and a little group of Tongans already aboard
the launch which was to take us down the harbor to
the distant island of Ovaka.

"Come on," they cried. "Everyone else is here.
We're only waiting for you."

They had not long to wait. We jumped hurriedly
onto the little boat and clambered up to the top of the
cabin where Farquhar made room for us.

"This is the best seat in the boat," he said, as we
settled down beside him. "We can see everything
from here."

In the clear, bright outlines of the morning light,
the islands on either side of us were like Rousseau
landscapes, with every tree and every bush and every
twisting vine standing separate as if it were posing all
alone for its portrait instead of being only a part of

the thousands that made up the scenery. The sea, too, had a clarity of its own. When we passed over reefs, we could stare down through depths of luminous green water to the bright-colored coral that grew on the sandy bottom.

On our launch, which chugged its way along past 'Utulei and around the cape and down the long island-guarded harbor, someone began to sing. Soon the air was full of the music which the Tongans so accurately call "sweet song."

Now and then, Tu'ifua with her strong, true soprano joined in, but more often she explained to Farquhar and me the meaning of the songs or told us the occasions for which they had been written; for most of the things they sang were original Tongan compositions—some of them so old that no one now alive could even tell what the words meant and some of them so new that they celebrated loves which were only beginning to blossom. As we went farther down the harbor, beyond the places I already knew, she began to point out the villages and the islands we passed—'Utungake, Otea, Oto, Ava, Sisia, Taunga—names that were music to blend with the song and the bright day.

At last, pointing straight ahead to a round island, she said, "There's Ovaka." As we drew closer, we knew at once why Tolani decided to have a show. Nature herself had given him the idea. The area around the Ovaka landing forms a natural amphitheater. There is a strip of white beach and a square of green grass, on one side of which is built the one-room frame school, and all around rises the gentle, grass-covered slope.

The actors were already on the stage when we
arrived. Lined up on the beach there they were—the
fifty or so children of the Ovaka government school,
ranging from toddlers to teen-agers, dressed alike
in neat white shirts and valas with bright red belts
and caps. Beside them, stiff and soldierly, stood
Tolani. As our launch with stilled engines glided
close to the island, he walked around and faced the
boys and girls and in another minute we heard him
singing the pitch note, as Tongans, whose true ears
make them spurn pitch pipes, always do. Then he
nodded his head and the children, taking a good
deep breath, burst gaily into a song of welcome. It
was a happy tune with happy words. Tolani was
pleased when, as he came to greet us, we guessed
correctly that he had written it for the occasion, but
he said in the deprecatory way of all polite Tongans,
"It is nothing. I am sorry we have no good song
for you."

His words continued to be modest and self-effacing,
but they could not conceal the pride which shone in
his face. "We welcome you to Ovaka," he said. "It
is a small island and poor, but we hope you will like
our show."

We all said that we were sure we would like it very
much and we commented on the beauty of Ovaka, and
on the order, too; for the whole place looked as if
it had been freshly clipped and swept for the day.
There wasn't a dead leaf to be seen on the grass, or a
coconut shell, or even a bit of driftwood on the
beach.

"Well, then," said Tolani when he had heard us
out, "please come first and meet our chief."

As Farquhar and I were the only two white people present, we were, automatically, the guests of honor. Tolani, walking between us, escorted us up the center of the amphitheater to the topmost point of the slope where, half hidden by a wide-spreading mango tree, stood a small European house.

"Go in, please." The young teacher held the door while we walked into an enclosed verandah whose floor was covered with a fine, closely woven mat. Along the rear wall were ranged the straight-back uncomfortable chairs which are the inevitable furniture of all Tongan-owned European houses. Directly in the center of the room, stood a small round table covered with an elaborately embroidered scarf on which was a cheap glass vase filled with delicate white spider lilies. Aside from that the room was empty and bare —unless, of course, you count the innumerable friends and relatives of the family who smiled out from faded and tattered snapshots which were tacked up on walls and shutters and even, in places, on the ceiling.

"This is our chief's house," Tolani announced, not even trying to conceal the pride he felt in it. Although native thatched houses are cooler and easier to keep, every Tongan dreams of living in just such a frame house.

"Sit down, please. The chief will come soon." He beckoned Farquhar and me to chairs. Tu'ifua and some of the others who had come on the boat sat beside us on the floor. They would not have been so presumptuous as to sit on a chair in the presence of a chief.

The chief, a well-formed young man, and his beautiful wife both possessed the height and the ample proportions which Tongans associate with rank. As they entered the room, Tu'ifua and the others greeted them, using the special words which are reserved for people of the chiefly class. The greetings were returned with the calm, friendly assurance of position, but when they were introduced to us, although they smiled and shook hands and sat down beside us, it was obvious that they were ill at ease. We felt so ourselves. There is nothing which inhibits the free exchange of conversation so quickly as sitting stiffly lined up on straight-back chairs. We were further hampered by language difficulties. When they had said "How do you do" and commented on the fact that Farquhar came from Scotland and I came from America and asked us how we liked Tonga, they were at the end of their English. Our Tongan was not much more extensive. Tu'ifua soon came to our rescue and interpreted for us, but we were all relieved when Tolani, coughing slightly to attract our attention, said, "Excuse me, but it is time to start the show."

We stood up to say our good-bys. The chief, apologizing because a meeting he was obliged to attend in Taunga would keep him away from the show himself, thanked us for coming and bade us enjoy ourselves. His wife, smiling all the while, echoed his words.

We left them and followed Tolani outside where we found assembled all the other men and women of Ovaka waiting to welcome our groups from Neiafu. Joining company, we made a gay crowd, chattering and laughing all the way over to the school building. As many of us as could—and then a few more— squeezed in to see the neat exhibits of handwriting, map making, and drawing. Tolani urged us to inspect the notebooks carefully and the parents pushed close to hear what we said, smiling happily whenever we found one to praise. But we did not linger in the schoolhouse. It had soon become obvious that to teacher and villagers alike this routine academic part of the show was of minor interest. The best, as far as they were concerned, was yet to come.

Nothing loath to follow their lead, we soon found ourselves in the open again. While we had been inside, some of the men had erected a typical feast shelter halfway up the slope above the green. A long structure with thick bamboo poles for supports, it had an open front. The back was walled with tapa cloth as a protection against the strong rays of the afternoon sun and the top was made of shade-giving woven coconut fronds. Within was a double row of mats and it was on them that we all sat down to watch the show.

Into the center of the green below us marched Tolani. A smart salute, a deep bow, and he began a brief speech in which he spoke of the little school and the work of its children. Then, still with modest words and proud looks, he announced the drill, blew a whistle and summoned the boys and girls onto the field.

Drill is one of many things which Tongans have taken over from papalangis and made uniquely their own. The outdoor life of these islanders develops in them at an early age a muscular coordination which makes the most intricate tricks of the *Infantry Drill Manual* and the most involved exercises of the Swedish gymnasts as simple as play for them. Yet, here in Tonga, there is none of the robotlike snap and precision which characterizes drill teams in other countries. Music lovers that they are, these people set their drill to song or to the gentle strumming of guitars.

"I'd rather be here than in any theater I know," Farquhar said. I nodded agreement. Content lay deep as sunshine on us.

As soon as the drill had finished, the Ovaka mothers sitting amongst us jumped up at once and hurried into the schoolhouse to help their young ones get dressed for the costume parade. This is a favorite Tongan item because everyone has a hand in it. Fathers and uncles debate the sort of costume that is to be produced, mothers and aunts sew it, and the children contribute ideas and help. From the schoolhouse escaped a good deal of talk punctuated by peals of laughter before Tolani once more stepped to the center of the green to announce that they were ready. Music of guitars drifted in from somewhere. The school door opened and out came—not the white uniformed children of the drill team, but all sorts of wonderful people.

First, from the old times before white men came and brought with them their store cloth, were all the traditional dresses of old Tonga. Girls and boys, their skins glistening from the scented coconut oil which had been rubbed into it, rustled by in grass skirts or walked sedately in big mats. Larger girls wore fringed dresses made of tapa, the beaten bark cloth, decorated with heavy dark designs which had been handed down from mother to daughter for untold generations.

In the next group, the Tongan gift for mimicry was given full play; for here were all the types of white people who ever set foot in the islands. Girls in stylish gowns, with their usually bare feet squeezed into high-heeled shoes, tottered daintily along applying lipstick as they went. Hiccoughing loudly, a carelessly dressed boy in an aloha shirt swigged from a half-empty gin bottle and wove unsteadily in and out of line. He was followed by a disapproving youth in long black trousers and frock coat who carried a Bible and, as he impersonated a missionary, walked with a dignified aloof air and refrained from smiling. Teachers, doctors, traders, tourists, bums—there were all the papalangis of the South Seas.

There were costumes, too, from distant lands—from the other islands of Polynesia, from New Guinea and Spain and China. There was even an American Indian with a chicken-feather headdress and a gingham plaid blanket who let out from time to time the most blood-curdling war cries imaginable.

"How good they all are!" I exclaimed to Farquhar. "I'd hate to have to try to pick the best of them."

He laughed. "You do have to pick the best," he reminded me. "You're forgetting that you were asked to judge the costumes."

"So I was," I cried, turning a newly critical eye to the costumes—the old and the new, the pretty and the clever. Now a colorful one made entirely of the red and yellow labels of tinned corned beef caught my fancy. Now I burst into laughter as two big boys, converted into wild animals by a thick covering of coconut-fiber "fur," broke out of line and came tumbling and roaring toward the spectators.

Choosing would have been difficult, indeed, had not my eyes happened to light on the smallest of all the children—a tiny, serious-eyed baby called Ane who was scarcely old enough for kindergarten. Her dress, made of tapa cloth, was completely covered with crinkly white shells the size of ten-cent pieces which had been sewed like sequins onto bodice and skirt. A tight-fitting cap was similarly ornamented and there was a purse to match as well as tiny shell bracelets and anklets. I thought of the hours that must have been spent on the reef gathering the shells and of the other hours consumed in sewing them onto the tapa base and I looked at the entrancing little result and named her the First Prize.

My choice was a popular one. Tolani had no sooner announced it than all the people clapped their hands and called thanks. Equally delighted, the costumed children gamboled about, bumping into one another in their glee. Only the little Ane herself looked overwhelmed as she peeked shyly at me from behind the vala of her mother, who came to meet me. I congratulated her on her work and on her little daughter, too, and she beamed with pleasure.

"It is for you," she said. What she meant I did not realize until she turned and, stooping down, began to peel the costume off her serious baby. I could see Ane's lips quiver as if tears were near.

"Tell her not to take it off," I begged Tu'ifua. "Let her leave it on Ane."

But Tu'ifua shook her head. "It is yours," she said. "It is our custom. The first prize always goes to the guest of honor. It would be rude of you not to take it because the people want to give it to you."

"Maybe the people do," I said ruefully, "but just look at poor little Ane."

Tu'ifua's gaze rested for a moment on the baby who stood before us. Dressed now in nothing but her soft brown skin, she stared with wide eyes as her beautiful shell dress passed from her mother's hands into mine.

"She'll be all right," Tu'ifua said. "She'll be proud."

Happily enough, Tu'ifua was correct. When I asked her to say that I would send Ane's costume to America so that my mother could show it to the children there, all the people clapped their hands again and Ane, with her naked little chest puffed out, went strutting among the children smiling and shrilling, "Ah-may-lik-ah, Ah-may-lik-ah. My dress is going to Ah-may-lik-ah."

We had left the shelter and walked about in order to see the costumes better. When we returned to sit down again, we found that in our absence the men had carried in the feast on long stretcherlike trays made of woven coconut fronds and set it down between the double rows of mats.

Food is the most important part of any island celebration; so it was no time before all the places were filled, grace had been said, and the banana leaves which serve as covers had been lifted, revealing a tempting array of food which was still steaming from the earth oven in which it had been cooked. For a while, the busy silence that characterizes all Tongan feasts reigned. Then, as appetites were satisfied, conversations began and later there were speeches to listen to and the children's dancing to watch.

All afternoon Farquhar and I sat with the crowd watching the children and talking with their parents. Yet some part of us drew away from them as surely as if we had risen and wandered far down the white sand beach. There in the sunlight with laughter all about us, we were suddenly alone together. Without any exchange of words, we knew that it was good to be so.

Our happiness lay deep within us as we climbed back onto the launch and said "good-by" to Tolani and the kindly people of Ovaka. The day had grown old. We noticed with surprise that the school children lined up on the beach to sing us their farewell song cast long, dark shadows on the sand before them.

A wave of hands, the engines started, and the little round island with its singing children was left behind. Going up the harbor, we could see that the clear outlines of the morning had softened and blurred until tree and bush and vine seemed to be woven together into one inseparable covering of green. The breeze which had rippled the harbor all day died and stillness lay on the water.

Tu'ifua was inside the cabin talking to an Ovaka woman who was traveling back to Neiafu. Farquhar and I sat alone on the narrow stern seat which was so close to the water that we felt a fine spray from the wake that rose just below us.

Up in front, the homeward-bound crowd began to sing softly. We listened in silence for a while and then Farquhar leaned toward me. "There," he said, waving his hand out toward the still water, "is what Homer meant when he talked of the wine-dark sea."

I looked and saw the sunset captured in the sea and felt the thrill of beauty shared.

We were almost back up the harbor—just passing Farquhar's house in 'Utulei—when he turned toward me again. "Was the day successful?" he asked, and smiling and lowering his voice, added, "And is your heart comfortable?"

I looked up into his eyes. "Yes, thank you, completely comfortable—and yours?"

"Comfortable," he said and his hand, as if by chance, touched mine and our fingers locked in a tight clasp.

Neither of us spoke the obvious word, but we both knew then that it was together our hearts were comfortable, and having that knowledge, we had no need of further words. And now, if I were asked to explain the happiness that is ours, I should know of no better way than to say that God has granted Tolani's wish. Our hearts are still comfortable.

6 A Sort of Wedding Journey

Farquhar came to Tonga to retire, but when the Crown Prince, Tungi, who was Minister of Health at that time, asked him if he would be willing to act as consultant to the medical department in Vava'u, he consented and added that he would be glad to help the government in any way he could. We were married early in May and before the month was out, he was reminded of his promise. The Chief Medical Officer in Nuku'alofa had put in his resignation and, as his departure would leave the capital city without a white doctor, Farquhar was asked if he would go down in June and fill in until a new man could be found.

"Not in June!" I cried when he told me the news. "That's my holiday. You said we'd start to fix up our house then."

"I know," he replied gently, "but I have promised I'd help out when I was needed and I must go."

Forsaking cherished plans quickly and gracefully is something every doctor's wife must learn to do, but I was new at it then and it was hard to see our month in 'Utulei disappearing.

My gloom was thick as Farquhar repeated, "I must go," but it began to lift when I heard him saying, "but there's no reason why you can't come, too. It will mean putting off the work on the house, but we'd have a month together before you had to be back in Vava'u for the college opening."

He watched me turning the proposition over in my mind and added coaxingly with a little laugh, "It will be a belated sort of honeymoon trip."

So Farquhar wrote Tungi that he would be in Nuku'alofa in June and, after the college was closed, we packed our bags and waited for the *Hifofua,* the interisland boat. The afternoon of the night we were to sail, he came down from the hospital with a sterilizer full of dressings and instruments. "You'll have to make room for these in our baggage," he said.

"Whatever for?" I asked. "Aren't there any instruments in Nuku'alofa?"

"Of course there are," he replied, "but I may need these on the boat. Melenaite is traveling down with us."

Melenaite is the wife of Tu'ipelehake, the younger of Queen Salote's two sons, who was at that time the Governor of Vava'u. I knew she was expecting a child and had heard that it was the wish of the family that she go to Nuku'alofa for the birth, but I thought I remembered Farquhar's having told me a week or so earlier that he had advised her to go south at once.

"Yes," he said when I asked him about it, "I did recommend that she go down a fortnight ago, but

Tu'ipelehake was busy here and they decided to wait until this boat." He shrugged his shoulders and added, "The royal family has the same casual attitude about birth that all Tongans have. It's not a bad thing on the whole, but I certainly hope Melenaite's child doesn't decide to be born on the *Hifofua*."

I had not, at that time, traveled on Tonga's notorious little craft, but I was able to understand Farquhar's reluctance to attend a confinement—especially a royal one—aboard her; for she had the reputation of being eighty tons of dirty rolling discomfort—a reputation which, I have since discovered, she deserves all too well.

That night, however, she seemed a trim enough little boat as she lay in the moonlight beside the Neiafu wharf. With Farquhar at my side, I pushed through the crowds on the wharf, feeling all the excitement of a big sailing.

"Wait," called a familiar voice, and I turned to see Tu'ifua running after us. She thrust a basket into my hands. "I had nothing for your trip," she explained, "so I made these little cakes for you."

"And I had nothing either," said Manu, another of the college tutors, who appeared behind Tu'ifua, "but my family send you these oranges." She pointed to a crate of the sweet, juicy Vava'u fruit which a boy at her side was carrying.

"My wife has made this oil for you," an 'Utulei man told me as I passed him, and another held out a piece of tapa while a third presented me with a mat. So, midst presents and farewells, we reached the

Hifofua. Since she did not boast a gangway, we heaved our cases across from the wharf to her deck and, after another good-by to everyone, leaped after them.

Our tickets for the trip were first-class ones, but as I discovered in a very few minutes, the mental picture evoked by the words "first class" had little in common with the facts of *Hifofua* life. Leaving the fresh air behind, we descended a steep ladder into the depths of the boat. On the way down, we passed a dark, smelly little cupboard which the steward who was accompanying us told us was the galley. A few steps after that came the end of the ladder. We entered an irregularly shaped room which was so full of bedrolls, baskets, and suitcases that I whispered to Farquhar that we must have got into the baggage room by mistake. Having been in Tonga almost a year longer than I had and having, in that time, acquired a bit of *Hifofua* experience, he laughed at my innocence.

"This is the dining room for the first-class passengers."

Abruptly I turned away from the room and from the disconcerting thought that my reputation as a good sailor might well vanish at it. "If this is the dining saloon," I asked, "what's all this baggage doing here?"

Once again Farquhar laughed. "You mustn't confuse the *Hifofua* with any preconceived notions you may have about ships in general," he said. "The baggage is here because, in addition to being the first-class dining saloon, it is also the place where the second-class passengers sleep."

My thoughts about the odd combination were interrupted by the steward, who threw open a small door a few feet from the dining table.

"Here's your cabin, sir," he announced to Farquhar, "the best on the *Hifofua*," and with that he shoved our cases in at the door, gave Farquhar the key, smiled politely and asked, "Is there anything else I can do for you?"

Farquhar shook his head. "No, thank you."

"Good night, then." He crossed the room and disappeared up the ladder.

Farquhar stepped into the cabin and held the door open. "Come in," he said, "if you can." The afterthought was well taken. When I tried to follow him, we found that we had to push the bags together and pile some of the cases on top of one another before I could find standing room.

"It's not exactly spacious," Farquhar said, with feigned joviality, trying to take my mind off the oversize cockroach which, scuttling down the cobwebby wall, had crossed the gray sheets of the upper berth and slithered down a pipe to the lower berth where he was sitting quite comfortably in the middle of the soiled and spotted pillow.

It was not, however, Farquhar's speech which diverted my mind from the cockroach, but my own awareness that my normal processes were being interrupted.

"I can't breathe down here," I gasped out and, spying a porthole in the wall above the upper berth, said, "Let's open that."

"We can't," Farquhar replied. "We'd have the sea in on us. But never mind. You'll get used to breathing without air. Everyone who travels in the *Hifofua's* cabins does!"

"Perhaps I will," I said doubtfully, "but do we have to stay here now?"

"No, of course not. Get a wrap if you want one and we'll go up on the bridge."

"Aren't you going to shut and lock the door?" I asked when we had gone out of our cabin.

"I should say not," Farquhar replied. "We'd never get in again." Even as he spoke, a man unrolled a pile of mats at our feet and lying down on them in the most unconcerned manner imaginable, drew a piece of tapa over his face and proceeded to go to sleep. "You'll see, when we come back, the place will be covered with sleepers. It's better to have the door open and hear them snore than to be shut up in that cabin."

If the first-class passengers must share their dining saloon with the second-class sleepers, they have compensation. The captain shares his bridge with them. He has no choice in the matter. With every inch of the decks full of passengers and their children and their baggage, the bridge is simply the only place you can find room to sit. It is an unsheltered open runway so narrow that one can sit up on the rails on one side of it and brace one's feet against the rails opposite, but it runs the width of the ship and the air is delightfully fresh.

Up there, I breathed again. I turned to my husband. "Is it true what the steward said?" I asked. "Is our cabin really the best on the ship?"

"The very best," he assured me.

"Then what are the others like?"

He lit a cigarette and said, "Oh, much the same."

"But what about Melenaite and Tu'ipelehake?" I asked. "If we have the best cabin, what about them?"

He nodded toward the afterdeck, explaining as he did so that usually that part of the boat was, like the forward deck, full of deck passengers, but that whenever the Queen or any member of her family traveled, it was reserved for the royal party.

"Then they don't have a cabin at all?" I asked.

For answer, he merely said, "You've seen the best cabin and the dining saloon. Can you imagine the royal family down there?—or even," he added, "getting down there?"

I thought of the narrow ladder and the tiny cabin and laughed. "I see what you mean." It had been a tight squeeze for the two of us who are only moderate-sized papalangis. For the more majestically proportioned members of the Tongan royal family, it would be a virtual impossibility. Still, I thought, the afterdeck isn't much of a place for a prince and princess. I turned to stare down at it and was surprised to see that it was swarming with even more people than the forward deck.

"Perhaps Melenaite and Tu'ipelehake aren't going after all," I said. "It seems as if they've let deck passengers on down there."

Farquhar looked down and shook his head. "Those aren't deck passengers. They're just Melenaite's and Tu'ipelehake's men and women."

"Surely they're not all going along!" I exclaimed. "There's not room for them all."

"There's room to spare so long as there's a passageway to lie in or a rail to lean against." Farquhar was right. I watched fascinated while the men and women of the prince's retinue, like a hundred moving sardines, stacked themselves and their possessions into the deck below. At the very stern of the boat next to the rails was the "room" prepared for Tu'ipelehake and Melenaite—a canopied square hung with tapas which, when they flapped in the breeze, revealed piles of fine mats spread for the royal beds.

"It's not very private," I remarked.

"Nothing in Tonga is private," Farquhar replied.

Turning from the royal deck, we stared out over the crowd on the wharf, picking out, one by one, the friends who had come to see us off. Now that they saw us looking their way, they called out last-minute messages and we carried on one of the many long-distance conversations which were making the air all around ring.

Beep, beep, de beep. The blatant horn of a truck drowned all our little noises as the truck itself came bouncing through the crowd and skidded to a stop on the wharf just beside us.

"It's the last of the prince's things," someone called as twenty or thirty men, carrying rolls of mats and tapa, baskets, vegetables, bottles of oil, and all the other paraphernalia of Tongan travelers, climbed off the truck and began streaming onto the boat.

"And here's the prince," called someone else, and the town's one automobile, a shabby brown taxi, rattled up behind the truck. The door creaked open and Prince Tu'ipelehake followed by his wife, the shy Princess Melenaite, clambered out of the car.

When the national anthem had been sung, they crossed over quickly onto the *Hifofua* and had not been long aboard before the convulsive throbbing of the engines shook the boat, sending her, even while she still stood at the wharf, into the steady roll from which she never recovered until the trip was over.

As we pulled away from the wharf, there was a final roar of good-bys and then the haunting strains of "Ofa Anga 'Ae Otua" came to us across the water. I had not heard the song since that day in Nuku'alofa, my first in the country, when the people had sung it to Queen Salote. It had been beautiful and moving then, but it came to me now with more significance. In the five months which had elapsed since first I heard it, all my life had changed. I had found a husband, a friend, and a whole new world. No longer was I merely an interested observer of Tonga. Now I belonged to it. For me, my belonging was symbolized that night by the sound of Tu'ifua's voice which rose clear and true above all the other voices on the wharf. "Ofa Anga 'Ae Otua," she sang to me, and silently I replied to her and to all the other people of Vava'u, "Yes, and God be with you, too, until we meet again."

The engines gained speed and the singing voices faded in the distance. My mood of solemn happiness was intensified a few minutes later when Farquhar, taking my hand in his, whispered, "There's home. We're just going by 'Utulei."

Through the darkness, I made out the bulk of our house and the curve of the cape. While I watched, the moon came up over the hill and turned the world into luminous silver.

"How beautiful it is!" I exclaimed. The voices of the villagers calling good-by from the 'Utulei beach mingled with Farquhar's as he replied, "Yes, it's a good place."

For almost an hour, we sailed down the island road of Vava'u harbor, passing from silver to shadow and back to silver again, staring into all the little inlets which in the night light seemed more than ever places of mystery. At last we came to the sentinel island of Kitu whose sheer rocky sides shone like steel. Just as we were passing them, there was a terrific crash and, for a moment, I thought that they were indeed steel and that we had run onto them. The whole boat quivered. I grabbed at Farquhar to steady myself.

"What was that?" I gasped. "Have we hit something?"

"Only the Pacific," he said. "We've come out to the open sea."

"Hmm," I said, and was too busy wrapping my legs around the rail beneath me to say any more.

"Are you all right?" Farquhar inquired solicitously, after a time.

For a minute, I watched the moon spinning madly from port to starboard. Then, gulping down a stabilizing mouthful of air or two, I managed a reply. "Yes," I said then, "I'm all right. It's just that I'm not used to such a wobbly world."

"Would you like to go down and go to bed?"

"No," I cried, fighting down the waves of nausea that swept over me at the mere thought of our airless little cabin. "No, I'm all right." Soon I really was.

The *Hifofua* rolled heavily, but she did it so regularly that once I got used to her rhythm, sitting the rail was like a new and strenuous sport. I rose on it with every roll as a horseman, adapting his pattern to his horse's gait, rises in the saddle.

When Farquhar was quite sure that I had regained my equilibrium, he said, "You may think we're rolling now, but this is nothing." Pointing to the ship's boats which were swinging on their davits just ahead of the bridge, he said, "See those boats. I've seen them water-borne. Every time the ship rolled, they went down into the sea and acted as a sort of outrigger for her. They were the only thing that kept her from rolling clear over."

I looked down at the dark lumps of sleeping passengers on the deck below and tried to imagine their plight in such heavy seas. "What happened to them?" I asked. "Weren't they soaked?"

"They certainly were," Farquhar said. "But Tongans," he reminded me, "although they are wonderful navigators, are notoriously poor sailors. By the time the sea washed over them, most of them were so sick that they wouldn't have cared if it had drowned them."

I had been conscious while Farquhar was speaking of a man who had climbed up the ladder on the opposite side and come onto the bridge and I'd noticed that the boy at the wheel straightened as he stopped beside him for a minute.

"Good evening, doctor," the newcomer said as he came toward us. "A beautiful calm trip."

"Yes," agreed Farquhar, "it's a fine clear night,"

and, turning, he introduced me to Captain George, the master of the *Hifofua*.

He was a square sort of Tongan with a stocky, powerful body. His face which was turned toward me in the moonlight was powerful, too. The nose, in some long-past battle, had been broken until it was only a remnant of a nose, but the keen brown seaman's eyes above it shone triumphant and the generous Polynesian mouth had an unfamiliar firmness about it which had come, perhaps, from years of knocking about the distant corners of the earth; for George had seen far more of the world than most Tongans ever do.

His English—ungrammatical seamen's talk that it was—bore no trace of a Tongan accent. It had faintly familiar echoes which I recognized only after he told me he had learned the language in America.

"For eight years, I shipped out of San Francisco," he said, and the mention of my native city made me feel an immediate bond with him.

"I remember," he went on as we stood there on the swaying bridge in the warm moonlight, "Stockton Street. I had a room on the far side of it and I used to walk down through the tunnel every morning on my way to town."

As he spoke, the silver Pacific night faded and memory carried me back. And once again I, too, remembered the Stockton Street tunnel and heard the clang of streetcars rushing through it.

"We may have passed each other in the tunnel," I said to George.

"Perhaps," he mused, and his voice sounded so

distant that I knew he, too, was hearing again the roar of the tunnel traffic.

And so up there on the bridge of the *Hifofua,* the long night passed. Sometimes George and I talked ourselves back to San Francisco and sometimes Farquhar and I talked of our plans for the future. More often, we kept silent, listening to the boy at the wheel who sang softly to himself as he kept his watch. Suddenly I realized with a start that Farquhar had been speaking to me for a long time and I had not heard a word of all he had been saying.

"I'm sorry," I said. "I think I dropped off to sleep."

"You certainly did," he affirmed, "and sitting on the ship's rail isn't the best place to do it. It's three in the morning. We'd better go to bed before it's time to get up again."

Too sleepy to offer any resistance, I followed him off the bridge and down the steep ladder to the dining saloon, whose floor was covered, as Farquhar had predicted it would be, with sleeping men and women. Once, when the ship gave an especially heavy roll, I stumbled and tripped over a man.

As he grumbled into wakefulness, I apologized.

"Sai—all right," he replied good-naturedly and, turning over, went off to sleep again at once.

We had decided when we had first seen our cabin that the gray sheets and matted blankets were far too dirty to lie on; so we spread our coats over the beds and, without undressing, lay on top of them. In the upper berth, bracing myself against the motion of the ship, I knew I could never sleep, but before

Farquhar had switched out the light, I had drifted off.

Sometime later, a noxious smell insinuated itself into my dreams. I stirred, trying to escape it, but it came again stronger and more pervasive than ever until dreams—and sleep, too—were driven away and I lay with eyes shut trying to imagine what dead or dying animal or what collection of decaying rubbish could give off so revolting an odor. Yet, try though I would, I could not identify that smell. Now, being a seasoned *Hifofua* traveler, I know that it came from the galley and that it was the soapy, rancid stench of overcooked purple yams boiling for breakfast. Then, recognizing only that it was something to flee from, I struggled to wake up sufficiently so that I could get out of my berth and run into the fresh air.

"Cup of tea?" asked a voice so close that my sleep-shut eyes snapped open at once to see the steward standing beside my bed. Into my hand he thrust an enormous stained white cup. I mumbled thanks, although when I looked at its contents, I found it hard to feel grateful. *Hifofua* tea boils in an iron kettle which, I suspect, has never yet been washed, but only has fresh leaves and water added to it from time to time. The resulting product is black mineral water with a particularly foul taste, but I drank it. It was hot and the biscuit with it, though unpalatable, was edible.

"Are you awake?" I called down to Farquhar, but there was no answer. Swallowing the last of my tea, I leaned over and discovered that his berth was empty.

I suppose he's gone up on the bridge, I thought to myself. I felt a great longing to be there, too; the purple yam smell was growing stronger and seemed to be forcing its way down my throat so that I felt constantly the necessity to swallow. Tumbling down from my berth, I balanced myself against the ship's sway while I ran a comb through my hair and shook out my clothes. Farquhar appeared in the doorway just as I was searching for a towel.

"I thought you might be waking up," he said. "I've been up on the bridge. It's fine and fresh up there. Come on up."

"I will as soon as I've washed."

"You'd better not wash," he suggested. "You won't like the bathroom."

"I must wash," I said firmly. "After sleeping in my clothes, I feel filthy."

"Well," he said, in the tone of a man who knows he is right, but doesn't want to argue, "go and try it then. It's at the top of the ladder. Turn right instead of going out onto the deck. And come up when you've finished."

The sanitary facilities of the *Hifofua* are widely discussed in all of Tonga, where they have played their part in hindering much of the travel which might otherwise flourish between one island group and another. My first glimpse that morning of the small, dark room with its obscure corners and its fetid floor was so brief that Farquhar laughed when, almost on his heels, I bolted up to the bridge.

"Did you have a good shower?" he inquired placidly.

"Don't be hateful." Unwashed as he was, I settled down beside him on the bridge.

"How long have you been up?" I asked. He shrugged his shoulders. "Not long. They came to call me to go and see Melenaite."

"And how is she?"

"Sick."

"Baby?"

"No, sea. We're going to put in at Ha'apai so she can rest for a while."

"I'll be glad of a rest from this boat myself," I confessed, and added, "If you don't mind, I'll not go down to breakfast." On my way up, passing the galley, I had seen the purple yams.

"I'm not anxious to go, either," he said. "We'll have breakfast here." He brought out a basket into which he had packed Tu'ifua's cakes and some of Manu's oranges. In the fresh sea air, our ravenous shipboard appetites returned and, sitting there on the bridge, we made a leisurely breakfast, munching cakes and oranges while we watched George maneuvering the *Hifofua* in and out of the reefs surrounding Ha'apai with all the skill of a tightrope dancer.

By the time we had finished our meal, George had the ship tied up at the wharf at Ha'apai's main village of Lifuka. As soon as the royal party had gone ashore, we, too, went off and strolled up the white sand beach until we came to the group of frame buildings that is the Ha'apai hospital. There we found a clean place to wash and tidy ourselves and Farquhar picked up some medicine for Melenaite.

"I'll just go along and see how she is," he said; so we walked back along the beach to the big old house that is the Queen's favorite residence. As we approached the place, some of Melenaite's girls came out to meet me and, while Farquhar went inside to see his patient, I went with them to the seaward verandah where they served me a welcome cup of good tea and amused me by singing and dancing. It was pleasant sitting there in the sunlight with the salty breeze coming over me and the reassuring knowledge that the earth beneath was solid and still, but I jumped up as soon as I saw Farquhar reappear. I was anxious to hear what news he had.

"She'll be all right," he said when I asked him. "We're going right on." He sighed. "I'll be relieved to have her safely in Nuku'alofa."

Soon we were back on the *Hifofua* and somehow all that day and all the night passed, rolling and swaying away until it was the gray time before dawn and we were again up on the bridge, straining our eyes toward the horizon for sight of land.

"There she is," George sang out, coming to stand beside us. His seaman's eyes were better than mine. It was almost ten minutes more before I, too, could make out in the distance the pencil smudge-line of the island of Tongatapu.

"See, Farquhar," I cried. "Nuku'alofa!" But his eyes were not on the island we were approaching. He was staring down at the afterdeck where the Princess Melenaite lay. "Thank goodness," he said.

7 A Royal Month

Largest of all the islands in this country, Tongatapu, some ninety-nine square miles in extent, contains more than fifty villages in addition to the capital, Nuku'alofa. Its interest, however, lies not in its size, but in the fact that, from the earliest times, it has been the center of religious and social life and the seat of kings. Its very name—Tongatapu, Sacred Tonga—is witness to the importance it has held in the minds and hearts of countless generations.

The month I spent there with Farquhar was a busy one for us both. He had to meet and work with a whole new hospital staff and I had conferences with the mission directors and the director of education about the college program. There were, too, a flood of social events at which we met most of the Tongan nobles and all of Nuku'alofa's Europeans. Yet it is not any of those tasks or pleasures which stand out in my mind. The really significant events in that first visit to the royal island were, fittingly enough, all royal ones.

We did not have to wait long for them to begin. Our first day in Nuku'alofa we spent in getting settled into the chief medical officer's house on the edge of the hospital grounds. Although we had taken with us so few of our possessions that we spoke, not of living in the house, but only of camping there for a time, the moving in was tiring, as moving always is. The weariness of our *Hifofua* trip was still on us, too, so we decided to go to bed early.

The bedroom was bare. It had neither curtains nor floor coverings and the furniture was sparse and un-attractive, but it did have two evidences of civiliza-tion which were lacking in Vava'u.

The first was a real luxury—electric lights! In all my life before I came to Tonga, I had accepted electricity quite casually as a standard part of the equipment of living. Like water in the tap or the morning bottle of milk at the door, it was some-thing I had always had and never bothered to think about. A brief residence in Vava'u had sufficed to change all that. The kerosene lamps we use are, I am told, a vast improvement on their old-fashioned prototypes. It may be so, but I'm sure that the person who first spoke of the Perversity of Things had them in mind. Certain it is that, in spite of the excellent performance which their manufacturers claim for them, they never behave for me. They leak on my best tablecloth, flare up alarmingly or smoke shame-fully after I have spent a good half hour cleaning them—and, if ever I try to read in bed by their erratic light, generate so much heat that I imagine my sins have found me out and plunged me into the fiery regions.

Small wonder, then, that a well-behaved electric

light that would shed its steady glow hour after hour for no more trouble than it took to push on the switch, was a welcome sight. I piled up the pillows at my back and had opened my book and started to read when I was aware that Farquhar, who had just come in from his shower, was grumbling away about something.

The book was a good one; so I went on reading, but the grumbles broke into my story until at last I put it aside and asked, "What's the matter?"

"Look there," cried Farquhar, and he pointed an accusing finger at the room's second sign of civilization—an ugly black telephone which stood on its table beside the bed.

"I thought I'd escaped such things when I went to Vava'u," he lamented, "and there it is again—the doctor's curse!"

"Don't worry," I said brightly. "No one knows you're here yet. You're safe tonight anyway."

But, as it happened, he wasn't. Sometime, long after I had stopped reading and fallen into a deep sleep, I heard the insistent ringing of the telephone. At first it was only a distant tinkle, but it came closer and closer until it sounded like a gong in my ear. Sleepily, I reached out, groping toward the table where the noxious instrument stood, but Farquhar was already up.

"I'll get it," he said and, in another minute, I heard his always calm voice saying, "Yes. The palace? Yes—yes, at once."

Almost before he had rung off, he had begun to put on his clothes and soon he was kissing me good-by.

"You heard?" he said as he went out. "That was the palace. It's one o'clock. Now go back to sleep."

The sound of his footsteps crunching across the gravel on the driveway came to me, but even as it died away in the distance, I sank back to sleep.

When I woke again, the sky outside was gray with dawn. I had had a good sleep. Its single interruption had been forgotten, but when I reached my hand across the bed and found Farquhar's place empty, the midnight telephone conversation came back to me. When would he return, I wondered as I lay there, and what sort of entrance was the new member of Tonga's royal family making into this world?

Boom . . . a long, slow blast like thunder shook the room and echoed through the house. I shuddered apprehensively, wondering what could have caused it.

As if in answer to my thoughts, Farquhar opened the front door and crossed to the room where I lay. "Do you hear the cannon?" he asked. "It's to tell the people that Tonga has a new little princess."

Sensing the questions to come, he said rapidly, answering them before they had been asked, "Everything went off easily. Melenaite is well and the princess is a fine fat little baby."

Our royal calendar had begun with the newest possible event—the birth of the Princess Fusibala. It was to be continued by a glimpse into the most remote past.

One morning during our second week in Nuku-'alofa, Farquhar came in from his hospital rounds and told me that he and one of the TMPs (Tongan Medical Practitioners) were going out to Niutoua on the easternmost end of the island to visit a patient.

"You come, too," he said. "Peni says there are some interesting things for you to see and it's a fine day for a drive."

I needed no second invitation. Soon, sandwiched in between Farquhar and Peni, the TMP, I sat in a government land rover which rolled out of the hospital grounds and past the outskirts of Nuku'alofa into the countryside.

Tongatapu is everywhere very flat, but the landscape is not without interest. For one thing, there is the lagoon sunk deep in the island's side which gives endless views of reef and sea and breaking white surf. For another, there is the luxurious tangle of tropic vegetation with its verdant, glossy look of newness.

European towns built of wood and stone breathe antiquity, but Tongan villages with their woven reed houses which are built anew every year or so have all the freshness of a new creation. Indeed, the whole world seemed very young that sunny morning as we passed through one little village after another— Havelu, Bea, Vaini, Malapo, Alaki. But Peni talked to us as we went along and we learned that, belying its appearance, the land we drove through was Tonga's most historical country and that on this same bright earth had occurred in the long-distant past battles and stirring events which would live forever in Tongan memories.

"Here is Mu'a, the old capital," Peni announced as

we drove into a pleasant village at the edge of the lagoon. A limestone church built by the Catholics less than a hundred years ago which, weathered by tropic rains, looked as if long centuries had passed over it, seemed at first glimpse to be the only old thing about Mu'a—the only old thing, that is, except memories.

"Sometime in the early thirteenth century," Peni was saying, "there was a king called Tuitatu'i who lived out at the far end of the island near the present village of Niutoua where we'll be going later today. He had a beautiful place for his royal compound, but his daughter did not like it. She complained, always, saying that she could not sleep or rest there because the constant noise of the surf breaking on the shore disturbed her. At last, she asked her two brothers to build a house for her here by the lagoon. They did so and when their father died, they, too, came and lived here and after that for many years the kings of Tonga stayed in Mu'a.

"When the king's daughter died, her two brothers built for her the first of the 'langi,' the terrace tombs."

I had become so interested in what Peni was saying that I had not noticed we had turned off the main road until, suddenly, we jerked to a stop beside a clump of bushes.

"We'll have to walk the rest of the way," Peni said. "I'm taking you to see the BaeBae 'o Tele'a— that's the terrace tomb of King Tele'a. It was built some four hundred years after the first langi, which puts it about the beginning of the seventeenth century. In all of Tonga there are over forty terrace tombs. Most people think this is the finest of them all."

We followed Peni a short distance until the bush path ended in a clearing on the far side of which the langi rose in tiered terraces. Wild bush plants grew in the soil of each successive level as if nature had been trying to make the langi as fresh and new as the surrounding landscape. She had not succeeded, however. The langi's coral sides were no exception to the fact that coral, once it is away from the sea, weathers quickly into the most ancient-looking dull gray. In spite of the bravely bright plants, here at last was something old enough to match the distant memories of the people.

"It's like a pyramid without the top!" I exclaimed, and Farquhar called, "Come and look at these coral blocks on the side of the tomb."

As thick as a man's body and more than twice as long, the blocks which formed the facings of the terraces and the L-shaped corner pieces were monoliths of great size and weight.

Peni jumped up on the first terrace and sat facing us. "We Tongans used to believe that these blocks of coral were brought from faraway 'Uvea in the Wallis Islands in a big canoe," he said.

"But, Peni," I objected, "they couldn't have been. Look at the size of them. They wouldn't fit in any canoe and even if they did, they'd never get here safely from 'Uvea."

The TMP smiled good-naturedly. "Papalangis always object to that story," he said. "Some white scientists came down here and discovered that the type of coral in 'Uvea is not at all the same as this coral. Then they found places out on the Tongatapu reef where slabs like these had been cut; so we've had to give up believing the canoe story, too, which," he said regretfully, "is a pity because it was a good story."

"Wherever the coral came from," put in Farquhar, who had been examining the sharp, true edge of the terrace, "it was most skillfully cut."

"Yes," agreed Peni, "and remember, in those old days we had no knives or steel and had to work with tools made of wood and shell."

"And how do you suppose they got the slabs here once they had been cut?" I asked.

For that question Peni had a simple answer which everyone agrees must be the correct one. "I think," he said, "that they raised them onto logs and rolled them here. That's the way we move any heavy thing."

We lingered there for a while longer, pondering, as do people who see the pyramids for the first time, on the power of the old kings who could command such monuments to be built and on the endless hours of toil of the common people who worked on them. Then, once more we were in the land rover and Peni was driving us back to the main road and away from Mu'a which, since we had seen the langi, had become for us, as it is for the Tongans, truly the old capital.

On we went until we came to the little village of Niutoua at the eastern end of the island near where the noisy surf once disturbed the old king's daughter.

There we stopped in front of a neat house that stood
in the center of a garden hedged by bright shrubs.
"Here's where our patient lives," Peni said. While
he and Farquhar went in to make their examination,
I sat in the car holding a halting conversation with the
crowd of wide-eyed little children who seemed to
have appeared out of nowhere the minute we stopped.
They soon exhausted their small supply of English
and I had run out of Tongan, but that did not seem
to matter. They stayed on, and when Farquhar and
Peni, still discussing the case they had just seen, came
out again, they found me in the car with a staring
circle of silent children smiling at me.

"What are you staring at so much then?" Peni
shouted. His words recalled to them the fact that
uninhibited gaping is rude. Because they were little
Tongans, their sense of shame awoke and they slunk
away, but because they were little children, they
laughed as they went and some of the bolder ones
crept back and followed along behind when, presently,
the three of us walked across the road and down to
an open space in which stood the most famous of all
South Sea monuments, the trilithon known as the
Ha'amoga. Looking like a bit of Stonehenge trans-
planted to Polynesia, the gigantic arch is made of
three squared coral blocks which are said to weigh
forty tons each. The uprights stand about sixteen
feet above the ground and the crosspiece, let down
into perfectly cut notches, is some nineteen feet
in length.

I had learned the figures on the Ha'amoga in that
distant library where I was first fired by a desire to
come to Tonga. There, too, I had read some of the

stories told about it—the most amusing of which, perhaps, is that of the prankish young artist attached to Captain Cook's expedition who sketched it with great accuracy and then, to add a touch, drew a round tin basin on the middle of the crosspiece. For years scientific gentlemen on the other side of the world tried to fit that basin in with what they knew of Polynesian material culture. Their problem was never resolved until one of them took the trouble to come and see the Ha'amoga and discovered that the basin had never existed anywhere except in the young artist's fancy!

But there are mysteries enough about the Ha'amoga without fabricating new ones. It was built at the order of that same Tuitatu'i whose daughter loved the peace of the quiet lagoon at Mu'a. That fact has been preserved in Tongan memories since sometime around the year 1200 when Tuitatu'i ruled, but how it was built and why have been forgotten in the long years. Scientists believe that the heavy coral blocks were dragged up a heap of piled earth and dropped into position in much the same way that the stones of the Egyptian pyramids were set in place, but exactly where the stones were quarried and how the labor for transporting them was organized are still matters for conjecture.

One Tongan legend says that Tuitatu'i, in building the Ha'amoga with its heavy crosspiece borne by the two uprights, sought to show his two sons the harmony in which they, bearing equally the burdens of state, should live. A more modern guess is that it was built as a gateway to the royal compound. Yet another idea comes from 'Alo, the brilliant head of the TMPs who, having made a careful study of the position of the Ha'amoga, believes that, like the Egyptian pyramids and Stonehenge, it has astronomical significance. There is much to be said for his theory. Not only did the celestial bodies figure largely in early Tongan religion, but they had also a daily practical use for these people who constantly made long ocean voyages guided only by the stars.

Whatever its original purpose, the Ha'amoga has become today the symbol of Tonga—of her old power and of the loyalty with which her present-day people support her.

"Come," said Peni after a time, plunging into the tangle of bush behind the Ha'amoga. "There's something else down here." He led us over a path so overgrown that it was remembered rather than seen, to a place where a great block of coral rose out of the earth. "This was Tuitatu'i's sitting stone," he said.

"It doesn't look very comfortable," I said.

Peni laughed. "Perhaps not, but it gave him a sense of security which was very comforting. You see, he sat down on a mat on the ground and leaned his back against the stone and then no one could sneak up behind him and club him."

"And was there much danger of that?"

"There certainly was," Peni said. "Royal people didn't very often die on their sleeping mats in those days."

I had heard the boom of cannon welcoming the Princess Fusibala to this world and I had climbed to the top of the terrace tombs where the old kings lay buried. I had stood beside the Ha'amoga and marveled at it as so many other people have done, but still my zest for royal things was not sated. Day after day I walked from our house in the hospital grounds across the town to the beach beside which stands Queen Salote's palace, a two-story frame building in Victorian gingerbread style surrounded by spacious gardens which are shut off by nothing more forbidding than a low limestone wall which a child could easily climb. The main gate, opening on a hibiscus-edged road which leads straight to the palace verandah, was always open and through it passed an endless stream of Tongan men and women, all of whom wore, as a mark of their respect for the Queen, the waist mat. Watching them going in and out so freely, I was filled with envy. I wanted to follow them and wander about in the garden to see if I could catch a glimpse of the old chief. One day, I did see the little Princess Siuilikutapu, older sister of Fusibala, being carried about the grounds by her nurse, but that was the only sight of the palace people I ever had, though I peered over the wall into every shady nook as I passed.

At last, when my desire to walk inside that low walled garden had grown to an overwhelming urge, I remembered that I knew someone inside the palace who might help me. This was the Queen's social secretary, Ve'ehala, a merry-hearted young noble whom I had come to know in Vava'u. He had been staying there with his old schoolmate, Prince Tu'ipe-lehake, while the Queen was in New Zealand. Something of an antiquarian, he has made a study of old

Tongan dances, which he himself performs with a fluid grace. Anxious to pass on his knowledge, he used to come every afternoon to the college to teach a group of the girls an intricate and beautiful laka-laka. After their practice, he always stayed awhile to talk to the tutors and to me, and it was then that we had come to know each other. Still, it was not without misgiving that I took down the telephone receiver and asked the operator to give me Number One.

I had—to state an obvious truth—not been used to calling up palaces. When she repeated the number questioningly after me, I almost abandoned the project, but before I could hang up, I heard her ringing through. In another minute the phone was answered by Ve'ehala himself.

His voice, as friendly as ever, was so reassuring that it was not long before I had confided to him my great desire to come into the palace grounds to try to get a sight of the old resident.

"When would you like to come?" he asked.

"Why, whenever it's convenient," I replied.

"Then come along this morning, if you can," Ve'ehala said after a reference to the engagement book.

The Queen lives in the big old white palace beside the sea front and when the royal princes are in Nuku'alofa they live there, too, with their wives and families. There are those who say that Queen Salote is the boss of the palace, but there are others who claim that honor for the old chief, and they may be right; for I've heard it said that when he comes to the royal kava circle, she moves aside and lets him have whatever place he chooses even if it be her own. I've heard, too, that when, with the rudeness of the aged, he crosses her path or stops dead in front of her, she gives way gracefully and passes on with a smile or, if she has time, stops and says indulgently, "Well, good day, Tu'i Malila, and how are you?"

That is why I was so anxious to see Tu'i Malila. Ve'ehala quite understood my desire. The old chief has a fame that has spread far beyond the limits of this little kingdom.

"I saw him around by the chrysanthemums a while ago," Ve'ehala said as he came to meet me at the palace gate later that morning. Down the grassy hibiscus-edged road we went and into a little path that led to the ocean side of the gardens, but when we reached the chrysanthemums, there was no sign of the venerable old fellow we sought.

"Perhaps he's gone along to the ferns," Ve'ehala suggested. "He's fond of going there on a sunny day."

And that was where we found him. "Come, Tu'i Malila," said Ve'ehala, "and see the doctor's wife." But Tu'i Malila only blinked and shook his head and wandered slowly back to his beloved ferns. It wasn't much of a reception, but I was satisfied; for Tu'i Malila, the oldest of all the chiefs in Tonga, is not a man, but a land tortoise. He must be among the most ancient of living things. He was already full-grown when Captain Cook, who brought him to Tonga in 1777, presented him to a high chief of Tongatapu. Where he came from originally no one now knows, but certain it is that ever since he's been in Tonga he has enjoyed the highest honors—a title, a place at the royal kava circle, and the freedom of the palace gardens. Time has not, however, been entirely kind to him. Once he was caught in a bush fire and once a truck ran over him. He carries the marks of both disasters in his scarred and cracked old shell. Nowadays, he leads a quiet life wandering among the flowers or straying across the road to visit the palace neighbors.

There was a pleasant storybook feeling about walking in the sunny palace gardens with the handsome young noble at my side, but I had achieved the object of my visit. I had seen Tu'i Malila and now it was time for me to go. I began to bid Ve'ehala good-by, but he was speaking to me, saying words which seemed to come right out of the pages of an old romance.

"Her Majesty invites you and the doctor to lunch at her country estate at Kauvai on Thursday," he said. Thoughtfully he added, "Discuss the time with the doctor and if it is convenient, call and let me know."

Somehow I thanked him and covered the distance between the palace and the hospital office, where I burst in on Farquhar with the news. Much to my surprise, he did not receive it as joyfully as I had expected he would. Instead, he shook his head sadly and said, "I'm afraid you're going to be disappointed, but you can't possibly go. I've just been around to the *Hifofua* office and bought your return ticket for Vava'u. The boat sails Wednesday."

The days of June had run out almost imperceptibly, and now, indeed, it was time for me to be getting back to the college, but—

"What about the *'Aoniu?*" I cried. "Maybe I could go back on her and get there in time."

Farquhar shook his head again. "The *Hifofua* is your only chance," he said. "The *'Aoniu's* laid up and no one seems to know when the *Hifofua* will make another trip, either."

"And you're sure it sails on Wednesday?" I asked as if my questioning could somehow change the fact.

"Quite sure," Farquhar said with a note of finality. "Captain George was in the office and he said he'd had orders from the government to sail then."

I was resigned at last. "Well, that's that." I went off to call Ve'ehala to ask him to convey our regrets to the Queen.

When I had explained the situation to him, he said in what I thought a most unfeeling and offhand way, "Oh, that's too bad, but we'll see." I was still feeling deflated when, a couple of hours later, the phone rang. It was Ve'ehala again. "There will be a car at the hospital for you at 11:30 Thursday morning," he said, quite as if I hadn't already told him I couldn't come. Perhaps he had forgotten, I thought, and I cried, "But I'll be halfway to Vava'u by then. . . ."

"Her Majesty," he broke in, "asks me to tell you that the *Hifofua* will sail for Vava'u at ten o'clock on Friday morning."

"What?" I asked, and then as his meaning came to me and I knew that we would be able to go to Kauvai after all, "Oh, thank you," I called and ran off to tell Farquhar.

Whether the sailing had been postponed for some routine reason or whether the Queen did not like to have her social engagements upset, we had, that day, the feeling that Higher Powers had intervened in our behalf—and a pleasant, exciting feeling it was, too.

Thursday morning found Farquhar in the long white trousers, starched coat, and neat tie which here in Tonga are a man's "dress up" clothes. I had put on my newest frock and done my hair with more than usual care and was still running in to look at the mirror every few minutes to see if I was "all right" when, punctually at 11:30, the car arrived.

For a while we followed the same way we had taken when we went to the Ha'amoga, but long before we reached Mu'a, we turned off onto a well-kept side road that led through neat groves of coconuts. A short distance brought us to an opening beyond which lay the calm blue waters of the lagoon. In the center of the clearing was a large Tongan house which was so beautifully proportioned and so skillfully woven that it gave me the keen sense of pleasure which I feel for any fine work of art. In the old days, the majority of houses in Tongan villages must have evoked in their beholders that same delight. Now, alas! that is no longer true. Here, as elsewhere in the world, the old crafts are dying out. Most of the people do still live in Tongan houses, but they spend little time and less care over building them; for everyone dreams of living in a frame house with a tin roof and is apt to regard his woven reed house with its thatch roof as a mere makeshift.

We had, however, little time to admire the house

or to philosophize about the changing trends in local architecture. As the car came to a stop, the door of the house opened and the Queen, her face wreathed in smiles of welcome, came out to us. Barefooted and clad simply in a quiet dress topped by an old cardigan, she was the easiest and most natural hostess imaginable.

"Come in, come in," she said, and her clear rich voice fairly singing with friendliness drove away the last bit of uneasiness we had felt about being in the company of royalty.

In Nuku'alofa, Queen Salote's life is no more her own than is that of any other ruler. There she belongs to Tonga, and all her waking hours are spent in its service. That she is a loyal and unselfish worker for the good of her people everyone here knows well—but every now and then queens, like more ordinary people, want a change and feel the need of "just being themselves." Her favorite spot at such times is Kauvai, for which she cherishes the same affection and the same pride that any householder feels for the place he calls home.

When I told her we had been admiring the building, she smiled with delight and, drawing us inside, pointed up to the high, perfectly arched roof whose beams were tied with coconut-fiber rope and covered with a thick thatch. "Twenty years and more that has been on and never leaked and never needed renewing," she said.

The house is, in reality, a combination of Tongan and European styles for it has glass windows and timber doors and floors, but the structure itself is purely Polynesian of the sort sometimes referred to as "bird-cage architecture." With its high roof and its twisted reed sides, it does somewhat resemble a gigantic bird's cage—certainly it is so delightfully light and airy that it has all the advantages of one.

Divided into two chambers by a low partition overhung by a native curtain woven of fau thread (a raffialike fiber made from a variety of hibiscus), studded with thousands of the tan and brown shells which are found on the beaches of distant Niuatoputapu in the far north of Tonga, Kauvai's furnishings also reflect both native and papalangi cultures. There are fine mats on the floor, but there is a European-style bed in the smaller room and European chairs and tables and sofas in the larger room. The general effect of the furnishings—as of the house itself—is Polynesian. They are plain and do nothing to detract from the basic simplicity and spaciousness of the place.

We went first into the bedroom where we left our things and then followed the Queen into the living room. There she sat down on a little sofa and, patting the empty space beside her, said to me, "Come and sit here so we can talk."

I had no sooner sat down than I heard behind us a sound as if some small animal were scratching his claws on the upholstery. I suppose I must have jumped involuntarily; for the queen laid her hand on mine and said with a laugh, "It's only my grandson, Taufa Ahau. He's feeling shy today." She leaned back and called softly in Tongan, "Come, Taufa, come." A minute or two passed and a little boy's brown face loomed up over the arm of the sofa. A pair of bright, dark eyes peered at me, turned away, and stared at Farquhar. I don't know how Farquhar looked at Taufa. His years of medical practice which have taught him a secret or two about driving fear and shyness out of children may have come to his aid. At any rate, it wasn't long before a very active little boy scampered out and crossed the room to him. Although Farquhar's Tongan was fragmentary and Taufa had not yet learned to talk, they seemed to come quickly to an understanding. Soon there were peals of laughter coming from the two of them.

"And here is Taufa's mother, Mata'aho," the Queen was saying. I looked up and saw standing before me a handsome young woman with a clear olive skin, straight shiny black hair, and a graceful bearing. She smiled and spoke and her voice and her manners reflected the gentleness of the kindly Vava'u nuns who had educated her; for Mata'aho, the wife of Crown Prince Tungi, comes from a Vava'u family. Perhaps it was that fact which created a bond between us. I do not know; but I was, from the very beginning, drawn to the charming young woman whom I have come to know better than any other member of the royal family.

That day at Kauvai, the Queen and Mata'aho and I talked of many things and Farquhar joined in the conversation whenever he could spare a minute from the endless games in which he and Taufa were engaged. We spoke of old Tongan customs and new American outboard motors, of books and clothes and of the many similarities between Highland clans and

Polynesian tribes. And always our talk was mingled
with the rich, full laughter of the Queen who, fond
and loving grandmother that she is, kept looking
across the room to see what new pranks her little
Taufa was up to.

After a time, a pretty young maid in waiting
entered the room and, bending low, approached the
Queen and announced that lunch was ready. Kauvai,
like most Tongan houses, is built in separate units.
We left the main building and, crossing over a
stretch of grass, came to the dining house—an open
structure with a thatched coconut-fiber roof. The
walls on three sides were hung with tapa, but the
fourth was left open, giving an unobstructed view
of the lagoon whose waves lapped gently at the shore
only a few feet away. The main building had been a
mixture of Tongan and European things; this dining
house was entirely Tongan. Its floor was covered with
fine mats, down the center of which had been placed
a "pola," or woven coconut stretcher, filled with all
the foods for a feast—pig and chickens, fish and yam,
kumalas and bananas.

Queen Salote took her place at the head of the
pola and the rest of us grouped ourselves around her
at its sides. Taufa and Farquhar, as is proper for men,
sat cross-legged while we women had drawn our legs
modestly to one side. I had often heard it said that
the Queen was most skillful at organizing feasts.
That day at Kauvai I learned that she owed her
reputation—as indeed fine hostesses everywhere do—
to an infinite concern with detail. The meal, whose
preparation she had herself supervised, was perfectly

cooked. We ate it, as Tongan meals are always eaten, with our fingers, but there were little pricks made from the midribs of the coconut frond with which we could spear succulent pieces of meat or hot vegetables and there were tapa cloth napkins to wipe our hands on. Pretty serving girls who knelt beside us carved the pigs and chickens and sliced the vegetables with an amazing deftness. They kept the fresh banana leaves which served us as plates well filled and fanned us with scented fans which filled the air with fragrance. When we had finished eating from the pola, they brought coconut-shell finger bowls and tapa towels and we washed our hands. Then there was fruit salad served in polished, intricately cut coconut shells which we ate with little shell spoons.

Just as we were finishing, one of the serving girls knelt behind me and fastened about my neck a lei woven of small waxy red flowers which gave a strong sweet perfume. "This is the necklace the Queen gives to all her guests," she whispered in my ear, and the Queen herself said, "We call that little flower the heilala. It has always been a chiefly flower here in Tonga and many poems have been written about it."

Late that afternoon, with Kauvai far behind us, Farquhar and I drove back to Nuku'alofa. The town was already deep in shadow, but the fragrant heilala lei glistened on my neck and our minds glowed with the memory of that day which for us both was the climax of our stay on the royal island of Tongatapu.

8 A Swimming Story

Farquhar had spoken of our journey to Nuku'alofa as a wedding trip, and with all the time we had had together and all the royal events we had shared, it had turned out to be the finest sort of honeymoon. It had only one flaw, but that was a serious one. The bride had to come home alone. When it was time for me to return to the college, there had been no word of a new doctor for Nuku'alofa so I had to sail away from Farquhar with the unhappy knowledge that it might be long months until I saw him again. It was, as a matter of fact, five months before he was again free to return to Vava'u. All during that time, whenever a boat came up from Nuku'alofa, I ran to the post office looking for his letters which were little bridges to help me over the separation. The time without him seemed very long, but it would not be quite accurate to say that I was lonely; for that's an impossible emotion for anyone who lives in the midst of a hundred lively girls.

Back at the college, I plunged into the usual busy round of teaching which left me little time to bemoan the fact that half my first year of marriage was being spent without a husband. We followed the curriculum prescribed by the mission authorities, with one addition which I had made soon after I first arrived—a swimming class. My stern predecessor had found no place for swimming on the college schedule and the authorities, who were suspicious of all innovations, opposed it for that reason, but I felt the girls needed some active recreation and it didn't seem right that so much fine blue Pacific water as there was in the harbor should be going to waste when my hundred girls might be splashing happily in it; so I held out until I won.

On two afternoons a week, anyone who chanced to be looking could see, winding through the streets of Neiafu, the long serpentine of college swimmers. In matters of dress, Tonga has never recovered from the prudery which is part of its legacy from the early missionaries, who considered the human body quite the most shameful thing the Creator ever made. Consequently, the girls were clad, not in the brief bathing suits that we wear, nor yet in the still more abbreviated grass skirts which rustle through white men's dreams of the South Seas, but in their everyday tunic dresses and ankle-length skirts. Some of them, to be sure, did wear grass skirts, but they were only the apronlike things which young ladies of Tonga put over their other clothes when they wish to be really well dressed.

On the way down to swimming, then, the girls looked no different than they would have, had they merely been out for a stroll, but on their return what a sight they were! Sodden skirts flapped about their

feet while soaking dresses clung to firm young bodies,
outlining and emphasizing their full curves in a way
that would have scandalized a worthy early missionary. Their hair, which on the way down to the sea was
carefully bound in neat braids, on the trip back to
the college escaped and hung in wet confusion about
their shoulders or stood up at right angles like
Fijian hair.

Yet, in spite of their bedraggled appearance, I
always felt particularly happy when I walked along
with the swimming-class girls; for it seemed as if the
sea had washed away their mission-bred coat of smug
propriety and turned them into the gay wild things
that young people have a right to be. Even after the
girls were back in the classroom and the last of the
giggles was suppressed, I could detect the value of
the swimming period; for they no longer sat, as they
had when I first came to the college, like docile lumps
of dark clay. Instead they struggled to bring to their
studies the same animation and energy they had
given to their play.

From a teacher's point of view, the swimming class
was very easy; it involved no teaching at all. Teen-
aged Polynesians just don't have to be taught to
swim. As babies in their island homes, they begin to
lead amphibious lives and forever after water is as
much their element as earth. Still, a hundred girls,
suddenly let free in the sea, need some supervision.
Therefore, when I decided to take the college swimming, I told the tutors they would have to come along
to help and I assigned two or three of them to each
class. Sometimes they swam with the girls, but some-

times, with the self-consciousness of adults trying to be different, they would stand on the wharf and merely watch over them.

On one particular sunny day, the eighteen-year-old Fusi, who was the youngest of the tutors, and Sesa, who rather prided herself on being the prettiest of them, were two who chose to stand on the wharf while Pita, the man of the staff, to whom the swimming class was the happiest of duties, splashed in and out of the water with the careless abandon of one of the flying fish whose silvery leaps break through the blue ripples of the harbor water. To the importunate pleadings of the girls who called them to "Come on in," Fusi and Sesa turned deaf ears. Ordinarily they would both have enjoyed a swim, but not on that particular day; for, as it happened, each of them had on a new dress and each fancied that, from the wharf, she showed herself and her dress to great advantage. Yes, and each of them hoped that Pita who, it must be said, was an exceptionally handsome young man, would admire her. So there they stood together under the shade of a big black umbrella exchanging a soft flow of gossip which they pretended was their only interest.

With new dresses and beguiling looks, Pita was completely unconcerned. He was still in the first proud period when a man, though he break a hundred hearts and make countless sighs echo on the air, never, himself, spends so much as a second's anguish in wondering how some beloved girl will greet him, what favors she will admit and what deny. That is not to say that he was by any means insensitive to

feminine adoration, but merely that he was not yet
ready to suffer for it. For the time, the flattery of the
college girls satisfied his vanity and contented him
wholly. For them he swam with quick, sure strokes
far out to the distant buoy and, when he returned,
without so much as stopping to catch his breath,
climbed to the top of the wharf, stood for an instant
exhibiting his arrow-slim body, and then, in a swift
perfect dive, plunged himself back into the midst of
the admiring girls.

It was only after he had gone through that exhibi-
tion a dozen times or so and had begun to feel the
need of a moment's rest that Pita lingered long
enough among the swimming girls to be aware of their
pleas to Fusi and Sesa to come in. He looked up then,
and seeing the two young tutors on the wharf above
him, observed their preoccupied chattering, observed,
too, the shy half-smiles on their lips which he found,
as it was intended that he should, provocative.

"The water's good," he shouted. "Come on in." And
he gave them a broad smile and waved a wet brown
hand at them.

By way of reply, they smiled politely, turned their
backs, and set to gossiping more busily than ever.

Now, Pita was not used to having girls turn their
backs on him; so perhaps it was wounded vanity
which spurred him on or perhaps it was some mischievous Polynesian devil which took possession of
him. At any rate, before another minute had passed,
he whispered something to the girls closest to him
which sent them into gales of laughter.

"Watch Pita dive," they screamed to their distant

companions. "Watch Pita dive." By the time he had scrambled to the top of the wharf all eyes were on him—all, of course, except Fusi's and Sesa's. They gossiped on quite unconcerned by all the excitement, although I did hear Fusi say, "Foolish boy," and I did hear Sesa reply, "Showing off his good swimming."

If Pita heard them, he gave no sign of it; for he stood as he had done before, poised on the edge of the wharf, ready to dive. Suddenly he gave a triumphant shout, leapt into the air, made a twisted sideways lunge toward Fusi and Sesa, and with one quick, strong motion pushed them both—new dresses, gossip, umbrella and all—into the water below.

A hundred shouts of glee went up from the girls and everyone burst into laughter. And I who should have represented decorum and propriety laughed with the rest, for never had I seen a show of indifference so completely and so quickly upset. Yes, everyone laughed and Pita most of all, and everyone laughed twice as hard when Fusi, spluttering with fury, clambered dripping back onto the wharf. When she stamped her foot and turned on Pita, shouting angrily, "Bad man, man like an animal," everyone roared—everyone, that is, except Pita, who saw in her dark eyes a fire that made him suddenly burn with shame and remorse.

But laughter and shame and remorse all gave way in the next minute to fear, for Sesa did not climb angrily up the wharf as Fusi had done. She did not climb up at all, but hung limply to the bottom of the ladder, gasping, "I'm almost drowned. Help! I'm almost drowned."

Now, I knew very well that people who are almost drowned rarely feel up to mentioning it; yet, by the time Sesa had been hoisted up onto the wharf by the pushing and shoving of a dozen frightened girls, the hysteria of the group had infected me. However, I did my best to hide the anxiety I felt as I knelt beside her to examine her.

I was able to dismiss at once all possibility of drowning. As she lay on the wharf, her breath, though it escaped from her body in great groans as if she were torn by some tremendous emotion, came regularly enough.

"She's very pale!" a second-form girl whispered into my ear.

"I don't think so," I replied firmly, although I was not then sufficiently used to brown faces to know whether she was or not.

"Her hands are dead," Pita gasped in horror.

I started in alarm at the expression and stared at her hands. They looked dead enough, for they hung unmoving at her sides, but when I felt them, they were reassuringly warm and the pulse was as regular as my own.

I felt my calm returning and when I glanced at her eyelids which fluttered ever so slightly over her tightly shut eyes, I stood up and said quietly, "She's all right, but we must get her back to the college. Then she must lie down."

"I can't walk," Sesa wailed, breaking her silence.

"Of course not," I agreed, although I had begun to suspect she could walk as well as anyone. "Of course not, but you can stand and someone can carry you."

"I'll carry her," the chastened Pita volunteered, but Sesa shook her head and wept.

"No, no," she cried. "Don't let him come near me. He almost drowned me." Pita flushed with shame and slunk away. In the end, some of the older girls made a chair of their hands and started back to the college with her. The trip was slow, for Sesa sighed and gasped and said her heart hurt. At regular intervals, she feared she would faint and begged the carriers to go more gently, but at last the dripping procession reached the college.

By that time, I more than suspected that Sesa was making the most of her troubles. Still, I felt very uncertain of my own medical knowledge and very sure of my responsibility to the college; so I sent off a note to the hospital to Lutui, the head TMP whom Farquhar had assured me would help with any college health problems arising in his absence.

When Lutui arrived, Sesa had been dried and put to bed, but she'd been put to bed in no ordinary way. The girls, who, like schoolgirls everywhere, loved a dramatic situation, had made the most of this one. They had dressed her in Mele Seini's new pink silk nightgown with lace ruffles and at her head they had put a pillow covered with embroidered roses and violets through which, in fancy yellow feather-stitch, twined the motto, *Love Is All.* Her hands, still limp, were being rubbed with Tongan oil by two girls from the third class, while a very proud little thing from the second was fanning her face with a fan fringed with white chicken feathers. At the foot of the bed sat Emili, the music tutor, strumming a guitar and singing softly in her husky, melodious voice while all around sat groups of girls gossiping away at a great rate in an effort to entertain their poor Sesa.

It was to such a sickbed that I showed Lutui. As he entered with his stethoscope dangling professionally from his hand, the gossip died away to a whisper and only the most muted chords escaped from the guitar. He sat beside the bed and took Sesa's pulse and listened to her heart. He asked a few questions and left without breaking the atmosphere of somber quiet which he had brought with him. Not until he was back in my office did his stern face relax and break into smiles.

"She's quite all right," he said reassuringly.

"But her heart?" I asked. "What of that? She complained of pains there."

Lutui laughed aloud. "Hm!" he said. "Maybe her heart aches, but it's not the sort of ache the Medical Department cures." Then he added, "No, there's nothing wrong with Sesa at all."

"You mean," I asked in relief, "that she's really quite well? That there are absolutely no bad effects from her having been pushed into the sea?"

"None at all," said Lutui.

"Then she could get up if she liked?"

"Of course, she could. She's quite as well as you or I."

Lutui got up to go then, but before he left, he turned back to me. He had studied his own people and now he gave me a bit of advice out of his knowledge. "Nothing's wrong," he said, "but I shouldn't try to make her get up just yet anyway. When we Tongans decide to be sick, we're going to be sick no matter what any doctor or TMP says. Probably Sesa has her own reasons for pretending to be sick. You'd only wear yourself out trying to make her get up."

I smiled my thanks to the clever young TMP and I took his advice; for I was vastly more interested in observing people than in reforming them. And observing was fun in the week that followed!

First, there was Pita's formal call of apology. He came to see me that very night as I was sitting alone correcting the fifth form's English compositions. I noticed, as he entered the room, that he was dressed in fresh white clothes and that he wore the trim waist mat without which no Tongan man is formally dressed. I realized that this was for him a very serious occasion, indeed.

"Yes, Pita," I said, trying to make my words sound friendly so that he would feel at ease.

But Pita could feel no ease. He reddened and began in his slow, painful English to speak. "I have done a very wrong thing," he said. "1 am ashamed. I ask you to be patient and forgive me. I am shamed before Fusi and Sesa, before you and all the college, I am ashamed."

Again and again the words of humiliation and contrition poured from him until I longed only to comfort him. The foolishness of what he had done I readily conceded. I even managed to speak a bit sternly of the duties of a tutor as an example of good behavior to the girls, but I ended by telling him that —inasmuch as Lutui had said there was nothing

seriously wrong with Sesa and as Fusi had been all
right from the beginning—it was all just an unfortu-
nate incident that we would forget.

Pita thanked me profusely for my kindness and
understanding, but, if Sesa was not to be talked out
of her sickness, neither was he to be separated from
his shame. For months he wore it, a gentle mantle of
solemnity which, by making him slightly mysterious,
only increased the attraction he held for the girls.

During all the next week, the whole college routine
was upset; for Sesa announced, from one day to the
next, that she really felt too weak to get up to teach.
Pita, eager to make amends, volunteered to take her
classes. Manfully he struggled through periods of
drawing and domestic science which, added to his
own hours of mathematics and history, were a heavy
burden.

Once a day he asked my permission to visit Sesa
at her bedside and once a day I gave the permission;
although it came to my knowledge that the visits were
a sore trial to Pita. Sesa, it seems, developed a great
horror of him. She really couldn't bear to see him at
all, but she graciously allowed him to sit each day
for a miserable half hour on the floor beside her
bed. When the girls, observant young creatures that
they were, noticed that, in spite of her expressed
dislike of Pita, she always combed and braided her
hair and rubbed oil scented with the heady sweet
mohokoi flower on her body just before the time of
his daily visit, they accused her of loving him. She
giggled then and looked coy; but when they turned

and teased Pita, he merely bowed his head, already
bent beneath so much shame.

Naturally, from such a beginning, the story grew
that Sesa and Pita were most devoted to each other.
The college girls, liking nothing better than a romantic tale, wove the story into a beautiful idyl which
always ended in a great and wonderful wedding with
Sesa and Pita dressed in so many fine mats they
could scarcely move and enough fat pigs at the feast
to feed all the college and everyone else in Vava'u
too.

But schoolgirl dreams are schoolgirl dreams, and
life rarely follows the pattern they set. And a good
thing, too, I thought to myself a year later, as I got
dressed for Pita's wedding; for what, after all, would
a nice young man like him want with a silly giggling
wife like Sesa who pretended to be sick whenever she
wanted her own way? What would Pita want with
a wife who lay back and let him do her work as well
as his own?

Didn't Pita marry Sesa then? you ask, and if he
didn't, what has happened to the story? It has been
going on behind our backs. Well, most stories do
go on behind their readers' backs, but remember,
please, that Pita pushed not one tutor, but two off
the wharf. Fusi was the name of the other one—or of
the one that came up spluttering in fury. Naturally
Pita didn't have much to do with her; for what can
a man have to do with a woman who shouts at him
and stamps her foot and says he behaves like an
animal? And, of course, his attention wasn't drawn

to her as it was to Sesa. No, for Fusi, in spite of her ducking, was quite capable of teaching her own classes, thank you, and she needed no help from anyone. Only once during the remainder of that year did Pita ask me for permission to go into the women's study and speak to Fusi. I granted his request and ten minutes later Fusi came storming into my office demanding with flaming face that she be consulted before "foolish men" were sent to talk to her.

And that is all I, who was right there all the time, knew of the affair between Fusi and Pita until I got the invitation to their wedding. It is all anyone knew; for they were both shy young things and whatever they said to one another they said in private.

And one thing more. As I went through the crowded churchyard, I heard Sesa entertaining a group of girls with tales of her romances. They laughed and asked her why she had lost Pita.

"Oh," she said, with a toss of her head, "Pita. I could have had him if I'd wanted him." But we all knew better.

9 At Home in 'Utulei

With Farquhar away in Nuku'alofa and the college making so many demands on my time, I did not attempt to live in our house, but kept on in my little cottage on the college grounds in Neiafu. Only now and again, on holidays or at weekends, did I find time to cross over to 'Utulei. Then, if I felt ambitious, I would dig a bit in the garden and if I felt lazy, I would sit on the verandah and read or merely sit and watch the traffic of Vava'u passing up and down the harbor. Somewhere in my subconscious, I must have realized that the house itself presented problems too great to be solved in a bit of spare time; for I passed quickly through the inside, giving the rooms only the most casual of glances.

Not until December, after Farquhar had returned to Vava'u and my year of teaching was over, did we really begin to live in our own house. The moving itself was simple. Farquhar's possessions were already there, and I had only my clothes and the few books and pictures which I had had at the college to take over. But the moving was the merest beginning. When we came to look critically, we saw that, like

113

most European-style houses in Tonga, ours was merely a shell. True, in the few months that he had lived there before we were married, Farquhar had had men in to line the rooms, so there were walls everywhere. There was little else. The place was completely lacking in closets, shelves, and cupboards. Fortunately there were plenty of doors and windows, but unfortunately no two of them matched and, as for the floors, they would not have done credit to a barn.

The furniture situation was little better. The kitchen, containing a wood-burning stove, a kerosene refrigerator, and an ant-proof meat safe, was adequately outfitted. The bathroom was also satisfactory, but the other rooms were woefully bare, and the big central room that looked more like an untidy railway station than the dining and living rooms it eventually became was furnished with nothing except the papers, boxes, and miscellaneous rubbish which always seem to accumulate in empty rooms.

Our first reaction to our home was one of complete helplessness. As city dwellers, both Farquhar and I always before had lived in houses or apartments which, though they may not have been ideal dwellings, were so complete in themselves that it never would have occurred to anyone to hammer a shelf into their well-finished walls or destroy a room's symmetry by knocking up a cupboard. If alterations had been required, there was always a corps of plumbers, painters, decorators, carpenters, and miscellaneous handy men no farther away than the telephone. In

Vava'u the situation was not so simple. There were no telephones and even if there had been, we couldn't have called a host of workers. The workers we needed simply didn't exist in Tonga. After all, people who live in houses of woven coconut fronds wouldn't have much use for them.

Fate was kind to us, however, and we discovered in Neiafu one good carpenter, a kindly old Norwegian named Jack Hoel who had lived in Vava'u ever since, as a mere lad captivated by the islands, he had jumped ship here. Saws and planes fitted naturally into his hands and he had a rare ability for transforming a pile of rough lumber into well-finished necessary objects. When he had done the jobs we gave him, the library had proper shelves, our bedrooms had a wonderful series of wardrobe closets, there was a storage cupboard in the kitchen, and the big main room was divided into dining and living areas by a central line of shelves and drawers. In the living room was a large L-shaped sofa big enough so we could both lie down and read at night, and beside it, to hold our books and our teacups, an L-shaped coffee table.

With such a sizable chunk of the work done, we felt encouraged to go on. Perhaps because we were greatly inspired by the joy which old Mr. Hoel had taken in the objects he had created with his hands, we tried to do for ourselves many things which in the days when we lived in cities, we would never have dreamed of doing. Perhaps our helplessness merely disappeared because there is no place for such futile feelings in Vava'u. At any rate, Farquhar and I emerged soon as designers, decorators, carpenters, and general handy men.

We stuffed pads for the L-shaped sofa with the springy fiber that surrounds ripe coconuts and teased kapok that bursts furry from its pods on trees growing all around the village, for bed and sofa pillows. The floors we stained with the dye of mangrove bark or covered with the beautiful mats which our neighbors weave. Bedspreads and draperies were made of tapa, the clean, earthy-smelling cloth which Polynesians beat out from the bark of the paper mulberry tree and decorate with the rich, deep colors made from native plants—brown of the koka tree, red of mangrove, black of candlenut.

As time went on, our library grew and Farquhar, who had acquired a good workable collection of tools and taught himself to use them, made new shelves. Barrels of things I had collected long ago arrived from California, and there were presents from Farquhar's family in Scotland and from friends everywhere, and soon what had been the shell of a house assumed the familiar lines of our comfortable home.

There was work to be done outside, too, for, although the garden contained breadfruit trees, avocados, custard apples and lemons which were all very welcome when it came to solving the food problem, it was completely devoid of flowers or other ornamental plants. Its barrenness was due to the fact that in 'Utulei, as in all outlying villages in Tonga, pigs are allowed the freedom of the town and wander about rooting wherever they please. Consequently, the first step in making a garden was to build a strong fence, for nothing—hot wind or rain or drought or all the host of sucking and biting and chewing insects—can do so much damage to growing plants as a single little pig let loose for an hour or two.

When the whole place was fenced, we set off a smaller area for a vegetable garden, and there I tried for a couple of years to grow everything that flourishes in California. The results were dismal, to say the least. What seeds the ants didn't carry away burst forth in spindly stems and sick-colored leaves which waved impotently in the breezes for a while and then collapsed. Nowadays, taught by experience, I have resigned myself to planting native vegetables and only such exotics as have been proved in the tropics. The garden has rewarded me by growing almost as well as the vegetable gardens which sprout in the pages of seed catalogues.

Another small area we wired off for a chicken yard. It was no sooner completed than the kindly people of the village came down. "A chicken yard needs chickens," they said as, one by one, they presented us with hens and roosters to start our flock. Their gifts and the solicitous care we lavished on them have not, alas! sufficed to give us a fowl run to brag about. Tongan chickens are a deceptive fluff of feathers. When they are plucked and ready for the table, they are a pile of bones held together by a few stringy shreds of flesh. As for laying eggs, they do it so infrequently that one almost suspects them of having discovered a new way to reproduce their kind.

The rest of the garden was more immediately re-

warding. Generally speaking, tropical plants grow
quickly and bloom generously. I was delighted to
discover that I could grow in my garden so many
flowers I had formerly seen flourishing only in hot-
houses or in florists' windows. Tu'ifua comes from a
family of garden lovers who, as the Tongans say, have
"living hands." She kept me supplied with an endless
stream of cuttings, bulbs, and little plants. There
were branches of frangipani—fragrant white and
delicate pink—cut from her Aunt Vaea's trees, big
white gardenias from her own home and little native
ones from the bush, jasmine and bouvardia from her
cousin Lose's and from friends, shell ginger and red
ginger and a whole host of lilies for which I know no
names except their Tongan ones.

For everything I found a place, and Farquhar, who
suffers from a sort of vegetable claustrophobia which
makes him fear he'll wake up some morning to find
himself trapped in a jungle of my planting, groaned
audibly every time he saw Tu'ifua and me going
toward the garden. The things grew over his objections, but honesty compels me to admit it is perhaps
fortunate that I agreed to respect his wishes when
it came to trees. Had I not done so, his dire predic-
tions that we would have to move the house to
make way for the garden might well have come true,
since Tongan trees never seem to know when to
stop growing.

If I have given the impression that, after a period
of effort, we achieved the perfect house set in the
perfect garden, I have been misleading. Our house is
a good one that grows and changes along with us,

but in it, as in us, there is never-ending room for
improvement. As far as the garden goes, along with
the vegetables and the flowers it brings a full set
of emotions: disappointment when a sudden wind
breaks a favorite tree, frustration when too little
rain dries out new seeds or too much rots them, joy
when all the red lilies burst into fiery bloom at once,
and hope that the endless tiny green shoots will grow
into sturdy plants. Like all living things, it is always
beginning and never finished.

House and garden, important though they are,
were only a small part of getting settled in 'Utulei. To
move into a village all of whose inhabitants belong
to a race and a culture very different from one's own
is to move to another world. Unless one is prepared
to understand the people and to try to see life from
their point of view as well as from one's own,
happiness is quite impossible. Even when one has,
as both Farquhar and I had, the best intentions, it
is a bit of a job settling in; for houses are far easier
to arrange than minds, and gardens can be changed
with less trouble than habits.

In the beginning, I found it very difficult to get
acquainted with my neighbors in 'Utulei. That
they were filled with kindly feelings for us was
obvious. Scarcely a day passed that one or another
of them didn't come down with a yam, a ripe pine-
apple, a bunch of bananas, or some other food gift.
When we walked along the beach, the men and women
we met smiled and greeted us politely, but they
always passed by quickly and seemed to have no
desire to enter into conversation.

Somewhere in the back of my mind, I suppose, I had expected that the people of this little Tongan village would come to call as people in small towns at home would have done, but no one came. When we had been here several months, and had been left strictly to ourselves, I began to feel that the village must have taken a dislike to us. One day I voiced my fears to Tu'ifua. She laughed and asked, "How could they dislike you? They don't know you well enough to know if they like you or not."

"That's just the trouble," I agreed, "but they don't even want to know us. They never come or—"

"Naturally they wouldn't come to see you," she said. "They're ashamed to come."

"Ashamed! Why?"

"Why, because Farquhar is the doctor and you are rich papalangis."

"But we're not rich papalangis!" I exclaimed. "As a matter of fact, we're rather poor ones."

In the years that have followed, I have been able to convince Tu'ifua that money is something which has to be considered carefully in this house, but at that time she shared the almost universal Tongan belief that all white men possess unlimited capital. They regard money as a papalangi invention and innocently suppose we all come supplied with endless amounts of it.

Then Tu'ifua only said, "Well, rich or not, your husband is the doctor, and you are papalangis."

"And what's wrong with that?" I asked belligerently.

"Nothing at all," she replied soothingly, "but the

doctor is important to Vava'u and papalangis—well, you know, sometimes they are very proud of themselves and don't like to talk to Tongans."

"But we're not like that," I protested.

"No, I know you're not," she said, "but the village people aren't sure about you yet, and they are ashamed to start talking."

The Tongan sense of shame, such an incomprehensible thing to newcomers who only desire to be friendly with the people, is no doubt partly a result of the haughty attitude adopted by those white men who still feel their fair skin gives them an automatic ascendency over all dark peoples. Tongans are proud of their country and proud of their Polynesian blood. Like all proud people, having been snubbed once, they are reluctant to expose themselves again.

However, the complete explanation of this, to us, unnatural shyness is not to be traced to white arrogance. Its roots go much deeper—far into the age-old social structure of the Polynesians. Noble, chief, or commoner one was born in the old days and, but for the rarest exceptions, noble, chief, or commoner one died. The rigid stratification of society was maintained by the abject awe with which each man regarded all those who were of higher rank than himself and by the duties imposed on him by his superiors. That men allowed themselves to be trapped in the ranks in which they were born was due, in Tonga, as it has been elsewhere in the world, partly to police power and partly to the paralyzing effects of their religious beliefs. Chiefs and nobles were surrounded with guards whose spears and war clubs could quickly change a rebel's mind. An even more potent weapon in the hands of the mighty was the old Polynesian religion. It taught in the genealogies that all the great families of the land were the direct descendants of one or another of the gods. Naturally enough, no ordinary man would risk divine displeasure by rising against a member of a god's family, since although the old Polynesian gods were sometimes quite pleasant and helpful in their dealings with mortals, they were, when provoked, like the Old Testament Jehovah, quick to wrath and speedy to seek revenge.

An unending sense of inferiority was also given commoners by the teaching that, lacking souls, they found in death nothing but complete annihilation while their chiefs and nobles went on to enjoy the society of the gods in Pulotu, the Polynesian afterworld.

Nowadays all Tongans, commoners included, look forward to spending their afterlife in that greatest of all democracies—the Christian heaven. In the meantime, their earthly condition is considerably improved, although chiefs and nobles still have a great deal of control over the lives of commoners. The old feelings of subservience and awe persist to an extent that is difficult for one who was born and bred in a modern democracy to realize. Because white people —especially those who, like Farquhar, work for the government—are treated as chiefs, they, too, are shown a great amount of respect; and commoners keep their distance until they are convinced that their society is really wanted.

When Tu'ifua had made me understand this background of Tongan "shame," I realized that, if we were ever to become a part of 'Utulei, it was up to us to make the first move.

Accordingly, the next day I walked up to the village. When I saw 'Ugatea sitting under a tree weaving a basket, I walked over to her and said in the proper Tongan manner, "Thank you for weaving."

She looked up at me and smiled and replied, "Yes, thank you for walking up here."

The conversation could easily have ended there, but because I was determined not to let it do so, I mumbled something about how hot it was.

"Very hot," 'Ugatea agreed. Then, jumping up and spreading out the mat on which she had been sitting, she invited me to sit down and rest. I did so and begged her to sit down again, too, and go on with her weaving. After a bit of persuasion, she came and sat beside me, but her weaving made little progress. Once having decided that I really had come for a friendly visit, she lost her shyness and devoted all her attention to me.

Our talk proceeded slowly, and there were many gaps which had to be filled in with reassuring smiles, since 'Ugatea had no English and my Tongan was still very sketchy. Still, in our first conversation, we learned a great deal about each other.

"How old are you?" she asked by way of a beginning.

The question seemed rather an abrupt one with which to start off, but I supplied her with the correct answer and was immediately rewarded by being told her age. In exchange for Farquhar's years, I learned those of her husband, of her adopted son, and of her mother-in-law.

Seeing that I continued to answer her questions with a smile, she soon launched forth into the genealogical catechism so dear to Tongan hearts.

As an only child, I made comparatively dull conversation, but Farquhar, who was one of eleven, kept 'Ugatea going for almost an hour. At the end of that time, I had recited in proper order by ages, the names of all his brothers and sisters, giving details of their marriages, children, whereabouts and fortunes in general. 'Ugatea repeated everything I said carefully as if she were committing it to memory (as, indeed, she was) and turned the strange Scotch names over and over until she had converted them into proper Polynesian sounds. From Donald, Duncan, James, and John, she brought forth Tonaleti, Tunikane, Semisi, and Sione.

When at last I walked back down the hill, my head was awhirl with 'Ugatea's family tree. All the time she had been extracting from me facts about my family and Farquhar's, she had been supplying me with information about her own.

In the weeks that followed, I acquired a similar knowledge about all thirty of the families of the village; because, once 'Ugatea had reported that we seemed possible people, the shame and shyness disappeared as if by magic and everyone was anxious to talk to us. Needless to say, my mind was for a time a hopeless muddle of who had been married to whom and which children belonged to which family, but after a while the information settled down. Nowadays when Farquhar comes home and asks, "Do you know anything about a man called Sione 'Ofa whose mother was an 'Utulei woman?" I am able to reply at once, "Yes, of course. His mother was Lola, the youngest daughter of Seini's great-grandmother. She married Seme from Kapa, and they had one son, but he died. Then Seme died and she married 'Akima'u from Ha'apai, and they had Sione 'Ofa and Sione 'Ofa married Mele Lalo from Tu'unuku."

In addition to my talks with 'Ugatea and the rest of the women, there were two other factors which hastened our acceptance by the village. The first was their discovery that Farquhar is the sort of old-fashioned doctor who always has time to see a patient. Although his agreement with the government demands only that he act as consultant to the TMPs stationed at the hospital in Neiafu, it was not long before our verandah was the scene of a morning sick call for the village. Tongans are a pretty healthy lot, but there is a never-ending number of cuts and scratches to be attended to and, after every big feast, the inevitable stomach-aches for those who sat too long. To the children, coming to our verandah was, at first, a terrifying experience. Tongan parents, seeking a quick and satisfactory way to quell the exuberance of their offspring when they are around white men, have the habit of telling them that, if they don't behave, the papalangi will eat them. From the screams they let out when Farquhar approached them, it was obvious that they thoroughly believed their parents' tale. However, as time went on and we showed no inclination to gobble up brown babies, the young things of 'Utulei lost their fear of us and developed in its place a wholesome curiosity.

Nowadays, they don't wait for their parents to bring them. When they fall in their play, they rush at once to the verandah to ask for treatment for their cuts and bruises. The wounded one is invariably accompanied by a group of his friends who come along to see whatever is to be seen. If neither Farquhar nor I are on the verandah, the bigger children, following their elders, do not knock at the door, but sit down patiently on the verandah and attempt to attract our attention by coughing at discreet intervals. The younger ones, taking advantage of the opportunity to see what the inside of the house looks like, stare through the glass doors into the living room until someone inside spots them.

The other thing that made the village decide we were quite human in spite of our white skins was our friendship with Tu'ifua. At first, when she used to come down and plant in the garden or bake cakes for us, they assumed that it was the usual white-Tongan relationship in which the Tongan, however well he is treated, is in reality nothing but a servant. However, as time went by and they observed (and they did observe, for everything one does is noticed and discussed) that she slept in the guest room, ate with us at meal times, and sat at nights in the living room reading our books or playing cards or talking, they lost their distrust and came to understand that the color of one's skin was no preoccupation of ours.

10 Love Is the Same

The day was the sort of soft warm one that invites you to pass it in idleness. Tu'ifua and I, accepting the invitation, were sitting out on the verandah in easy chairs with no more serious occupation than that of following with our eyes the slow progress of an occasional cutter as it made its way up the harbor to Neiafu. Now and then we exchanged a word or two. More often we lapsed into drowsy silence. At last, after a pause longer than usual, I roused myself and made a demand which, in most places in the world, is sufficient to call forth any number of tales.

"Tell me," I said, "some love stories about Tonga."

But Tu'ifua was not so easily stirred into narration. Without bothering to open her eyes, she replied, "It is the same."

"The same? The same as what?" I prodded.

She sat up then and looked at me as if I were a child to need an explanation of so obvious a remark. "Why," she said, "love in Tonga is the same as in the rest of the world. Sometimes a boy loves a girl. Sometimes they marry. Sometimes not. And if they do—or if they don't—they are happy or not."

The subject, I confessed to myself, could scarcely be covered more completely or more concisely. Yet, on a day when time seemed to move no more quickly than the still air, a bit more detail was desirable. "Tell me," I began again, but Tu'ifua was not listening. She was staring fixedly at a big cutter which for almost an hour had been directly across the harbor from us, its slack sails waiting hopelessly for a breath of wind.

"They're getting out the oars," she observed at last.

Annoyed at having been turned away from the subject I had chosen, I said crossly, "Well, if they want to get up to Neiafu today, I suppose that's all they can do."

"Oh," she said definitely, "but of course they want to get to Neiafu."

The positive tone of her voice surprised me. "How do you know?" I asked.

"Why, because it's the new bride. She's taking her things up to Neiafu for her honeymoon. Naturally she wants to get there."

"Naturally," I agreed, "but what new bride?"

"Haven't I told you?" Tu'ifua asked innocently.

Upon being assured that she hadn't, she began, and I settled back well pleased. I realized that the story I had requested was about to be told.

The beginning wandered about a bit. As usual when she tells a story, Tu'ifua wanted to be perfectly sure that I had the scene well in mind. "You know Tu'anuku?" she asked.

"Of course." We both turned and looked far down

across the harbor, following the curving line of the main island to the place where the green land was broken by the irregular line of the houses of the village of Tu'anuku.

"And beyond Tu'anuku, on the other side of the ridge, you know Longamapu?"

"Yes, I know it, too." In my mind was a picture of another village, of one at the very end of the island where houses nested high in the hills above the open sea.

"And the lake that lies in the hollow between Longamapu and Tu'anuku. You remember it?"

The question was purely a rhetorical one. Only the week before when I had been in the midst of one of my occasional fits of sightseeing, we had crossed the harbor in the motorboat and walked together from Tu'anuku over the ridge and down past the village gardens through the vine-tangled bush to the shore of the lake. Tu'ifua moves with the stately grace of a queen, but neither she nor any other Tongan ever regards walking as a pleasure. My ideas of the joy of hiking she thinks simple madness, but she bears with them because it is one's duty to put up with the eccentricities of one's friends.

The way to the lake was long and hot, and once the village and the gardens had been left behind, the path was slippery with gray mud. In addition, there were flies everywhere which bit our legs and arms and buzzed about our heads, and we were oppressed by the rotten-sweet smell of decaying vegetation which hung thick on the air. My relief was almost as great as Tu'ifua's when, finally, we saw some reeds

rustling in a breeze that swept up off the lake that
soon revealed itself to us. Stretching far along the
base of the ridge and then curving suddenly out of
sight, the water presented an aspect of wildness. There
was no house built beside it and none of the gardens
reached to its shores. Edging it were only the green
tangle of the bush, the singing reeds, and some
grotesque outcroppings of jagged rock.

The picture was fresh in my mind. "Yes, I remember the lake."

"Well, then," said Tu'ifua, "I can go on with the
story. The girl lived in Longamapu. Her name was
Hina and she was very beautiful and—"

"The boy saw her and fell in love with her," I
suggested.

"He did," Tu'ifua agreed. "And his name was
Siua and he lived in Tu'anuku."

Tu'ifua had said at the outset that the girl was a
bride. I began to fear lest the tale was coming too
soon to its happy ending; but I was not long in dis-
covering that Tonga is no exception to the rule that
true love has often to run a very rugged course.

"Hina's mother was dead and her sisters all went
up to Neiafu to the girls' college, but her father
wouldn't let her go. She was his favorite daughter and
he kept her with him always. When he went fishing,
she went in the canoe with him. When he went to the
bush to weed his garden, she gathered flowers while
he worked, or sat in the shade of a tree and sang
sweet songs for him."

"A most possessive parent," I murmured, translat-
ing Tu'ifua's story into papalangi terms.

She frowned at the interruption. "Oh," she cried, "all the people were very pleased to see that man and that little girl, because they knew he loved her very much." Then, out of consideration for my ignorance, she explained, "It is often that way. A man will have a lot of children. He will love them all and take care of their food and their clothes and teach them how to do the right things, but only one will be his favorite—only one he'll love very much and want to keep with him always.

"Sometimes it is very sad for a man when his favorite grows up, because all the boys come to see her, and he knows that soon she'll find one she likes and then she'll get married and go away."

"I suppose that's what happened to Hina," I said.

"No, it didn't," Tu'ifua replied, and she plunged into her story as if she were conscious of having lingered too long over its beginning. "It didn't happen to Hina because Sione—that's her father—wouldn't let the boys come around. He told them she was too young. He shut the door in their faces and told them to go away.

"At first, Hina didn't mind very much because there wasn't any boy she especially liked and she was happy enough with her father. But she was very beautiful and very nice, too, so the boys came back again and again in spite of all Sione could say.

"After a while the people in the village began to talk. They said Sione shouldn't shut his daughter up. They quite understood that she was his favorite, but she was growing up. She should be allowed to talk to

the boys. Sione heard what they said, but maybe he
didn't care. At any rate, he pretended not to care.
So long as Hina went everywhere with him, it
didn't matter to him what anyone said."

In Tonga, as elsewhere, anyone who does not con-
form to the prevailing social code gets talked about,
and sometimes the talk is neither charitable nor
nice. So Tu'ifua lowered her voice as she went on.
"Then the people in Longamapu began to say a very
bad thing about Sione. They said he wouldn't let
Hina see any boys because he wanted to keep her for
himself. That wasn't true," she hastened to explain.
"It wasn't at all true, and the people knew it wasn't,
but they thought if they said it, Sione would be
ashamed and would let her see the boys. But he
still pretended he didn't care what they said and
still he kept her always with him.

"So the people grew very angry, and when they
knew Hina loved Siua, they were glad."

"Wait," I demanded. "You're getting ahead of
yourself. You haven't even told me Hina knew Siua,
and now you tell me she loves him. How did she
ever get a chance to see him if her father kept her
with him always?"

Tu'ifua shook her head irritably, implying that
I had asked a senseless question. "How should I know
how she saw him?" she demanded impatiently. "Those
things happen. Siua had a horse, and he and some of
the boys used to race along the track between Longamapu and Tu'anuku. Maybe she saw him come
riding into the village with his friends one day. Or

maybe his garden was next to Sione's garden, for the
Longamapu gardens and the Tu'anuku gardens are
side by side in the bush. Or maybe they met in
church. I don't know, but it doesn't matter because
it always happens someway. The boy will meet the
girl, and they will love each other."

I had to be content with that explanation which
was, after all, perhaps as good as any that could be
made, so I leaned back in my chair and listened while
the story moved on.

"Siua is a young man anybody would like. He
works very hard in the bush, cutting copra and growing vegetables. He is clever at fishing, too. He has
a boat of his own. He has a nice family, and he is a
good son to them. He belongs to the Tu'anuku church
choir, and he knows all our old Tongan customs."

Tu'ifua was describing not only the hero of her
story, but also the ideal young man of Tonga.

"He wanted to do things the right way, so he
went to Sione.

" 'I love Hina,' he said. 'Please let me come and
see her. I want to marry her. I have told my parents,
and they will come and talk to you about our wedding.'

"But Sione was very angry when he saw that young
boy standing there asking for his favorite little
daughter. 'Go away,' he shouted. 'Go away and never
come back. I don't want to see you or your parents
either. I forbid you to talk to Hina. Go away. Go
away.'

"Siua was a polite young man. He didn't shout

back at Sione. He only turned and went quietly away, but as he was going, he said calmly, 'There is one thing I will tell you. Hina loves me, too.'

"Nothing else Siua could have said would have hurt Sione so much as those words. 'Liar!' he shouted. 'Liar, go away!' And even after the young man had gone, he kept muttering to himself, 'He lies. It's not true,' but deep within himself was the haunting fear that the fellow had spoken the truth. At last he went to Hina and asked her outright.

"She had never lied to her father, and she did not lie then. 'Yes,' she said simply, 'it is true. I love Siua and I want to marry him.'

"Now, when Sione heard those words, a terrible thing happened to him. His heart became darkness, and there was no longer any love in it for Hina. There was nothing inside him but anger. He stopped treating Hina as his favorite daughter. Instead he was very unkind to her. He beat her with a thick stick and everyone in the village could hear the blows and everyone could hear Sione shouting.

"Of course, it wasn't long before Siua heard about the way Sione was acting toward Hina and he was very sad. He wanted very much to do things in the right way, but he thought to himself that unless he and Hina ran away, they could never get married at all. So he went to church—"

"To pray?" I asked, struck by the thought that piety was to be added to all the young man's other virtues.

But Tu'ifua shook her head. "Of course not to pray. He went to church in Longamapu to see Hina."

"And did he see her?"

"Naturally. A boy can always manage to see a girl in church. He saw her, and he asked her if she loved him very much, and she said she did. Then he asked her if she loved him enough to run away with him. She said she did again, so he told her he'd think of a plan and let her know about it.

"Now Sione didn't hear what they said, but he knew they had been talking together, and he knew very well that Siua might try to run away with Hina. He kept her closer to him than he'd ever done before. He even borrowed the neighbors' dogs and tied them near the house, so they would bark and warn him if Siua came. Yet, in spite of all her father's precautions, Hina found a chance one day not very long after the talk in church to slip away from him and walk through the village and down the path to the graveyard above the sea. Maybe it was just a chance meeting or maybe it was planned. Anyway, a friend of Siua's was sitting there half hidden by the flame tree that grows over the old chief's grave, and he had a message for Hina. That very night, he said, Siua and his friends would come for her."

"Siua and his friends," I repeated. "Why his friends? You don't want friends when you're eloping."

"Certainly you do." Tu'ifua was positive. "You always want friends. They are necessary. They help."

I reflected on the extent of Polynesian gregariousness and found nothing to say but a rather weak "Oh."

"You'll see," went on Tu'ifua, justifying the Polynesian point of view, "that it was a very good thing that Siua had friends in Longamapu and in Tu'anuku, too. The plan would never have worked without them."

"And what was the plan?" I asked.

"Well, it was decided that after Sione went to sleep, Hina would steal from the house and go to Siua who would be waiting outside. They would ride over the track to Tu'anuku and then around by the new road to Neiafu and in the morning they would go to the courthouse and get married.

"The idea was a good one, but that night it seemed to Hina that Sione would never go to sleep. He sat on the doorstep of the house, and he made Hina sit inside. He didn't talk because he was still angry at her for loving Siua, but he watched her. Every time she got up and walked across the mat, his eyes followed her. So, at last, she lay down and pretended to go to sleep. She knew he was still watching her, still listening to her. She couldn't even sigh for fear he'd hear her. So she lay still and listened. Outside she could hear the dogs which her father had borrowed from the neighbors. They moved about restlessly, pulling against the ropes with which he'd tied them. Sometimes one of them would give a low whine. Once she thought she heard the beat of horses' hooves in the distance, but then there was nothing but silence. Silence, and still Sione watched her and the night was passing. The stars had moved far across the sky when Sione said, as if to himself, 'I will sleep now.'

"Hina's heart was happy when she heard his words, but not for very long, for, instead of going to sleep

in the far corner of the house where his sleep mat was
kept, he went and got the mat and pulled it to
where he had been sitting. Then he threw himself
down on it, lying across the open doorway so that
no one could come or go without disturbing him.
Though her heart sank when she saw where he lay,
Hina said nothing, nor did she move. Even when his
breathing grew regular and heavy and she knew that
he slept, she lay still. She was afraid lest she wake
him. His breathing deepened into snoring, but still
she didn't move. After a very long time, she heard
outside the soft pad of footsteps on the ground and
the low panting of dogs and then, so close that he
might have been in the house with her, the voice of
Siua. 'Come out. We are ready,' he whispered.

"His voice was a rope to pull her. She stood up and
went to the side of her sleeping father. For a minute
she looked down at his face, then she stepped carefully over him. Only when she was safely outside and
Siua had lifted her into his arms did she turn to see
if Sione had been disturbed. He had not stirred. She
was free."

"But what about the dogs?" I asked. "Didn't they
bark?"

"No," said Tu'ifua with a smile. "You see, I was
right when I told you friends were always necessary.
Siua had friends in Longamapu, and they happened
to be the same people from whom Sione had borrowed
the dogs; so, when Siua came for Hina, his friends
came and crept up to their dogs and brought them
food and petted them and the dogs were quiet.

"When Siua and the boys from Tu'anuku came

riding up on their horses," Tu'ifua continued, "some of the Longamapu people were awakened and some of the people got up and lit their lamps and tried to see who was coming into town in the middle of the night. Now, a lot of the people in Longamapu were Siua's friends, but some of them were Sione's friends. Even though most of them thought him a very bad father, still, there are always people to take the father's side. When the boys saw the people looking out at them, they were afraid they would be discovered, and they said to Siua, 'The horses make too much noise. One of us had better take them back to Tu'anuku and wait there. You and Hina had better walk over the track.'

"To Siua, however, the idea seemed only half good, for, if he and Hina walked from Longamapu to Tu'anuku, Sione would certainly wake up and miss Hina and come after them with dogs and horses and men to help him in his search."

When she reached that point of her story, Tu'ifua smiled with the indulgent smile that the most practical people reserve for romantic ideas. "I suppose," she said, "that was when they decided to swim across the lake. They knew Sione would never think of looking there for them. Maybe it sounds silly—their thought about swimming—but it must have been a good idea because it worked.

"Hina and Siua and two of Siua's friends ran through the village and down the twisting track to the lake. It was very dark, and I think maybe Hina was afraid, but she loved Siua; so when he told her they would have to swim the length of the lake, she got into the water with the three boys, and they began to swim. I don't know how far it is from one end of the lake to the other, but I know they swam a long time, and it seemed even longer than it was. They all kept wondering if Sione had awakened and begun to look for them. Hina got very tired, but the two friends sang to her and Siua talked to her and after a while, she did not think any more about being tired or about being frightened, but only about going away with Siua. By the time they reached the Tu'anuku end of the lake, the sky was light and the birds were singing their morning songs. Waiting for them on the lake shore was the boy who'd taken the horses back. He told them Sione had wakened and had come to Tu'anuku with men on horseback and a whole pack of dogs. He had shouted and banged on the doors of all the houses in the village looking for Hina and Siua, but of course he couldn't find them, and after a while he'd given up and gone back home.

"When Siua and Hina heard that Sione had gone back to Longamapu, they were very happy, but even so, they were afraid to stay long in Tu'anuku, for they never knew when he might start the search all over again. So they only rested a minute before they got on the horses and set out on the road to Neiafu. Galloping along with the dawn breeze in their faces, Hina and Siua and Siua's friends forgot all about being weary from their long swim because they knew they were safely away from Sione, and they were free and happy in their hearts. They galloped through the villages of Tefisi and Vaimalo and through Leimatu'a and they never stopped until they came to Neiafu. It was after nine o'clock then, and the judge was already in his office—"

"So they got married and lived happily ever after," I said, putting the usual end to the story.

"Well," Tu'ifua said prosaically, "they got married, but that was only last week, so I don't know about the rest. Maybe they'll always be happy and maybe not. No one knows."

She turned and looked at the cutter which, during the telling of the tale, had moved up the harbor and was already tying up at the government wharf in Neiafu. "Hina and Siua are having a honeymoon in Neiafu this week. That's why she went to get her things. Next week they'll go back to Tu'anuku, and Siua will build a new house for them."

"And what about Sione?" I asked. "Did he try to have the marriage annulled, or has he forgiven them?"

"Not one or the other. He sailed on the *'Aoinu* last night for a holiday in Nuku'alofa."

"For a holiday!" I exclaimed, surprised at such unorthodox behavior from an outraged parent. "Why a holiday?"

"I don't know," Tu'ifua said, "but I heard him say that they were married, and he couldn't help it, and he was tired of both of them."

"A most philosophical man, after all," I observed. "And, as for the story, thank you for telling it. It's as romantic a one as you'd find anywhere."

"Of course, it is," said Tu'ifua. "I told you it was the same everywhere—love in Tonga and love in other places."

11 Fish Stories

Although Vava'u seems to me to be as close to paradise as I could possibly get on this earth, I am no blind devotee. Well do I realize that there are some people to whom it would offer nothing at all. Chief among them are those who long for the amusements of society—for balls and concerts, for new pictures every night and the latest television shows, for bus rides and long-distance telephones, for window-shopping and lunch in town. It is useless to tell them, as some too fond lovers of the islands foolishly do, to come along anyway, and it is futile to imagine that, once they are here, they will revel in it. They won't. They will hate it and they will complain and grumble and make life miserable for themselves and everyone else until the steamer comes and mercifully carries them back to the bright lights and the clatter on which they thrive.

There are even people content with more natural diversions who would find this place little to their taste. Mountain climbers would probably not be stimulated by the ascent of our lofty Talau which brushes the heavens 430 feet above sea level, nor

would my friends who live from one skiing weekend
to the next be held long by 'Utulei where the only
ice and snow anyone has ever seen is to be found
inside my refrigerator. As for hunters, there is nothing
here worth the trouble of loading a gun. True, some
of the eager young papalangis go down to the lake
for doves or pop away at flying foxes, but they soon
grow tired of it and leave their guns to rust forgotten
in the bottom bureau drawer.

In the old days before ever the Europeans came,
there was a bit of hunting here, but the common
people had no share in it. The sport was reserved for
chiefs and nobles. Like most activities limited to a
single class, it has long since died out and no one
seems faintly interested in reviving it. A certain
amount of skill was required for the handling of the
tiny foot-long arrows which were discharged from
child-sized bows, and gentlemen whose tastes were
luxurious rather than sporting could gratify themselves with beautifully ornamented woven quivers
or with finely carved bows or bright feather-tipped
arrows. Nevertheless, Tongan hunting was doomed
because the essential element of danger was lacking;
the prey was nothing more ferocious than the meek
little gray bush rat. There are those who scoff at the
old nobles and their fine sport of rat hunting, but it
is only fair to remember that they had no choice.
Aside from the rats, a native variety of pig seems to
be the only mammal that was indigenous to these
islands. In the old days, as now, the pig was far too
important an item of diet to be made an object of
sport.

If this land itself is disappointing from a sportsman's point of view, what matter? Nature, as usual, maintains an even balance. It is the sea that is important here. To anyone who likes to be on the water, or in it; to anyone who is content merely to watch its ever-changing aspects, Vava'u cannot fail to be a place of enchantment. With its many islands and its endless inlets, it is an ideal spot for sailing or motorboating. I myself usually get about in a little yellow outrigger canoe which Felipe, one of the village men, made for me the first year I came to 'Utulei. It has carried me on some ambitious harbor trips, but for the most part, I am content to paddle out over the reef in front of the village and float lazily over the colorful coral world below. I have quite come to believe that Water Rat was right when he said, "Believe me, there is *nothing*—absolutely nothing—half so much worth doing as simply messing about in boats."

There are times, too, when the water looks so inviting that being on it is not enough. Then—over the side and into it! We swim here in all sorts of weather—when the harbor is glass-smooth and when the wind piles it into waves, when the day is bright and when it's dull. Tongans young and old alike enjoy a swim most when it's pouring and the raindrops bounce and leap off the surface of the sea, until it looks like a furiously boiling cauldron. There is much to be said for their choice; there's something invigorating about the bracing sting of salted raindrops and there's a fascination in hearing the insistent little thunder of water falling on water.

On the water or in it, Vava'u is a fine place; and under the water is a whole new world. Lately scientists and explorers, equipped with aqualungs and flipper feet, have traveled along the lower edges of some of our coral reefs. They have made interesting discoveries about submarine life and have found wondrous underworld caves whose existence no one even suspected. Although the regions beneath the sea around Tonga represent a whole new area of study for learned men, they hold equal attraction for less daring, more humble explorers.

My own equipment for underwater exploration consists only of a pair of goggles and a rather indifferent ability to hold my breath, but the delight of knowing another world has not been denied to me on account of that. On sunny days, at low tide, I swim out over the reef in front of the village. I have learned my local submarine geography well enough to know that, when I'm on a line with Kuli's house and the marking buoy, I can dive and, leaving behind the familiar sight of Vava'u harbor, float slowly down a long valley whose sides are coral mountains—green and pink and unbelievable cornflower blue. The "atmosphere" of this new world is the luminous green-gold water which sparkles and shimmers as I move through it. The inhabitants are legion. Some, unsociable or frightened, hurry away at my approach so that I know no more of them than a spiny tentacle slipping into a dark hole, a memory of color closed within a gray shell, or a bright flash of a tail plunging down to the depths where I dare not follow. To others, my presence is a matter of complete indiffer-

ence—to the big spotted leopard cowries who lodge
in coral nooks or move slowly over sandy places, to
the dappled green fish and the striped black and
white and yellow ones who swim past me as if I were
nothing more than a new sort of coral, to the trans-
parent jellyfish moving through the green light like
materializations in a spirit picture. Only the blue
miniature fish glinting like precious cloisonné in the
water show any curiosity about me. A whole school
of them follows me, glistening about my head, darting
through my legs. And all this curiosity and indifference and fright goes on in complete silence; for the
world under water is soundless, still, quiet.

I can know its beauty only in snatches. Soon the
necessities of my own world claim me and, spluttering
and gasping for air, I rise to familiar surroundings,
leaving behind me the mysterious world of the
deep.

For those who would rather catch things from the
sea than look at them, there is sport aplenty here—and
it comes in all sizes from "o" fish the size of my little
finger to whales. The "o" come only occasionally, but
when they are running close to shore, there's a village
holiday. Then all the people—young and old, men
and women and children—come down to the beach
and shouting and splashing run into the sea and
scoop up the "o" in their valas or haul them out by
the bucketsful.

Clustered around the beached canoes into which
the tremendous catches are put for safekeeping, are
the children who, dipping in and helping themselves,
gobble down the still-living "o" as if they were candy

chews. Their elders, too, steal a wiggly tidbit now
and again although most of the fish are carried off up
the hill to be fried for dinner. I share in the excitement when the "o" come, but not in the spoils. I
cannot deny my neighbors' claim that they are tasty
fish, but neither can I accustom my papalangi palate
to accepting pins and needles; and an "o," whatever
else may be said for it, is a living pincushion.

Small fish abound, but there are big ones, too—
tuna and barracuda and less commonly known game
fish. There are even whales, and down in Nuku'alofa
there is a family which still catches them; although
nowadays the oil which was highly prized in the old
romantic times of Pacific whaling is of so little value
that it is not even saved. The Nuku'alofa whales are
butchered on the beach and the meat has a ready
sale among the Tongans, but not among the Europeans, who are driven away by the overwhelming smell
which fills the whole town whenever the whalers come
home with a catch.

Here in Vava'u, no one has any whaling equipment,
so the big animals are left in peace. Often they come
in by Kitu and play about in groups at the harbor
entrance. One day a big old brown whale came
all the way up the harbor, puffing and spouting right
past our verandah. That morning, as it happened,
there was only one boat on the water—a rowboat
which held a solitary man, old Pongia, from the
neighboring village of 'Utugake. We could see him
eyeing the whale nervously. Whenever the creature
submerged, we knew he was praying it would surface
far away from his little boat. Around the curve of

our cape, clear up to Neiafu, the whale sported about Pongia's rowboat—and he, poor old man, worked the oars with terrified speed. But the whale was only playing. Pongia landed safely enough and when he stopped shaking, he said it had been great sport.

Possessing a far worse reputation than the playful whales, are the sharks. It is not often they come into the harbor, but the outer ocean abounds in them. In spite of his teeth and his hungry ways, the shark is really quite an amenable fellow when he is properly approached. If you will shake a rattle made of coconut shells to attract his attention and sing him a song or two, he'll be so pleased, he'll beg to be caught. You can get him on a line, but the really sporting way to take him is to slip into the water yourself and swim along until you come up to him. Then, if you face about and stare steadily into his eyes, the trusting shark will look calmly at you while your treacherous hand is plunging a knife through his head.

These ways of the shark I know—well, no, not from any hair-raising experience of my own nor even from any graphic accounts of my friends and neighbors here in Vava'u, but from innumerable books on island life whose pages are enlivened by tales of encounters with fierce man-eating sharks who, after a bit of music or conversation, become as friendly as puppies. That the tales are true, I haven't the slightest doubt; I've read them so often in so many different books. For that matter, I have heard them discussed here in Tonga, too. The late Akau'ola, who was as merry-hearted an old noble as ever lived, came from the island of Taunga far down the harbor which is noted for its skillful fishermen. He used to say that everyone knows that sharks are pleased when people get into the water and talk to them, but, he added, he himself never indulged in such conversations because he wasn't sure that he and the sharks spoke the same language.

The villagers here in 'Utulei, sharing Akau'ola's conservatism, don't fraternize with sharks. When they do catch one, they get him prosaically enough with a hook and line. Of course they talk to the sharks, but they don't single them out for special attention. They get only the same conversation that all the other fish rate.

On still, black nights when the harbor is dotted with fishing lights or on calm mornings before the dawn breezes ruffle the waters, I often hear the men out fishing. As they throw in their baited hooks they chant, "Kai mai, kai mai, kai mai," which is a polite invitation meaning, "Come and eat here." They repeat it again and again and if the fish are reluctant, they embellish the invitations with a description of the succulent tidbits which dangle from their hooks. Sometimes, when a group of high-spirited young fellows are out in their canoes, the invitations are shouted and, as time passes and the competition grows keener, they call out loudly, each one explaining to the fish the merits of his particular bait and disparaging that of the others. Needless to say, there is a great deal of laughing and joking, and here as elsewhere in the world, a fishing party is 90 per cent fun and 10 per cent work.

Yet, for all the fun, fishing is a serious occupation. In the old days before white men introduced the favorite South Sea island delicacy, tinned corned beef, fish was a daily essential. It is still an important item of diet and modern Tongans have lost none of the skill which their forefathers developed with line and spear and net. Nor do they disdain the newest methods. A shipment of sea-green nylon lines which the local stores received a few months ago was sold out at once and the men, like eager children with a new toy, were out day and night trying them.

Dynamiting fish is illegal here, but the men who make their living from the sea think it too sure a method to be overlooked. Getting the dynamite is difficult. Some of the members of the crew of the monthly steamer carry on an illicit trade in it, but the most favored method of procuring it is to steal it from the Public Works Department. Consequently, the really successful commercial fisher must have a willing accomplice in Public Works. Some time ago, a Neiafu man used to cross over to 'Utulei every morning with a canoe of freshly dynamited fish to sell. There are no police here, and so he thought it a better business location than Neiafu where the law might have interrupted him at any moment. He did a brisk business and always went back home again before noon with an empty canoe and a full purse. His trips ceased abruptly after a routine government supply check revealed unexplainable shortages and resulted in the dismissal of all Public Works men who had had access to explosives.

The medical department is another stumbling block

in the way of the dynamite-fishers; for its members are required to report to the police any injury due to explosives which comes to their attention. One afternoon, Farquhar and I were sitting on the verandah when we noticed a launch speeding down from Neiafu. It came in at our beach and one of the hospital boys jumped ashore and ran up to the house, holding out to Farquhar a note from TMP Semisi. *Please come at once,* it said. *There is a man here who seems to have blown off his hand.*

When Farquhar had gone over to the hospital and come back again, he told me that Semisi's note was a masterpiece of understatement. The man had blown off one hand completely and badly injured the other and he was in danger, too, of losing an eye. The whole time his injuries were being dressed, the man kept insisting, "A shark, doctor, a very big shark jumped out of the sea and bit my hand." He repeated the story so often and so convincingly that he was almost believed—almost, but not quite, for not even in the oldest Polynesian myths is there so much as a reference to a fire-breathing monster of the deep, and the outer edges of this man's injuries were scarred by the unmistakable mark of powder burns.

Dynamite is dangerous, but there is no denying its efficiency. Even the most skillful man, pursuing the fish under water with a spear or dropping a throwing net over them or hooking a few on the line hung out from a canoe, can hope for nothing more than a modest catch compared with the dynamiter's haul. Still, the more we learn of the ancients, the more we know that they were not so far behind us as time and our own self-importance might lead us to believe.

The old Tongans, for instance, had no dynamite, but they did have a way of getting a lot of fish at once which was quite as successful as dynamite and much safer. We had been here several years before we realized that the old method was still in use.

Then, one day, a village girl, Vei, came running down to the house. "There's to be an 'uloa today," she cried. "My mother sent me to tell you. She said I should take you if you wanted to go. You must come and see it."

"And what is an 'uloa?" I asked.

Partly in her bit of school English, partly in Tongan, but mainly by the curving of her expressive young hands, she made me understand that an 'uloa was a barrier fence made of woven coconut fronds. Two of them would be stretched from our island to the neighboring island at high tide and when low tide came and the water was nowhere more than knee-deep, the fish that had been trapped between the 'uloas would be easily caught. The fishing was to be a joint venture shared by 'Utulei and our neighbors on the next island whose village is 'Utugake, and it was obvious from the sparkle in Vei's eye that it was to be a sort of community holiday.

"You'll come?" she urged.

"Yes," I said, "I'll come."

She pranced in her eagerness. "Come then," she said. "My brother is going now in his boat. He'll take us."

"Now?"

"Yes, right now," and her impatience to be off fairly popped from her.

"But I can't go now," I said, shattering her mood.

"The doctor's over in Neiafu and he's bringing Tu'ifua back to have lunch with us. After lunch we'll go."

"After lunch!" Vei wailed in despair, thinking of all the fun she would be missing if she had to wait to take us.

I smiled down at her. "You go on now," I said. "You've told me where the 'uloa's to be and we'll come after lunch."

She did not need to be told twice. Pausing only long enough to flash on me a radiant smile and a happy "Malo, malo aupito—thank you, thank you very much," she was out the door, down the verandah, across the grass and into the waiting boat.

After lunch, Tu'ifua and Farquhar and I set out to follow her. Being staid grownups, we stepped into our boat more calmly than she had leaped into her brother's. Still, we had our own eagerness; for none of us had seen an 'uloa before—not even Tu'ifua, who is a Neiafu girl with all a city dweller's ignorance of country ways. As for Farquhar and myself, we had only read in books of the ancient Polynesian methods of fishing.

Down the harbor we sped, following the curving shore for almost a mile until, turning a sudden corner, we came into the baylike water that lies cradled between our island and the next one down. Far from us, where the distance between the two islands is shortest, we could see a great crowd of people standing in the shallow water and, knowing that they were at the place of the 'uloa, we shut off the motor and let the boat drift quietly toward them.

As we came closer, a familiar young figure broke away from the crowd and raced toward us, splashing up fountains of water as she ran.

"There's a fine place to leave the boat just over here," Vei cried as she came up. With amphibious unconcern for her dress which was soon soaking, she dashed forward and, grabbing hold of the boat, pulled it safely to a shallow, sandy place.

We took off our shoes and slid out of the boat, following our young guide through the water toward the crowd of people, but alas! we had gone only a few steps when the sand gave way to coral. Vei's feet, like those of all the villagers, have soles of iron. She runs over the reef as happily as she crosses the grass, but Tu'ifua's feet are town feet used to smooth roads and Farquhar and I have hopelessly tender papalangi feet; so we limped on painfully, grumbling because we hadn't had sense enough to bring sand shoes. When the coral sharpened into spikes, we stopped, unable to move, but Vei ran lithely ahead of us and disappeared into the crowd. From someone she begged shoes and a moment later she was back with them. Mine were two sizes too large, but I was grateful, nevertheless. Floppy though they were, they enabled me to get over the reef almost as comfortably, though by no means as gracefully, as the barefooted Vei. Coming up to the crowd, we could see that all the people were standing outside the enclosure made by the 'uloa—an enclosure roughly the size of four square city blocks. Each person held in his hand an empty basket which he hoped to take home that night full of fish.

"You're just in time," Vei cried in delight. "They're just now ready to start."

She had scarcely finished speaking when a group of young men carrying baskets of shredded bark entered the 'uloa and, throwing the bark into the water, churned it about, calling as they did so, "Here's kava for the fish. Here's kava for the fish." The bark which they had thrown into the water comes from the fue, a vine found deep in the bush. When it is put into the water, it acts as a drug on the fish, slowing up the movements of the larger ones and killing the very smallest ones.

When the bark had been given time to act, about ten young men, carrying spears made of sharpened wire mounted on long poles, entered the 'uloa enclosure. With great splashing and great shouting, they ran about and, as they ran, we saw the fish jumping ahead of them trying to escape their relentless spears.

"Why don't the others go in, too?" I asked, noticing that all the rest of the crowd—our neighbors of 'Utulei and the 'Utugake people, too—stood outside the 'uloa although they were also armed with spears.

Tu'ifua had never seen an 'uloa before, but she knew how one was conducted, so she was able to explain, "They don't go in because it's tapu to go now. Those men are gathering the biggest fish for the chiefs and the high people and when they've finished, everyone can go in and pick up what's left."

"Tu'ifua, Tu'ifua," cried a voice from the far side of the enclosure. "Go inside, you and the doctor and his wife, and choose what fish you like."

The invitation came from the man in charge of the

youths who were spearing the big fish for the chiefs. It was extended to Tu'ifua because, although she belongs to neither of the villages which were holding the 'uloa, she is a member of a chiefly family; to Farquhar and me because all white men are accorded the respect given chiefs. We all, however, shook our heads and Tu'ifua called back our thanks and said we had only come to watch.

"Come for a walk," begged Vei, who had been darting back and forth in her excitement. Leaving Tu'ifua and Farquhar behind, I went with her the length of the 'uloa, crossing over to the 'Utugake side, stopping now and then to exchange a word or two with some of my 'Utulei neighbors or to pick up one of the beautiful brown and coral-colored oliva shells which abound on the reef.

Here and there were very young children sitting in the water close to the 'uloa in the hope that a fish would find its way out of the tapu area. Now and again one did, and a child with nimble fingers caught it as it slipped through the green fronds of the net, and popped it into his basket. Near the 'Utugake side, sitting on jagged pieces of coral, half in the water and half out, were a pair of lovers who, oblivious to all the world about them, gazed soulfully into each other's eyes and uttered rapturous words over their empty baskets.

Vei and I had finished our walk and had come back to Tu'ifua and Farquhar just as a great cry rent the air. "The chiefly portion has been taken. Time for everyone to pick up fish. Time for everyone to enter the 'uloa."

With shouts as wild as ever their savage ancestors uttered as they plunged into battle, all the crowd which had waited so patiently rushed into the 'uloa. I looked about for Vei and saw her far away scooping up a drowsy green fish. All about her, men and women were turning over rocks and pushing aside bits of seaweed, ferreting into all the hiding places.

When it seemed that the last poor drugged fish must long ago have been caught, the people still ran about splashing and still they slipped the varicolored fish into their overflowing baskets. It began to grow dark. Tu'ifua and Farquhar and I turned back toward our boat. As we went, there was a shout, "Wait for your fish," and Vei came stumbling after us with a big, full basket. "It's a present from the people," she said, thrusting it into our hands.

We took it and thanked her and hurried into the boat, thinking of the fish dinner to come. Vei, with a shout and a leap, ran back to the 'uloa.

12 Tea for the Princess

For the most part the Vava'u climate is ideal, but occasionally we, like everyone else in the world, are afflicted by unusual weather. Among our more distressing unusual varieties are winds so high that we rush into the library every few minutes to look at the barometer to see if they are going to develop into hurricanes, and rains so heavy that we fear they will wash us right off the beach and down into the sea; but those frightful manifestations of nature are really rare. More frequent is "putting off" weather.

Pleasant it is then to swim lazily in the sea or to lie in a shady spot on the verandah with a book or to take part in conversations—the slow, tranquil sort that flow on and on even though one dozes halfway through them. All of living is delightful then, with the single exception of work—and work, be it physical or mental, hard or easy, long or short, is not to be considered, but only to be put off at all costs. That is why that good warm time is known as "putting off" weather.

It was definitely "putting off" weather on the Monday morning when I asked Lotu to find a man to help

157

him cut down the weeds below the garden and told the girls they had better wash the windows and scrub the verandah. Naturally, they all answered my requests politely enough. Tongans always say "Yes" when they sense your desire to hear it. I don't doubt, even, that they all intended to do the work eventually, but it was, as I have said, "putting off" weather. Consequently, Lotu snoozed in the coolness of the papaya grove and the girls sat in the kitchen door singing snatches of half-remembered songs. In the heavy, somnolent air, I felt no more inclination to activity than they did, but I had invited guests for afternoon tea on Wednesday and I was anxious to have 'Utulei appear at its best for them.

"Lotu, Lavinia, Tama'a—come quickly, come at once," I called in what I hoped was a tone of great authority. It may have been, too, because Lotu opened his unwilling eyes, the girls stopped singing, and soon all three of them stood before me.

"I asked you to do some work and you have done nothing," I began, but I could see that I was making little impression on them. There was none of the contrition and resolve I had hoped to see on their faces, which, indeed, showed no expression at all, but were completely shrouded by the blank look that Polynesians assume when they do not wish to be disturbed.

"I have invited people to come on Wednesday," I said. I may have stormed a bit because Lotu, losing his blankness for a minute, gave me the glance of amused disdain that Tongans reserve for papalangis who lose their tempers over nonessentials.

On and on I talked, but all to no avail, until, growing really angry, I shouted, "You must get to work. You must. Mata'aho is coming with Taufa Ahau."

If a blast of icy wind from the south pole had blown the "putting off" weather away from Vava'u at that second, they could not have come to life more quickly. Hooded eyes flashed open, flaccid limbs stiffened with determination and Tama'a, smiling sweetly, asked, "But why didn't you say that at first?"

Before I had time to answer, all three of them had gone off to work, leaving me to marvel at the magic that can be wrought by the mention of the royal family; for Mata'aho is the wife of the Crown Prince Tungi, and their son, the little Taufa Ahau, will in his turn be king of Tonga.

All the members of the Tongan royal family are most kind in their relations with us—as they are with all the white people who live in their country, but Mata'aho is the one I feel I know best. Ever since that day I first met her at Kauvai, the Queen's country place, and discovered that she, too, belonged to Vava'u, we have seemed to have a bond in common. These days, of course, she lives in the palace at Nuku'alofa, but she comes to Vava'u as often as she can and always when she comes, I enjoy some hours of pleasant companionship with her.

When I asked her down to 'Utulei for afternoon tea, I assumed that it was a private matter, but the people of 'Utulei were to take a different view of it. So quickly does news travel in this newspaperless country that within half an hour of the time I had told Lotu and the girls she was coming, I was besieged

by visitors from the village. Every man in the place
came to offer to help in whatever was to be done—
every man, that is, except Langi, the schoolteacher,
who, I'm sure, is the laziest man in all of Tonga. He
did come down to see me; for no one stays behind
when it is a question of the royal family, but the help
he offered was that of the school children, not his
own. While they swarmed noisily over the beach
picking up stray bits of driftwood and broken coconut
shells, the men reduced the garden to picture-book
order. Not to be outdone, the women turned to and
scrubbed the house from one end to the other in
spite of my protests that it really didn't need it.

When, at last, all the picking up and polishing and
sweeping and scrubbing were done, Ta'anaki, the
son of old Kuli, our village officer, came to see me on
his father's behalf.

Without wasting time on the usual polite Polynesian circumlocutions, he came to the point at once.
"What are you feeding them?" he asked.

"They're coming for afternoon tea," I replied.

"Yes," he insisted, "but what will you give them to
eat?"

"Why, sandwiches and cakes and tea and a fruit
drink for Taufa and—"

"No pig?" he broke in impatiently.

"Of course not," I laughed. "People don't eat pig
at afternoon tea."

Ta'anaki's brow furrowed into wrinkles. "Mata'aho
is Tungi's wife . . . and there's Taufa," he said. "It's
only right they have pig. Think how ashamed all of
us in 'Utulei would be if the other villages knew they'd
been here and had no proper food."

"I shall give them proper food," I insisted a bit huffily, but Ta'anaki only shook his head and muttered, "Pig, pig, pig."

In the end, we reached a compromise. Grudgingly the village agreed to let me feed my guest in my own paltry papalangi way, but they were determined that, when the royal party was ready to return to Neiafu, they would put into their boat some neatly packed baskets containing roast pig and chickens and yams and all the other things that go to make up a traditional feast.

I had, also, to talk them out of a plan they had of having the entire population line up on the shore of the beach to sing the national anthem as Mata'aho and Taufa stepped off the launch. Such a display would have smacked too much of the official life from which Mata'aho was enjoying a brief Vava'u vacation. I suggested, instead, that after we had had our tea, the school children's dance team come down and do a laka-laka on the lawn, and to that they finally agreed.

With the village restored to happiness, my preparations for the tea proceeded normally except for the fact that Tu'ifua, who came down to help me bake, insisted that we make twice as many cakes as I thought we needed and once, when Farquhar took her over to Neiafu to get something we'd forgotten at the stores, she came back with half a dozen watermelons. I suggested that they were a foolish purchase and most unsuitable for afternoon tea. She heard me out, replying patiently when I had finished, "You'll see, they'll be very useful."

Time has taught me not to argue with Tu'ifua, who

has a way of always being right; so I said nothing
further and Wednesday came. In the morning, I took
Lavinia and Tama'a aside and went over with them
for a final time the proper way to serve tea. They
listened attentively to all I said, but when I had
finished, Lavinia, the shy one, shook her head.

"I'd be too frightened," she said. "I think I must
refuse. I can't serve Mata'aho and Taufa."

And Tama'a supported her, saying, "Yes, we are
only village girls. You'd better have Tu'ifua serve.
She knows all the proper ways to act with the royal
family."

Fortunately, I remembered my Polynesian psy-
chology that time; so instead of getting angry with
them and telling them they would have to serve
whether they liked it or not, I cast down my eyes
mournfully. "Mata'aho knows well that Tu'ifua is my
friend. She will expect to see her here," I began.
Then, looking sadder with each word, "But oh, how
ashamed I will be if she comes and finds only Tu'ifua
to serve her. She'll think I have no little girls to
help me. Oh, what a poor house she will think this
is and how ashamed I'll be."

Shame is the most compelling of Tongan emotions.
The mere threat of it was enough to move the girls.
"Perhaps," said Lavinia, "I can serve after all, if
Tama'a will help."

To which Tama'a said stoutly, "Of course, I'll
help."

Tu'ifua came by just then and reassuringly said,
"Behave in whatever way you think best and you'll
be all right." At the time, the advice seemed excellent;

for both girls are normally polite young things who
have, since they have been with us, learned much
about the ways of conducting themselves in a papalangi house.

So all the arrangements were made and my mind
was at rest and soon Farquhar and I were walking
down to the beach to welcome Mata'aho and Taufa,
who came down by launch from Neiafu. With them
came our one other guest, Rosie Sanft, the trader's
daughter, who went to Vava'u's Sacred Heart Convent
with Mata'aho and has always been one of her warm-
est friends. Tu'ifua was here, too, but such are the
peculiarities of Tongan custom that she could scarcely
be counted a guest. Although she is both a relative and
a friend of Mata'aho's and, like Rosie, played with
her as a child, she would not think of sitting in a
chair in her presence—nor, in company, of initiating
any conversations; because Mata'aho is Prince Tungi's
wife. Consequently, while Farquhar and Rosie and
Mata'aho and I talked, Tu'ifua had to content herself
with seeing that the girls had all the tea things in order
and with talking to Taufa's nurse, Tuputupu—a
beautiful young girl who, as it happens, is cousin to
both Mata'aho and Tu'ifua.

The rigid stratification of Tongan society is something which, it seems to me, must be broken down or
at least relaxed before there can ever be, on a large
scale, truly intelligent and harmonious relations between Tongans and the white people who live in
their country—or, for that matter, before Tongans can
ever fully realize their own potentialities. Admittedly,
there are Europeans here who are so old-fashioned that

they are unable to regard Tongans—or other people whose skin is darker than their own—as anything but "dumb natives." They are the hopeless vestiges of old errors with whom it is useless to try to remake society. There are others of us, however, who have really settled in this country and made friends with its people, but whenever we try to share with them the sort of social experiences we have enjoyed elsewhere in the world we run afoul of custom. If we have as many as three or four Tongan friends, one of them is certain to outrank the others. That means that, although they may be his superior in education and intellect, they will not be free to express their opinions in his presence or even to sit or move at will while he is about. If he happens to be a member of the royal family, commoners would not even feel free to eat at the same time he did. In the upper strata of society, the gradations are infinite. I remember, for instance, an evening Farquhar and I spent in Neiafu with Mata'aho and Tungi. Since there were just the four of us present, the evening proceeded as any evening shared by two couples might have done, with us all sitting together in the living room talking in a friendly, normal way. When supper was served, however, custom divided us. Mata'aho took me off to the verandah where we had our meal; for her royal husband outranks her and custom does not allow them to eat together. You can, of course, side-step the issue by entertaining Tongan friends one at a time, but you can scarcely make a party of one, although it is a pleasant enough way to have afternoon tea, as we were doing that day.

We had for some time been sitting and talking when I nodded my head "Yes" to Lavinia, who kept peeking from behind the door to see if it was time to serve tea.

Mata'aho was sitting on the L-shaped sofa when the two girls, who were all too obviously trembling with excitement, entered the room bearing their trays of tea and sandwiches. Slowly, shakily, they moved to the center of the room where, to my great consternation, they fell to their knees. That, alas! was the result of Tu'ifua's well-meant advice to the effect that they should behave as they thought best. It is true, of course, that Tongan royalty—and other Tongans, too, for that matter—are generally served by kneeling girls, but then, they are usually sitting on the floor to eat. When they are sitting European-style in chairs, the kneeling position presents difficulties. For a second, seeing the two girls making their awkward waddling progress across the floor, I was seized with a mad desire to laugh, but when I looked at Mata'aho and saw her sitting as always, perfectly poised, I felt ashamed of myself and found my balance again. The L-shaped coffee table, usually a convenience to us, would have presented insurmountable difficulties to the girls had not Mata'aho reached over and taken their trays from them. As she did so, she asked them all the vital statistical questions that Tongans whatever their rank or station always ask when they first meet, until at last their trembling ceased and they passed her milk and sugar and offered cakes as gracefully as they could, considering their position and the coffee table they had to reach across.

Tuputupu was giving Taufa his tea on the verandah, but with typical little-boy curiosity, he came in
from time to time to see if we were having anything
he hadn't been offered. He was talking then and
chattered away at great length to Mata'aho, but he
had reached the stage of being shy with strangers, and
although he was most polite, quite refused to say a
word to Rosie or Farquhar or me.

Just as we were finishing tea, Mata'aho, who when
she is with Europeans politely tries to follow their
customs rather than her own, said with a laugh, "My
girls are cross with me. They all wanted to come to
'Utulei, but I told them they had to stay home because
I was visiting a papalangi and papalangis aren't used
to having a crowd turn up when they have invited one
guest. I only brought Tuputupu to look after Taufa
and the others are jealous."

Tuputupu, who was sitting in the doorway, half
in the room and half on the verandah, began to
giggle in a most disrespectful way before Mata'aho had
finished talking.

At the sound, Mata'aho turned and demanded
sharply, "What's wrong with you?"

Still laughing, Tuputupu pointed out toward the
sea. "Excuse me," she said, "but I think the girls
decided not to stay at home after all."

We stood up and, looking out, saw a long canoe
filled with a dozen of Mata'aho's attendants who
had paddled across the harbor from Neiafu and were
laughing now like schoolgirls playing hookey.

Mata'aho's dark eyes blazed angrily. "Tell them to
go back at once." I shook my head. "Let them come

up," I said. "There'll be some dancing soon and they can watch it with us." And, sounding very casual, as if a dozen unexpected guests perturbed me not a bit, I said to Tu'ifua, who had just come into the room, "Ask Lavinia and Tama'a to take the girls something to eat, will you?"

Tu'ifua had been right once again. Secure in the knowledge of extra cakes and watermelons, she gave me a knowing smile as she went off.

Soon she was back again to say that the laka-laka party was waiting, if we were ready. We all moved out to the verandah. The house is built up on piles, and seats on the verandah, six or seven feet above the ground level, always seem to be box seats for whatever is going on in the garden or in the sea beyond the garden. Chairs had been set out in a row that day and Mata'aho, Rosie, Farquhar, and I sat on them, while at our side, on the floor, sat Tuputupu, holding the little Prince Taufa on her knee, and Tu'ifua. The canoeists—who now that Tu'ifua had seen to their refreshment and Mata'aho had forgiven them for following her, were in fine spirits—were sitting on a mat down on the grass.

When we were settled, Ta'anaki came over the fence and stood in the middle of the lawn below us, bowing and giving the flourishing salute that Tongans keep for their royalty and chiefs.

" 'Utulei is a poor village," he said, beginning on the correct note of self-abasement, "but this is a day of great happiness for us. For the first time a member of the royal family who will one day rule Tonga comes to our village. Welcome Taufa Ahau to 'Utulei.

And welcome, too, to Mata'aho, our dear kinswoman who comes again to Vava'u. May you both enjoy the dance that our children will do for you. Our love to you."

As he finished, he waved his hands and the children came out from behind the frangipani trees where they had been waiting and formed a double line on the grass before us. In spite of the short notice, they had a gala look. Here costumes do quite literally grow on trees; so they had had no trouble outfitting themselves. The girls wore skirts made of shiny oiled leaves which, whenever they moved, sent a pleasant fragrance wafting through the air. The boys had anklets of the flat round seeds that the children call "money" and head decorations and armbands of leaves and flowers. Both boys and girls wore heavy frangipani leis.

There are better dancers in Tonga, I know, than the school children of 'Utulei, but I confess that they are among my favorite performers. They all have such a zest and such joy in their dancing that their delight is contagious. In the center of the line stand the girls who are almost grown, moving with a new womanly grace. The big boys, still awkward adolescents, have so much energy and vigor about their movements that they, too, are good to see. At the far straggly end of each line, like little afterthoughts, stand the babies, clapping their pudgy hands and bumbling through the motions of the dance an obvious minute or so behind their older brothers and sisters. That day, performing for Mata'aho and the little boy who will one day be their king, the children did their best. They had a good audience, too; for, one by one, all the village people had come down and were sitting on the lawn watching with us. Much to the villagers' delight, Taufa expressed the enjoyment we all felt by calling out, "Malie, malie—well done."

When at last they had finished and made a farewell bow, I noticed that Taufa had begun to fidget with the fastenings of his sandals. Having heard that the royal grandchildren, when the Sunday sermon grew boring, had lately taken to diverting themselves by removing their shoes, I merely supposed that now the dancing was over, he was amusing himself in his own way.

That I was mistaken, I discovered very soon. Tupu-tupu stood up and lifting the prince, who by that time was quite barefooted, in her arms, went down onto the grass where she stood holding him while the people of 'Utulei came one at a time to bow down before him and kiss his tiny foot. The old people came slowly with tears of emotion streaming down their cheeks, the young respectfully, and the little ones gaily. Sitting up on the verandah watching, I couldn't help wondering whether, in this changing world, little Taufa would go all through life having his foot kissed. To me there was—as I suppose there would be to anyone who has grown up in a society which teaches the equality of man—something distasteful about such a show of submission, but the ceremony is, after all, a Tongan one and perhaps it is fairer to look at it through Tongan eyes. Tu'ifua, with whom I discussed it later, said that, whatever the origin of the custom may have been, it is continued

today only because it allows the people to show their
love for the royal family. I quite believe her, but it
seems to me a strange way to express love. I couldn't
help feeling glad that Taufa was such a well-behaved
little boy. It would somehow have been much worse
if he had been an overbearing, rude child.

By the time everyone in 'Utulei had kissed Taufa,
the afternoon shadows were lengthening and Mata-
'aho's launch came down from Neiafu.

"We have no good present for you," Ta'anaki said
to her as a group of men came down the hill, stagger-
ing under heavy baskets full of roast pork, chickens,
fish and yams.

"Only this poor food," Ta'anaki finished, and the
villagers stowed the baskets into the launch and piled
on top of them presents of tapa and mats until there
was scarcely enough room for Mata'aho and Taufa
and Rosie to squeeze in.

Farquhar and I had gone down to the beach alone
to welcome our guests, but when they went away, all
of 'Utulei was there to wave good-by and to call out
their love for the little prince. It was our first
experience of "joint entertaining" with the village.
It was a good one, too; for it was pleasant to know
that everyone had had a fine day and that all of
'Utulei would go happily to bed that night.

13 The Spirits

Many Tongans believe in spirits, and it is not surprising. In the old days, Tonga was full of both spirits and devils. They were an audacious sort who, not content to haunt cemeteries and remote parts of the bush, had the disconcerting habit of coming into villages and upsetting people's daily lives. Some of them were rather useful; they frightened children who strayed too far from home, withered the hands of thieves, and put their mark on young girls who broke tapus. On the whole, though, they were a bad lot. One day, for instance, a couple of rascally young devils tore off the top of Talau, the mountain just across the harbor from our house, and ever since then it has been only a truncated half-mountain with a wide flat top instead of a proper peak. What they wanted with a mountaintop no one knows. They can scarcely have known themselves because when it began to get heavy, they simply threw it away and went off to look for some fresh mischief. It landed about half a mile down the harbor. It is still there today. The uninitiated refer to it as Lotuma island, although any sensible person can tell merely by looking at its size and shape that it is the top of Talau.

There were other tricks they played, too, such as leaving perfectly good fresh-water springs so close to the sea that at high tide they get all salty, or throwing jagged pieces of coral into the best channels. Still, annoying though the devils were at times, the Tongans had always managed to get along with them and would probably be doing so yet if the missionaries hadn't come. Even so, if those old devils had been content with rearranging the landscape, the early missionaries might have left them in peace, but they also attacked men's souls and that the missionaries couldn't allow; souls were their business. Consequently, there was open warfare between the two, and after a time the missionaries announced that there were no more devils. Some people think the announcement was premature. However, they must have bagged a few of the ringleaders because nowadays these islands —mountaintops and all—are satisfactorily stationary except when perfectly routine earthquakes set them shaking a bit. But a few of the devils and some of the craftier spirits must have managed to outwit the Christian gentlemen, for they do keep cropping up from time to time.

Only a couple of years ago when a lady anthropologist, who apparently longed to publish some shockingly erotic accounts of goings on in the South Seas, came to Vava'u inquiring for Fehuluni, she found that attractive devil operating as actively as if a missionary had never existed. Fehuluni, be it understood, is a she-devil whose stock in trade consists of a body so beautiful that if the shadow of it so much as falls across a man's dream, it robs him forever of

any desire for mortal women. Her main activity is
sleeping with men who should be properly at home
with their wives and children, but she gives some
time, too, to the initial experiences of innocent lads
and to misleading bald old fellows who ought to
know better.

The anthropologist, who carried a thick notebook
in which she was constantly making voluminous
entries, said the Fehuluni stories were all well authen-
ticated. She confessed she hadn't found any man who
would admit that he himself had been a victim of
Fehuluni's charms, but she had found plenty who
had watched their friends and neighbors being enticed,
and she had whole pages of testimony from irate
wives who said their unregenerate husbands had
gone off with Fehuluni, or if not with her, with
some equally vicious she-devil!

And Fehuluni is not the only devil about, either.
I know, because I often hear people discussing others.
Fortunately our village of 'Utulei is a poor one whose
people are all commoners, and no full-fledged devil
works this territory, so for the most part we live in
peace. Only now and then the spirits (who, as I understand it, occupy a rank in fienddom definitely below
that of the devils) stir up trouble. They used to
frighten our little house girl as she went home at
night, and that was a nuisance because it meant
that either Farquhar or I would have to walk with
her up the steep hill on whose side the village houses
are built. She felt perfectly secure with us; it seems
that Tongan spirits dislike papalangis so much that
they stay away from them. They are brazen creatures,

though, for, in spite of the fact that they wouldn't think of associating with Farquhar and me or any of our white friends, a whole band of them lives quite comfortably in our front bedroom. I was not even aware of their occupancy until one day when a Tongan friend came to visit me. When it began to get dark, I suggested that, instead of going back across the harbor, she stay the night.

"No, no, no," she cried with a vehemence that I felt was scarcely flattering to me as her hostess.

"Why not?" I asked.

"I'd be afraid," she said, and then, in a lowered voice, she informed me that my guest room was already full, adding, "I could never stay there—those spirits are noisy. They keep singing the old songs. They frighten me."

"Don't be silly," I said, laughing. "There aren't any such things as spirits," and I reminded her that she, as a minister's wife, should know better.

"Perhaps I should," she agreed gently, "but does being a doctor's wife make you know how to cure sick people?"

She went back across the harbor that night, leaving the singing spirits in sole possession of the room.

One day not long afterwards, Farquhar was called up the hill to see a young girl who was reported by her relatives as being very sick. As soon as he saw her, he remembered that he had examined her at the hospital in Neiafu the week before. Mele was a pupil at the girls' college, and the missionary had sent her to the hospital because she complained of dizziness, pains in her head, faintness, and a whole variety of ailments which made it quite impossible for her to do her schoolwork. Their joint conclusion was that she suffered from that universal malady which is so common in Tonga, "pretended sickness." He further expressed the opinion that inasmuch as she showed a marked dislike of the college and everything connected with it, she would probably not recover as long as she was there. The diagnosis annoyed the missionary, who could not conceive of anyone's failing to be grateful and eager for his particular brand of Christian education, but when Mele's parents began to demand that they be allowed to "take her home to die," he gave in and let her leave the college.

Farquhar was surprised to discover that, safely in 'Utulei, she still complained of the same troubles. "I think," he said to me, "that she must be afraid they'll send her back to the college." Nevertheless, to satisfy her relatives, he examined her carefully once again and once again he found nothing wrong. "It's nothing serious," he told them. "Leave her alone, and she'll be all right in a day or two."

Neither Mele nor her family could accept that opinion. Mele moaned when she heard it as if some mortal pain were pushing the last breath from her body. The family said politely enough, "Thank you, doctor, for coming," but they had on their faces that well-known Tongan expression which says so plainly, "White men are all right in their way, and very clever, too, but of course they don't know much about us." Farquhar had no sooner left the house than they burst into an excited babble.

In spite of their doubts about his abilities, the family called Farquhar back three times in the week that followed. On his last visit, he arrived somewhat earlier than he was expected. As there was no one about outside the house, he stepped up to the open doorway and looked in. He had expected to find Mele, as usual, groaning in bed with her weeping relatives sitting about waiting to catch her last words, but what a different sight greeted him! She was there, but she was all alone and, far from lying in bed, she was dancing in the middle of the floor—dancing wildly, turning her head this way and that, twisting her body through a whole series of gracefully grotesque motions, stamping her feet until the mats on the floor rustled like palm fronds in the wind. Above her head she waved her sheet and, as she did so, she chanted to herself. Now Mele, although her figure is too generously full to please the average European taste, is a beautiful girl in many ways and when the village has a celebration, she is always in demand as a dancer. Therefore, I daresay the performance Farquhar witnessed was rather a fine one. However, the hill to Mele's house is steep, and he was weary of attending a patient who wasn't sick, so he only gave an unappreciative snort, turned on his heels and came back home.

Tu'ifua came down for lunch that day, and Farquhar poured out his indignation to her. She listened politely enough, but she seemed strangely embarrassed by Mele's story; so we let the subject drop and talked of other things. We had just finished our ice cream and were about to go out onto the verandah for

tea when the still atmosphere was shocked into vibra-
tions by a tearing shout which came down from the
hill behind the house and filled the room. Ordinarily
our village is a quiet one. If ever a fragment of
sound drifts down to the house, it is likely to be
the voice of a lay preacher monotonously intoning
about the sins of the world or the song of the school
children singing at recess time. Sometimes, when the
wind blows around from the south, we hear old
Maumau, our nearest neighbor, and his aged cronies
who sit endlessly drinking kava and debating again
the problems of their distant youth; but let the wind
blow north or south and never a voice comes from the
place directly behind the house, for that is the village
cemetery. Yet that sound most certainly came from
directly behind the house—that shout and the others
which followed it in angry succession. I tried to follow
the words as they came hurtling down into the room,
but my comprehension of Tongan was limited to
words spoken slowly and enunciated clearly. It disappeared completely before syllables shouted in
passion and violence.

"Who is he and what is he saying?" I asked Tu'ifua.

"I think it's Noa," she replied. "Don't pay
attention to him. He's drunk."

The problem of alcohol is becoming a serious one
in some parts of Tonga, but so far it has been the
nobles and the townspeople who are the main offend-
ers. "Kava papalangi," as the Tongans call all our
intoxicating drinks, is rare in the quiet little villages
like ours, so rare that I replied to Tu'ifua, "No, I
don't think he's drunk."

"Oh well," said Tu'ifua, "think what you like, but he is drunk."

"Drunk or sober," I said, "what's the shouting about?"

She did not answer, and I heard the shouting voice joined by a lower, calmer one which seemed to reason with it. After a time the shouting died away as if the sober man led his drunken friend home to recover more quietly from his spree.

We finished our tea and Farquhar, who was going across to the hospital to give his weekly lecture to the TMPs, left us. When he had gone, I asked Tu'ifua again what Noa was shouting about, and she broke out angrily, as if against her will, with the information that he had been in the cemetery shouting and swearing at the spirits.

"Ah," I said, feeling that at last I was getting somewhere, "are Tongans given to shouting at spirits?"

"Of course not," she replied indignantly, adding a moment later, "We aren't so impolite."

"Noa was shouting," I said.

"But he was drunk."

"And if he hadn't been drunk," I pursued, "he would have talked more politely to the spirits?"

Tu'ifua sighed the sigh of final defeat. "All right," she said, "I'll tell you about it, but I don't like to because you'll think I believe the same things Noa does—and I don't."

"No," I promised, "I won't think that." Involuntarily I reflected how much I would dislike being classified with those of my own countrymen who find the color of a cat or the number of people who get a light from a single match a matter of deep concern.

"I was ashamed to talk about spirits in front of Farquhar, and I don't much like to do it with you. I," she hastened to explain, "don't believe in them myself, and I don't like to admit any Tongans do. I know very well that diseases come from germs. Most of us know that. We are taught it in school. But in the olden days, the Tongan people believed that diseases were sent by angry spirits. Some few people still believe that. Noa believes it. His sister, Mele, is sick, and that's why he came to shout at the spirits and ask them to stop bothering her."

Tu'ifua's lips curled scornfully as she said, "I think he'd be afraid to talk to the spirits ordinarily. That's why he got drunk—to make himself brave."

"If I were a spirit," I said, "I'd definitely resent being shouted at that way."

Tu'ifua laughed. "And I, too—and I think the spirits also, for they aren't used to being spoken to that way. You see, when somebody gets sick like Mele—"

"Wait," I interrupted, "you're forgetting that she's not really sick at all. She's only pretending."

"Yes, I heard you talking about that at lunch," said Tu'ifua, as if I had introduced a wholly irrelevant remark. "Maybe she's quite all right, but she says she's sick and she lies down and everyone thinks she's sick, so I'll call her sick."

I did not contest the point. I knew from past experience that Tongan ideas of sickness are inflexible.

When a Tongan decides he is not well, no one can talk him out of it. Like certain neurotic women of our society, he flits from one doctor to another until he can find one to agree with him and then settles down to enjoy his malady. When I was at the college, one of the primary schoolteachers came one day to tell me that he had to give up teaching because he was sick. He was a handsome, vigorous youth whose face, as he related his troubles, was wreathed in smiles.

"What's the matter?" I asked.

His reply was startling. "I've broken my back," he said. "It's fractured."

I looked at him standing straight as a young kapok tree and shook my head. "You can't have done that," I said, "or you couldn't be standing here or walking about or—"

"That's just what the doctor and the TMPs said," he agreed cheerfully, "but I knew it was fractured, and today I found an old Tongan doctor who told me I was perfectly right. He said I needed a rest for two months and then I'd be better; so I will not work for two months."

There was no use trying to argue with him. Against whatever I could say was the pleasing prescription for two months' holiday. I didn't even try to argue with him—nor did I again contest Mele's sickness.

"So I'll call her sick," Tu'ifua said. "Often when people are made sick by the spirits, they feel worried. They worry because they think the spirits are calling them. Maybe it was that way with Mele. Maybe she thought the spirits wanted her to go to their meeting.

If she's sick that way, she calls out the names of many people who want her, but all those people are dead. They are spirits. They tell Mele that her relatives must let her go.

"That's probably what happened when Noa went to swear in the cemetery. The spirits were probably saying her family should let her go with them. But if he hadn't been drunk, he never would have gone there and shouted as he did.

"The proper thing to do," said Tu'ifua in the tone of one who reads from a well-worn etiquette book, "is this. Some strong men of the family should come to hold the sick girl down. That's so she won't do what the spirits ask and go away with them. While they hold her, the head of her family goes to the man who is the chief of the cemetery. He explains to him that the girl is still young, that she has not yet been married, and that much of life still awaits her. He tells him how much her relatives love her and how greatly they would grieve if she died. Finally, he begs him to go and ask his spirits to leave the girl alone. Usually, the chief of the cemetery agrees to do as he's asked. He gets dressed in his best clothes and goes to the cemetery. When he gets there he talks to the spirits, but he does it very politely. He doesn't swear at them. He doesn't go when he is drunk as Noa did. Speaking very nicely, he explains everything that the head of the girl's family has told him."

"And does it do any good?" I put in.

"Oh, yes," said Tu'ifua. "If the spirits are told properly they stop bothering the girl. The next night she sleeps well and soon she's quite all right again."

Tu'ifua's family is an educated one and Fe'vale'aki, her father, is given to receiving all things and all ideas in the light of common sense. However, the family is also very conservative. Although they are loyal members of the Wesleyan church, their lives and their thinking are regulated by ancient Tongan customs. I couldn't help wondering how they would react to a visitation from the spirits, so I asked, "If you were sick and just happened to call out the name of someone who was dead, would Fe'vale'aki go to the chief of the cemetery and ask him to make the spirits stop bothering you?"

"No," she said slowly, "I don't believe he would because, you see, he doesn't believe in spirits. He'd call the TMP—that's all."

"And if Fe'vale'aki were sick?" I asked. "Would you go to the chief of the cemetery?"

"No," she said again, but this time she said it so definitely and so abruptly that I asked, "Why not?"

"Because," she explained, "I'm not an important person in my family. If anyone went, his oldest sister would go."

"And would she go?"

Tu'ifua considered the question for a minute and then replied frankly, "I don't know. If Fe'vale'aki had anything to say about it, she wouldn't, but if he were very sick, she probably would. My aunt," she added loyally, "doesn't believe in spirits, either, but if Fe'vale'aki were very sick, she'd be worried and she'd want to do everything she could think of to make him better. And even if she didn't think it would do any good to get the chief of the cemetery to speak to the spirits, someone else in the family would probably believe that it was something that just might help, and she'd have to go anyway. You see, when a person is sick, it isn't always what he believes that is done, nor even what his close family believes. It's what everybody else, all the rest of the relatives and friends, too, believe."

"Yes, I see," I said, and I did, for I well remembered solicitous relatives who had been responsible for some of my past ailments being treated by such diverse remedies as homeopathic pills and Chinese herbs.

Bringing my thoughts back to the events of the day, I asked, "And how do you think Mele will get along now that her brother has sworn at the spirits?"

"You already said," Tu'ifua reminded me, "that both Farquhar and the TMPs said there was nothing wrong with her."

"So I did," I agreed, "but who knows, perhaps after being sworn at, the spirits will fix her."

"I don't think so," said Tu'ifua in a voice which clearly indicated her own distaste for spirits and all their goings on.

Not to leave the story of Mele hanging in the air, I hasten to add that she did, in a very short time after her brother went shouting at the spirits, feel well enough to get up from bed. Those who adhere to the old beliefs will say that, in spite of the rude way in which Noa addressed them, the spirits relented. They say that it was for eyes from another world that Mele danced that day when Farquhar surprised her alone in the house and that if he didn't appreciate the dance, there were those who did. As a proof of their belief they have the undeniable fact that she is now very well indeed.

Every story, however, has innumerable explanations. I think, as regards this one, that there is much to be said for Farquhar's diagnosis of a bad case of pretended sickness brought on by her distaste for the girls' college with its overemphasis on religion and its total neglect of social life. As proof of that belief, I submit the fact that, although she completely regained her health, she never felt strong enough to return to school. As a matter of fact, before a month had passed, she had further demonstrated her desire for the nonacademic life by running off to the bush with Nafi, a handsome youth who had lured many maidens from the narrow path of virtue.

But who knows why she ran away? Was it a violent reaction against the narrow life of the college—or had the spirits, insulted by being sworn at, got into her ripe young body and worked their mischief? Believe what you will. Many Tongans believe in spirits.

14 The Drowning

One summer afternoon, Latu, a village man, was wandering up and down the strip of beach that runs along the side of our house, doing, as he often does, nothing more purposeful than dabbling his toes in the warm pools left by the falling tide and indulging in the idler's art of observing the world about him.

He stared up at our verandah, but we were away in Neiafu; so there was nothing to be seen here. Turning, he looked out at the water where Taufa, half asleep, half watchful, sat in his canoe waiting for a fish to hook itself onto the line which hung limply over the side. Beyond Taufa, across the harbor, he could see the bush-covered hills of the main island broken by the thin scar of a trail that leads to Kilikili, the landing where villagers who have been to Neiafu come to wait for a canoe to bring them across to 'Utulei. There were no people there when he looked, however. Indeed, but for himself and Taufa the world might have been empty. No boats moved up the harbor, no children laughed and ran on the sands of the beach, no men and women wandered about. Everyone, Latu reflected, must be sleeping to escape the afternoon heat. He would have gone to sleep himself, but walking up the hill to his house required too much energy. Since the beach would not make a particularly comfortable bed, he continued to splash about in the tidal pools, staring now up at our verandah and now out to Taufa and across to Kilikili.

Suddenly, in the still landscape, there was motion. A speck of white moved through the bush above Kilikili. As Latu watched, it grew into a man who came slowly down the trail and stood for a minute on the edge of the sea. Latu waited, listening for the man to shout over to ask for a canoe; but he did not call. Instead, he plunged into the water and began to swim.

The distance from Kilikili to our cape at 'Utulei is not great—certainly not more than a quarter of a mile. Nineteen-year-old Alipati who has just finished school and found a job with the Public Works Department in Neiafu swims it as easily as a city man walks to the corner drug store, but Alipati is bursting with a young man's energy. Few others swim it. Many could do so; for Tongans are people of fine physique and great strength, but most of them see no reason for wasting energy in useless displays of athletic ability. An additional deterrent to swimming across is, of course, the fact that, every now and then, someone spots a shark cruising about in the harbor waters. They aren't seen often, but the mere possibility of them is enough to keep swimmers close to shore. The old people say that long ago a great many sharks used to swim right up to the very end of the harbor. They churned about in the water near Neiafu and if a man so much as walked by on the path that ran above the sea, they would snap at his shadow and if he lost his balance and fell in among them—well, that was the end of him. Nowadays the sharks never come in great numbers, and the stray ones that do come very rarely attack anyone. The old people say they were driven away by the missionaries, and for all I know it may be true.

Although in the past Latu had seen Alipati and a few other men swim from the point, the occurrence was sufficiently rare so that he stood still and watched. The swimmer cut an easy path through the calm sea with strokes mechanical in their evenness. When he had almost reached the buoy that marks the channel, he stopped swimming, gave one loud, terrified call for help, and disappeared beneath the surface of the water. Latu, who had been staring at the whole performance as one stares at figures in a dream, shook himself and called to Taufa, the fisherman.

"Did you see that?" he shouted.

"Yes," Taufa replied, "I saw."

"Go and help him!" Latu cried across the water, but back over the waves came fear.

"No," Taufa said, "I won't go. That wasn't a man. It was a devil. I know because it shouted and then went into the water and didn't come back. A man would have come back up."

"Perhaps you are right," said Latu, half-convinced, "but it just might have been a man. You'd better go."

"Not I," said Taufa, and added, "at least not alone. If you want to go with me—all right, I'll go."

"Yes, I'll go," Latu said bravely, although now that devils had been mentioned, he felt less sure of himself and would have been glad if Taufa had refused to budge. Still, when Taufa paddled over close to shore, he climbed valiantly into the canoe. As they went gliding towards the buoy, they watched the sea, hoping to see the man come struggling to the surface, but he did not reappear. Nor, when they reached the buoy and circled slowly about it, staring down into the blue-black depths, could they find the slightest trace of him.

Taufa shivered. "I think it was a devil after all," he said. "A man doesn't just disappear. If a shark had come at him, he'd have struggled, but there was no struggle—and we'd be able to see blood in the water, but there is no blood. Even if a man drowns, his body comes up, or his shirt floats on the water. It was a devil, I tell you."

Latu nodded shivering agreement. "Yes, we'd better go back."

And they turned and came back to 'Utulei and from that day to this no body has come up—no, and not even a piece of clothing has floated to the surface. Still, for all that, it was not a devil Latu saw, but a man, a young man who was a fine swimmer. He came from 'Otea, a village on an island far down the harbor. His name was 'Ofa. Latu and Taufa saw him drown, and that was the end of him. It was, however, neither the beginning nor the end of his story, but only a bit somewhere in the middle. Actually that day—the day of 'Ofa's death—was to have been his wedding day. To be sure, his marriage would not have been that union of two innocent young things which poets sing and ministers praise. As we say here in Tonga, he had gone to the bush with Fusi, the girl, some three months before and lived with her off and on ever since. I knew Fusi, and it was hard for me to imagine why 'Ofa ever ran off with her in the first place, let alone why he later thought of marrying her. True, she had the careless good looks common to all young people, but that was the end of her attractions. Always rather dirty and very sloppy, she had, most days, the somnolent, puffy eyes of one who spends her nights in riotous living. Though I regret to say it of one who must, I suppose, be called the heroine of the story, she was far from being "a nice girl." Still, 'Ofa ran off with her.

Having thus destroyed the character of the heroine, it is perhaps only fair of me to confess that the hero was not exactly an exemplary young person, either. However, his sins, though numerous enough, were not particularly black. They were only the usual ones common to young men the world over who find themselves possessed of high spirits for which they have no adequate outlet. If he stole a bit, it was not because he was dishonest, but only for the adventure of the thing. If he lied at times and swore often, it was only because he found a thrill in shocking the staid members of society by his falsehoods and his curses. Of course, he went to the bush with Fusi, and he drank "kava papalangi," the white man's alcohol, but on the whole, he wasn't a bad boy. He was just one of the crowd.

The aim of 'Ofa's crowd was to have a good time

with as many adventures and as few responsibilities as possible. Consequently, when he announced to them that he was going to marry Fusi, the news was received without enthusiasm. Running off to the bush with a girl was all very well, but marrying her was quite a different sort of thing. Married men had to work in their gardens, they had to build houses and entertain their wives' relatives. What was worse, they never had time to take part in the doings of the crowd.

Why 'Ofa came to the decision to marry, no one knows; but, having come to it, he stuck by it. Still, he didn't like to break with his old friends; so he did his best to assure them that getting married was really a very good idea. If he had a house, the crowd could meet there. Nothing would change; for, after all, Fusi was part of the crowd, too. They were not quite convinced, but when he further told them that before the wedding he would give a big party up in Neiafu with enough "kava papalangi" so that everyone could drink as much as they liked, they changed their minds and decided that his getting married wasn't so bad after all.

'Ofa was as good as his word. On the appointed day, all the crowd gathered in Neiafu. The wedding was not to be held until five o'clock in the afternoon, so the day was free for the party—and the party promised to be the biggest the crowd had ever had. Brandy, whisky, gin, wine, vanilla, and lemon extract, everything alcoholic that the local store sold, 'Ofa had collected. Food there was, too, provided by the relative at whose house they were meeting and by Fusi's family.

Before noon of the wedding day, they were all—prospective bride and groom included—gloriously drunk. They were happily drunk; for the bright Tongan day outside and the cool house in which they made merry seemed to spin gaily about in time to the songs they sang.

Their laughter, though it was loud enough to make sober passers-by stop and stare, was friendly and light-hearted. After noon, however, the subtle changes that always take place in a prolonged party came into evidence. Having sung all the songs they knew a dozen times over, they fell into conversation. The conversation became discussion and the discussion became argument, and as often as not the argument ended in violent disagreement. The pleasant spinning of the world grew into a dizzying whirl. The cool house became oppressively hot. Several stomachs revolted, and their poor young owners had to stagger from the house and find a tree to lean against while they retched in agony. Once, mistaking another man for 'Ofa, Fusi pinched him familiarly and gave him a long, clinging kiss, and the crowd roared with glee and teased 'Ofa about his bride's infidelity.

'Ofa, however, gave no sign of jealousy and no doubt he felt none, for he was the sort of steady drinker who, while remaining to all appearances perfectly sober, becomes enfolded in a layer of unconsciousness which shuts him off from the world about him as completely as if he were suddenly translated to another planet. To the remarks of his friends he certainly made replies, but what he said he himself could not have told a minute later. The unnatural shine of his eyes and the slightly fatuous smile which rested on his lips that day were, perhaps, the result of drinking, but they might quite as easily have come from the ordinary dazed condition of a young man about to be married.

People commenting on the affair later said that 'Ofa and Fusi must have had a quarrel that afternoon, but none of the crowd remembered any angry words between the two. Fusi herself, although she was scarcely in a condition to give an accurate report of anything, said that she couldn't remember a word 'Ofa had said to her that day until late in the afternoon when he'd begged to be excused, saying he had left some things at home and that he would go and get them and return in time for the wedding. At the time, Fusi had simply accepted his statement and smiled good-by. Had she been slightly less befuddled, she surely would have questioned him. "Home" was 'Otea, fifteen miles and four islands away. As it was, she and the rest of the crowd were scarcely aware, a moment later, that he had gone.

What passed in 'Ofa's mind that afternoon no one now will ever know. Maybe, in a flash of sobriety, he took a second look at Fusi and decided a lifetime with her would be unendurable. More likely, he had no idea at all what he was doing. It is only known that he walked away from his friends and his bride, staggered through town, climbed the path to the point and plunged into the sea. Latu and Taufa know the end of that.

The week after 'Ofa disappeared was a sad time around the harbor. All his family and his neighbors from 'Otea came up to look for his body. Boats full of divers with hooks and poles and ropes circled the buoy. When they failed to find the least trace of him, they studied the currents and the tides, thinking he might have been drawn far away from the buoy. They widened their area of search from day to day until at last they had covered all the waters of the inner harbor, but it was all to no avail. On the steps of the wharf at Neiafu sat his weeping family and the once-gay crowd, sober and shamed and red-eyed, waiting for news, but no news came. At last, they had no choice but to go sadly back to their island village.

Some said 'Ofa must have been taken by a shark. Some thought his body had been wedged into a crevice in the coral. Others felt sure he had been swept far down the harbor and out to the open sea. But no one knew and days passed and Vava'u talked of other things and the crowd returned to its old ways and even those who mourned him most began to lose their sadness in the busy life of every day.

So, 'Ofa might have been forgotten had it not been that one night several months later, he talked to his father. He came in a dream, but the dream was as real as waking and the words that he spoke in his own familiar tones were as clear as any words he ever uttered while he lived.

"It is I—'Ofa," he said at once to allay the old man's doubts. "I come to tell you I am still under the reef beside the buoy. My body is caught there in the coral and it can't get loose. I don't like it there. I want to be buried in the earth. I don't want to stay under the reef."

His old father wept and begged him to tell him

what he should do. At once, the boy replied, "There is only one thing. You know my friend, Fai'iva from Kapa? He is a clever diver. He can get me out. Go to him and tell him to come down and get me. That is the only thing to do."

"All right," promised the old man, "I'll go." Then he added, "Your mother grieves for you. Her tears still fall." He longed to hear from his son some words of remembrance and affection which he could carry to his wife to treasure, but he longed in vain. In death, as in life, 'Ofa was completely preoccupied with his own problems and, having told his father what he wished him to do, he disappeared in the final irrevocable way of people in dreams.

Sighing, the old man awoke, but being a devoted and long-suffering parent, he did not pause long over his son's shortcomings. Instead, he dressed himself and saddled his horse in preparation for the trip to the neighboring village of Kapa. While 'Ofa lived, his father had disliked Fai'iva; for he thought of him as a bad influence, blaming, as doting parents do, his son's faults on his son's friends. After 'Ofa's drowning, he had thought of Fai'iva as a heartless creature; he alone of all the crowd remained at home and did not join in the search for the body. However, that morning, as the old man rode along the hilly path to Kapa, he lost all the bitterness he had felt. If Fai'iva would make it possible for him to give his son a proper burial, he would have nothing but praises for him.

When, at last, he reached Kapa and found his son's friend, the old father was convinced that Fai'iva was

a good young man after all. He listened politely to
the telling of the dream, and at every mention of
'Ofa's name he lowered his eyes and trembled so
that it seemed his grief was as great as the father's
own. When all that 'Ofa had said had been explained,
the old man, with tears in his eyes, turned to Fai'iva.
"You are the only one who can get him," he said,
"so you'll come. My boat is being brought around
now, and we can go up the harbor as soon as it gets
here."

Fai'iva started at the words and trembled more than
ever, but he managed to stammer out that he would
go if 'Uili, the minister, went along, too.

"Of course, 'Uili will go," 'Ofa's father cried, more
than ever pleased with Fai'iva for making the sugges-
tion. Too many young men these days—his own
poor 'Ofa included—found it easy to forget the
church and the great power of prayer. Surely, he
thought to himself, he had wronged Fai'iva in the old
days when he had regarded him as a wild youth. He
was, on the contrary, a model young man.

A model, indeed, he seemed later in the day as he
and 'Uili, the minister, together with 'Ofa's father
and some of the other 'Otea men, sailed up the harbor
toward the buoy near which 'Ofa had disappeared.
When the men spoke to him of the currents in the
harbor and the location of coral, he listened attentively without saying a word. When 'Uili started a
hymn, he joined in with a zeal unusual in young
men.

At last, reaching the buoy, they circled about it.
Leaning far over the side of the boat, 'Ofa's father

stared down at the black depths as if they were
windows through which he might suddenly see his
son. Fai'iva sat very still, saying nothing and not
even looking at the water. When, however, the men
began to haul down the sails and talked of anchoring
there, he suddenly shouted at them. "Stop, stop!" he
cried. "We must go to Neiafu for prayers. We must
have prayers first."

"Of course, we'll have prayers," 'Ofa's father said
soothingly. " 'Uili will say them right here and—"

"No, no, no," thundered Fai'iva. "Prayers must be
said at the mission house in Neiafu before I begin to
dive. They must be."

Some of the men tried to reason with him, explaining how much time they would save if they had
prayers in the boat, but Fai'iva would not hear of it.
"To the mission house. To the mission house," he
kept repeating with an insistence which grew to be
almost hysterical; so that, in the end, although 'Ofa's
father was beside himself with eagerness to get the
diving started, they gave up and sailed the rest of the
way to Neiafu.

At the mission house, Fai'iva asked for the European
minister, but he had gone off on a visit to a distant
village and was not expected back until the next day.
Fai'iva was inclined to wait for his return, but when
the other men said 'Uili was very well able to say
prayers and lead them in singing hymns and the
minister's wife agreed with them, he gave in and the
prayer meeting commenced.

To the great surprise of the others, Fai'iva seemed
unable to remember the words of the hymns although
they were all the old ones he had heard ever since

he was a child, and when they prayed, he choked as
if he were gasping for breath. Such behavior they
could not understand, but it made them less surprised
than they would otherwise have been when, just as
'Uili said the last "Amen," Fai'iva shouted in a broken
voice, "Go away! Go away all of you! I must confess
to 'Uili. I must confess now."

Something in his tone stopped their questions.
Without a word, they shuffled out of the room, leaving
him alone with 'Uili. They went on outside and sat
down in the shade of a mango tree. One of them
spoke of the young man's sudden desire to confess,
but they could make nothing of it and soon fell to
talking of other things. Only 'Ofa's father walked
up and down, up and down, grumbling at the delay
and complaining that the day would be over before
the diving even started.

The old man turned out to be right. The diving did
not commence on that day—no, nor on any day to
follow, either. After what seemed an endlessly long
time, the door of the room opened and Fai'iva and
'Uili came out. Together they walked toward the
mango tree where the men waited. When they got
there, Fai'iva sat down and buried his face in his
hands and 'Uili, standing very straight and using the
sonorous voice which he reserved for making sermons,
began to speak.

Fai'iva, he told them, could not dive for 'Ofa,
neither now nor ever. He was aware of the grief of
'Ofa's father and of his desire to have his son's body
to bury and he was sorry for him, but he could not
help it. He could not dive.

As 'Uili spoke, 'Ofa's father tried to protest, but

the minister lifted his hand for silence. The old man
fell back amongst his friends. A tearing sob and a
broken "Forgive me" came from Fai'iva and then all
was silence until 'Uili once more began to talk. He
told the tale simply, referring to Fai'iva as if he
were far away and not sitting right there with them,
his body shaking with sobs and his voice breaking in
from time to time with the oft-repeated words,
"Forgive me . . . forgive me."

Fai'iva, it seemed, and 'Ofa and a boy called Pauli
had been great friends. The three of them had done
many wicked things. They had been unclean in their
speech and in their thoughts. They had drunk kava
papalangi—lots of it—and they had stolen kerosene
from the church to fill their lamps for kava parties.
They had stayed away from services and, what was
worse, while their more pious neighbors were praying, they had stolen the food which had been prepared
for the minister's feast. They had not helped their
fathers to weed their gardens or cut copra, and they
had not cared for anyone but themselves. They had
sinned with girls, they had . . .

And 'Uili smacked his tongue against his lips as
he enumerated each fresh sin. When, at last, he had
come to the end of them, and gone over the worst
a second time, he shook his head righteously. "The
Lord punishes sinners," he said. "The Lord has
revenge on evildoers." He looked significantly at
Fai'iva and Fai'iva appropriately enough gave forth
a muffled sob, after which, in doleful tones, 'Uili
continued.

Two months ago, Pauli, who should have been

helping his father with the fishing, was lying indolently under a coconut tree sleeping off the previous night's wild party when, all of a sudden, a full-grown nut came crashing down on his skull, smashing it to bits. Accidents resulting from fallen nuts are frequent in fiction, but in life they are rare—so rare, indeed, that one could safely say that Pauli's death was nothing more nor less than God's punishment for his wickedness. Pauli was the first to go. And then poor 'Ofa, 'Ofa who lay at the bottom of the reef far below the buoy.

But 'Uili had no need to speak at length of 'Ofa, for at the mere mention of his name, his father burst into tears and the other men, because they were his friends and neighbors and sympathized with him, wept too. Tears were a part of 'Uili's professional equipment; so he, too, shed a few before he went on to explain Fai'iva's refusal to dive.

Pauli was dead and 'Ofa was dead and both before their time. To Fai'iva it was clear that their tragic endings had not come merely as a punishment to them, but also as a warning to him. Unless he stopped his sins, he, too, would meet some frightful disaster. When 'Ofa's father had come to ask him to dive for 'Ofa, he had agreed to because he felt sorry for the old man and wanted to help him, but as he thought of diving down far below the buoy, he started to grow afraid. 'Ofa was there, and 'Ofa was probably angry that he had drowned while Fai'iva who was every bit as bad as he was, if not worse, was still alive. The more he thought about it, the more he realized that 'Ofa was only trying to lay a trap for him. If he went down there, 'Ofa would catch him and hold him down below the black waters until he, too, had drowned. That was why Fai'iva refused to dive. He was sorry for 'Ofa's father, but he couldn't dive.

As 'Uili finished, Fai'iva lifted his head, revealing a tear-stained face, and for the last time uttered the words imploring forgiveness. White parents would, undoubtedly, have dismissed Fai'iva's story as the excuse of a coward, but Tongans are better acquainted with the malevolent nature of the dead and everyone, including 'Ofa's father, knew that even when he was alive, 'Ofa had not been the most amiable of youths. Consequently, all the men stepped up and shook Fai'iva's hand as a sign they understood his reluctance to dive, and forgave him. 'Ofa's father, who forgave him along with the rest, kissed him on the cheek and stood weeping by his side while 'Uili intoned a final prayer in which he praised Fai'iva for confessing his sins, and begged God to forgive him, even as they had done.

All that happened a year ago and more, and Fai'iva still lives; so perhaps his confession was accepted. Some of his neighbors say he has reformed and some say he is the same as he always was. I don't know, for Kapa is far away from 'Utulei. Fusi has, as Fusi would, run off with a new boy. 'Ofa has never again come to talk to his father. His name lives on in our village, for the children, swimming off the beaches, call to their too adventurous comrades, "Come back, come back. 'Ofa will get you, 'Ofa will drag you down into the sea."

15 The Second Tu'ifua

Farquhar and I had been married a very short time when I noticed a new question cropping up in all the conversations I had with Tongans. Eyeing my middle speculatively, they would ask, "And are you making a baby yet?"

Having been brought up in a part of American society which doesn't often mention such things and having, furthermore, come to Tonga from a British country which never speaks of them at all, I found the question a bit disconcerting. Still, since it came to me from nobles, chiefs, and commoners, from people I had known since I arrived in the country and from others I had just met, I learned to answer it with a polite, calm denial. When a year and more had passed and I was still answering the question negatively, people shook their heads sadly and exclaimed, "Oh poor couple! Who will look after you when you are old? Who will shut your eyes when you die?"

I tried to turn their concern aside with a laugh, but they wouldn't let me, for all Tongans believe that sons and daughters are essential if one is to have a happy life and a comfortable old age. To them, any house without children is a sad and empty one. As a matter of fact, ours was the only childless house in 'Utulei. Although there were two other village couples to whom no child had been born, they had each filled the lack by adopting a baby from relatives who were oversupplied. Adoption is a custom so widespread in Tonga, as in all Polynesian places, that when one tries to teach these people English and first uses the word "orphanage," he finds difficulty in making them imagine such a place. The idea of an unwanted child is wholly beyond their comprehension. A Tongan man and his wife who have many children will often allow one or more of them to be adopted by a childless couple (usually a couple belonging to their family). This represents no wish on the part of the parents to be rid of their surplus offspring. It comes about, rather, because Tongans seem to feel that children, like all the other good things of life, should be shared.

Actually adoption is today an essential part of the Tongan social system; for children are truly necessary in a native household. Here, every man is a farmer. From his seven or eight acres of leasehold land (for which he becomes eligible at the age of sixteen), he cuts copra to provide himself with cash for store goods. On the land, also, he grows all the fruit and vegetables and raises all the pigs and chickens that his family needs. There is no mechanized farm equipment to help him in his work and he does not even use horses for plowing. A hoe, a shovel, a knife, an ax, and a yam planter are all he has in the way of tools. With them he clears and plants his land, harvests his crops, and cuts his copra. Working by himself, a man is doomed to failure. Even if he worked steadily —as no right-minded Tongan ever does—he couldn't possibly get everything done. With a brace of children to do the weeding, fleet-footed little girls to chase chickens and nimble boys to run up coconut trees, the picture changes and life becomes successful and happy. Women, too, would find their tasks overwhelmingly heavy were it not for the young things who scrape coconuts, cut firewood, carry water, run errands and make themselves generally useful about the house.

Tongan children do a great deal of essential work, but it must not be supposed that they are exploited little victims of child labor. Nothing could be further from the truth. They have their chores to do, but they seem also to have more time left over to play than any other children in the world. Certain it is that, whether they are gathering sand for a new cement tank in the village, chasing pigs for the Sunday feast, or splashing idly at the beach, they lead a healthy outdoor life. That they are happy, no one who hears them shouting and laughing can doubt for a minute. Theirs is the security of the well loved, too, for parents and foster parents alike treasure each child and try to make him feel at home in this world.

Farquhar and I had no copra to cut and no land on which to plant yams and the yard boy and the little house girl managed very well with all the household jobs. Nevertheless, all our Tongan friends persisted in pitying us because we had no children to help us. They were even willing to supply our lack in the traditional way. One day, when I admired the curly-headed two-year-old daughter of my neighbor, Semisi, he said, "You like her? Take her then. I have many children. You have this one to be your daughter."

And Tupou, a good friend, who already had five fine, laughing children, was ready to give us her sixth when it was born. We did not accept their offers, tempting though they were. It was all too easy to see that a Tongan child who, while continuing to live in Tonga, was separated from the culture of his own people and given that of the white world would be doomed to a lasting sense of not quite belonging with either group.

Although we did not adopt a child, it was inevitable that children should come to fill a larger part of our consciousness than they had ever done before. There was almost always a wide-eyed little boy or a smiling girl on the verandah. They came on errands from their parents in the village to bring us a fish or a plate of bananas, to ask for a match or a bit of sugar. Others, with little coral cuts or bumped knees, came to Farquhar and when he had fixed them up went running happily away to show their companions the bit of plaster or the fine white bandage he had given them. Some, having learned my strange papalangi interest in collecting shells, came with fists full of shining cowries and some, pressing their flat little noses flatter still against the glass in the front door, came, as they quite frankly said, "just to look."

As each day came to its end, it found Farquhar and me sitting out on the verandah to enjoy the harbor's great show: sunset. When the tide was high, the boys and girls came down then for a swim and, as they splashed into the sea or ran along the beach, the last rays of the sun made shining silhouettes of their naked bodies. The pudgy babies with their fat stomachs and uncertain legs, the shy little girls who ran giggling into the water, the lanky little boys who turned somersaults and played tag, and the older ones whose shoulders were broadening into manhood —there they all were, a laughing, shouting panorama of the joy of living.

"What fun it must be to grow up in Tonga!" we said to each other one night as we watched them. "How wonderful to be little here where you can always be outdoors, where there's a sandy beach for running and a cool sea for swimming, where there's always a canoe to paddle about in and a reef to explore, where the bush is as full of mystery as a jungle, and fruit and nuts are to be had for the picking!"

It may be that you cannot live in a country without unconsciously absorbing some of the ideas and ideals of the people native to it, or it may only be that children are the inevitable wish of happy people everywhere. At any rate, it was not long before we were thinking that a white child was just what was needed to complete the group of sunset swimmers.

Then, the third year we lived in 'Utulei, I did not go to any of the New Year's feasts; for the thought, usually so pleasant, of sitting down before a whole pile of pork, chicken, fish, vegetables, and pudding was suddenly most repugnant.

Anaise who, by virtue of having washed our clothes every Monday since we arrived in the village, belongs to the family and exercises all the family rights of free speech, was not backward with her diagnosis. The first time she witnessed me parting abruptly and unceremoniously from my breakfast, she cried delightedly, "You've got the good sickness," and off she ran to tell all the village that the doctor's wife was, at last, making a baby.

Under ordinary circumstances, I would have kept the news to myself until time had given me the obvious undeniable shape, but with Anaise broadcasting the coming event and my uncertain stomach substantiating her story, any attempt at secrecy became impossible. As a matter of fact, my expectations soon became a matter of civic concern. When my continuing inability to face food caused Farquhar to put me to bed, old Kuli, the town officer, called a village meeting. After explaining my condition to the assembled men, women, and children, he decreed that from that time until the baby was born, the school children must bathe at the far end of the beach and whenever any of them came by our house, they must remember not to sing or shout or make any loud noise. He suggested, further, that it would be a good idea if all the village people would remember to try to find something with which to tempt my appetite.

The meeting had immediate results. Our cape

became a zone of quietness which was broken by
nothing save the hum of an occasional motorboat
making its way down the harbor. Now and then there
was a murmur of voices from the direction of the
kitchen and Tu'ifua, who had put aside all her
usual duties to come down and take care of me,
would come and tell me that someone had just
brought down a basket of something for me to eat.

A gourmet interested in South Sea delicacies would
have been delighted with the gifts I received at that
time, embracing as they did all that these islands
have to offer of good or rare foods. There were plates
of wafer-thin ai nuts, baskets of bright pink fekiki
apples, juicy pineapples, sweet oranges, and green
vi fruit. There were land crabs and all sorts of fish
and even an octopus on a pole with his tentacles
flapping out behind him like streamers in the breeze.

I need hardly add that I didn't take a gourmet's
pleasure in my food gifts. On the contrary, I found
it a trial having to hear about them, let alone see
them or taste them. Yet, in spite of my physical inability to enjoy the food, I thoroughly appreciated it;
for I well knew the kindness that came with each
offering.

When I once again began to feel better and got
up and went about as usual, I had a sudden rush of
visitors. All the villagers came to tell me how pleased
they were that we were to have a child, and the women
came back again and again to sit with me. I discovered
that I had arrived at a higher status among them.
Now that I was performing a wife's proper function,
they felt, as they never had before, that I was one

of them. In token of their new acceptance, they regaled me with accounts of all their own pregnancies and those of everyone else they had ever known or heard about. The tales were well mixed with imagination and some of them were frightening enough—or would have been, had it not been so obvious that, for all their talk, the village women thought childbirth the simplest of all natural processes. In spite of the fact that they came down frequently to consult Farquhar about all sorts of minor ailments, they rarely called him to a confinement. It simply didn't occur to them to bother him for that. Even if an occasional woman had difficulties, he wasn't asked to go. There was no need, since every old woman in the village set herself up as an accomplished midwife, and when a child was being born, as many people as could squeeze into the house crowded about to give their advice on the delivery.

Several of these village experts offered me their services. Anaise, who had diagnosed my case so accurately, assured me she knew as much about babies as there is to know. Litia, who spends many hours in our garden looking for the particular sort of grass out of which she brews her panacea, guaranteed a painless delivery. Others who specialize in coral dust, leaf poultices, and manipulation were equally anxious to be of use. However, we politely refused all their offers. Farquhar, assisted by Lutui, the head medical practitioner at the Neiafu hospital, delivered our daughter himself.

She was born on a stormy September night in the front bedroom of our house. By Tongan standards, there were few people on hand to welcome her, but it seemed to us that the house was overflowing. Lutui had brought with him one of the nurses newly arrived from Tongatapu, and Tu'ifua had, of course, come down to be with me. In the kitchen, the little house girl and her cousin kept up the fire and supplied hot water.

After the baby had been washed and wrapped, and I had been satisfied that she had the correct number of fingers and toes and was, in every way, a perfect physical specimen, I dozed off in the blissful satisfaction of my new maternity. I did not sleep for long, however. It was still dark when the noise of someone moving across the floor jarred me into consciousness. "What's the matter?" I cried out with a start. "Who is there? What time is it?"

I heard Tu'ifua's voice coming from the direction of the bassinet. "I'm sorry I woke you," she apologized. "It's just after three o'clock. I couldn't sleep because I was worrying about the baby. I just had to get up to see if she was still breathing."

"And is she?" I demanded, startled.

Tu'ifua laughed gently. "Of course. She's quite all right."

She came, then, and sat beside my bed. Too excited to think of sleeping any more, we whispered together of the new little mortal who lay in the bassinet across the room until the sky lightened and it was time for morning tea.

It was not long before Farquhar came in to see us. As both a father and a doctor, he announced himself thoroughly pleased with his daughter. Soon after breakfast he went off to Eniafu to send cables to our families and friends to announce the safe arrival of Tu'ifua Ann.

In the afternoon of the second Tu'ifua's first day on earth, some of the village people came down to see her. They peered in at her little face closed tight in sleep and exclaimed over her beauty in a way that elated me, and one and all, they thanked me for having produced such a fine baby. Everyone was happy that day—everyone, that is, except my friend 'Ugatea who, when she had finished admiring the baby, turned to me and said in a voice full of disappointment, "I didn't know you'd have her last night. If I had known I'd have come. I've never seen a white baby born."

I learned in the days that followed that there were many people who shared 'Ugatea's curiosity. Whenever Lutui or Tu'ifua or the nurse walked through the streets, they were stopped by men and women who implored them to describe "the way a papalangi has a baby." With the usual Tongan concern for details, they were especially interested in knowing whether or not I had behaved well. Fortunately for our prestige in the community, those who had been present were able to report that, as Tu'ifua expressed it, I did very nicely with no weeping and no screaming at all!

As usual here in Tonga, the people's curiosity was easy to bear because it was accompanied by so much genuine interest and by so much kindness. All during the two weeks that Farquhar kept me in bed, I was overwhelmed by visitors coming with gifts and good wishes, but the climax of all the visits was that which was made by the aunts.

When we named the baby Tu'ifua, Farquhar and I did so because of the great affection and respect we felt for our friend Tu'ifua. We both hoped that our daughter would grow to be a woman as intelligent, as loyal, and as loving as she is. As for Big Tu'ifua, she was delighted to have a small papalangi namesake and, from the beginning, she has been to her a sort of third parent who has shared with us both the anxieties and the joys which having a daughter involves. What neither of us suspected was that, with her name, we were giving our child not only a second mother, but also a second family. I began to understand that Big Tu'ifua's family felt quite genuinely that it had a new member only when she said to me one day during the second week of the baby's life, "The aunts are coming today to see our daughter."

"The aunts!" I exclaimed. Of all the members of a Tongan family, aunts are considered the most important. Whenever a whole group of them goes about on family business, you may be very sure that the occasion is one of great importance.

"Naturally they're coming," she said, making no effort to conceal her pleasure. "They must come to see you and to thank you for the baby. And they must welcome her, too."

That afternoon the aunts did come—all of them, dressed in their best church dresses with their finest mats fastened around their waists. From my bed, I could see them as they landed on the beach. I watched them while they straightened their hair, pulled down their dresses, smoothed out their mats, and gave all the other essential last-minute attentions to their toilettes. When they were quite satisfied with their appearance, Kalauta who, as the eldest sister of Tu'ifua's father, is the most important of them all, turned and spoke to a group of young girls and boys who were tumbling out of the boat after them. They listened attentively to her and then began to lift out of the boat bundles of mats and tapa and an enormous food basket. When all the things had been put down on the beach, Kalauta went over and inspected them. Apparently they met with her satisfaction. Nodding and smiling, she beckoned to the other aunts who, falling into a line behind her, proceeded to follow her down the beach and across the lawn up to the house.

A beaming Tu'ifua met them on the verandah and showed them into my room. Solemnly, one by one, they came to my bedside. Each in her turn first shook my hand, then stooped and kissed me Tongan-style, on the cheek, saying as she turned away, "Thank you very much for the nice baby."

When they had all greeted me in that manner, they sat down on the floor, making a circle about my bed, and Kalauta said, "We thank God for your safe delivery and for the health of your baby. We come to see you now because of our love for you."

Replying in the accepted manner, I thanked them all for coming and spoke of my love for them.

They smiled and Kalauta continued, speaking then in the disparaging way that all polite Tongans do of the gifts they make, "We have no suitable gifts for you. We have no fine papalangi presents for your little Tu'ifua. We are poor people. We have only our love to bring you."

Almost as an afterthought, she added, "There are some things we Tongan people always prepare for new mothers to eat. We thought you might like to try them so we brought you a little basket."

I thanked them while Tu'ifua went to see that the food was taken to the kitchen. I might add here that the basket contained chickens baked in coconut cream, the softest of all the yams, roasted drinking nuts, and a delicate arrowroot pudding. Kalauta had called it a little basket, but I was not deceived about its size because I had seen it down on the beach. That night it provided dinner for all our household and there was enough left over so that we were able to send shares to several of our neighbors.

Kalauta had spoken of the food because she knew it must be put away at once. The other gifts she dismissed with a mere shrug and a "Here are some poor things for the new Tu'ifua."

While she was speaking, the boys and girls who had been waiting on the verandah came in carrying their bundles and put them down in a corner of the room. As they piled them up one on top of another, I caught a glimpse of the finely woven double brown mats which are so prized here, and another of the gay varicolored mats which come from Samoa. I saw the deep fringe on a rare round mat and noticed fine white tapa and dark heavily printed tapa and I realized that all the family had brought forth its greatest treasures for our daughter. In accordance with Tongan custom, I refrained from looking at the gifts while their donors were present and contented myself with thanking the aunts profusely. They glowed with pleasure at the realization that I had appreciated the true value of their offerings.

When all the presentations were over, Kalauta turned to Tu'ifua. "Now, show us the little Tu'ifua," she said, and our friend who had been hovering protectively over the bassinet raised the net and proudly lifted out the well-blanketed little cocoon that was her namesake.

Undisturbed, the baby slumbered on while she was passed from aunt to aunt, from Kalauta to Kala, the big aunt whose hearty gay voice rumbled up from the depths of her two hundred and fifty pounds, to Lea, the sweet-faced one, and the retiring Vaca. When all the aunts had seen the baby, Tu'ifua took her again and exhibited her to the boys and girls who sat on the verandah just outside the door. The formal atmosphere which had prevailed during the presentations disappeared and a burst of chatter of the sort which greets new babies everywhere broke out. Big Tu'ifua's sister, who was one of the group of young people, said in the usual manner of little sisters, "She's a very fine baby, but why did you give her such a funny name? Tu'ifua's a silly name."

The boys and girls all laughed and Tu'ifua frowned and the aunts, all talking at once and all reproving, exclaimed, "Be quiet. This is no time for you to talk. It's a fine name and we are very proud that the baby has been given it."

Above the murmur, I heard Kalauta's clear voice. "Please give me the baby again," she said to Tu'ifua.

Tu'ifua stooped, and the old woman, who was widowed and childless, took up the little package that was my daughter and gazed silently for some minutes at her sleeping face. The other aunts stopped talking and the boys and girls were hushed. Then Kalauta, holding the baby in outstretched arms, said to her, "Welcome to this world, oh Tu'ifua! Welcome to your papalangi family and welcome to your Tongan family. So many people are happy because you live. May you, too, be happy."

Then, in a dreamy, caressing tone as if she spoke to the baby alone, she said softly, "Many times, I prayed for a baby. Every year my husband and I asked God to give us a child, but he never did and now my husband is dead, and I am old. Oh Tu'ifua, how fortunate are your parents!"

A tear ran down her cheek, but she tossed her head and finished in a firm voice, "Many people love you, Tu'ifua. May you in turn love many people. Oh, welcome to this world!"

When the visit was over and the aunts had gone away again, I lay back on my pillow and watched Big Tu'ifua settling little Tu'ifua back into her bassinet, and a great wave of happiness flooded through me. It seemed to me that never anywhere had any child received a finer welcome to this world than that which the aunts and our neighbors here in 'Utulei and all our other Tongan friends had given to our daughter.

16 The Kava Circle

Every land has its own particular sound which becomes for the people who live there the background music of their days and which, were it to be heard unexpectedly after years away in distant places, would evoke the country of its origin as surely and as quickly as a sudden sight of its towns or its peoples.

These islands have many sounds which cling to the memory. Visitors are immediately impressed by the church bells pealing endlessly not only on Sundays, but all through the week to summon the people to a constant round of services; and, following the bells, the vigorous singing of hymns which, though they started as the familiar old Wesleyan tunes, have been so altered by being given Tongan words and sung in Polynesian rhythms that they emerge as totally new productions.

There is dance music, too, that by its very phrasing brings to mind the intricate movements of the laka-laka, the sitting dance, and the beautiful girls who perform it with such skill and grace. And there are love songs sung softly on a still, black night or strummed on a haunting guitar. Oh, there is music everywhere here—in children's games and mothers' lullabies and in the rolling chants that the men sing as they work—but the sound that will always mean Tonga to me is far more prosaic than any song. It is the dull, heavy pound of the kava maker's stone.

Rainy days or sunny days, white nights or black, time of joy or sorrow—whenever and wherever you go in Tonga, the air echoes with the sound of kava making. So ever-present is that constant pound, pound, pound and so much a part of every event of Tongan life that a stranger could find no better introduction to island ways than a brief study of the kava drinking ceremony.

Kava itself is a strikingly beautiful plant—tall-growing, bushlike, with knobbed brown branches and large, bright green, heart-shaped leaves. It clings firmly to the ground by a tangled mass of fibrous roots which thicken and consolidate with each passing year until they are as thick as a man's arm.

The earliest of the explorers to reach Tonga found the natives making a drink from the dried roots of the plant. The kava maker divided the roots into pieces which he passed on to his helpers, a selected group of handsome and healthy young men and women. Each one put his piece of root into his mouth and thoroughly chewed it. When it had been reduced to a soft pulp, it was removed from the mouth and placed on a clean leaf. After a sufficient amount of the root had been chewed, it was collected on a larger leaf and carried to a big wooden bowl into which water was poured. The chewed kava was allowed to infuse for some minutes and then the maker, taking a handful of twisted fiber from the fou bush, squeezed out the pulp, leaving behind in the bowl a pale, mud-colored liquid. While all that was going on, the people who were to drink the kava sat in a circle about the maker, who announced to them when it was ready. At a signal from the chief or highest-ranking member of the circle, the liquid was served out. None of the wholesale drinking that goes on at cocktail parties was tolerated. Only one person drank at a time. The names of the members of the circle were called out by an attendant, and the order of calling was as rigid a social matter with them as the placing of guests at table is with us. As each name was called, its owner clapped, signifying his desire to drink. Then he cupped his hands before him and a polished half coconut shell full of kava was placed in them. Politeness demanded that he leave a drop or two which he tossed out behind him before he threw the empty shell back to the maker. Then it was filled for the next drinker. While each fresh lot of kava was being prepared the drinkers sang or listened to music or talked among themselves. In such circles were settled matters of state and of religion, affairs of the heart and all family business. There, too, were told again and again the old myths of the Tongan people, there the news of the day was discussed, and there the village gossip exchanged.

Kava now is made just as it was in the old days with one exception: the root is no longer chewed. Doctors have agreed that the dental health of Tongans in the days before they began to ruin their teeth by eating the papalangis' white bread and tinned meats instead of their native foods was so good that the average young person's mouth was as clean as a mixing bowl. Be that as it may, the first missionaries were so horrified at the idea of a drink made from matter that had been chewed that they never rested or let the people rest until the chewing had been replaced by pounding. Two volcanic rocks are used nowadays, a big flat one on which the kava is placed and a smaller one with which it is pounded. As a new lot of root is prepared for every round of drinks, the dull thudding goes on at intervals throughout every kava circle, and it goes on through all the days and nights of Tonga and through all my thoughts of these islands.

The kava circle itself is quite as important today as it ever was. Whenever the Queen travels from one part of the kingdom to another, she is honored in a royal kava circle, an elaborate ceremony in which the kava maker is involved in a series of motions which, more than anything else, resemble the figures in a ballet. A chiefly circle is also an impressive thing. Even the simple kava ring of commoners follows the age-old ceremonies.

To the average European it is scarcely comprehensible that a whole institution has grown up around a drink which tastes like nothing so much as lukewarm mouthwash. True, all sorts of fantastic tales have been written of its strange intoxicating powers, but they are all quite baseless. Young men who drink kava night after night are often pale and hollow-eyed and uninterested in the day's activities, but their trouble is not too much drink, but too little sleep.

Old men, after a lifetime of drinking, sometimes develop a rough grayish skin, but scientists suspect that time, rather than kava, is to blame for that.

However uninteresting and ineffective kava is to a white man's taste, it exerts a potent influence on Tongan life. As a British protectorate, Tonga has a parliament modeled on British lines, but it is a mere concession to papalangi custom. All the business of each session has been pretty well decided long before the members go to the meetings, in the numerous kava circles in the palace, in the homes of the nobles and the chiefs, and in the places of the representatives from all of Tonga. On the village level, too, both civic and religious matters are commonly settled around the kava bowl.

There are no newspapers in this land and, except for the Bible, virtually no books, but the lack is scarcely felt. News travels through the kava circles as fast as it is spread by printer's ink, and stories take shape and grow and are transformed in the same way that they were in Europe in the days of the strolling bards.

Generally speaking, kava circles are composed of men, although women sometimes have their own circles and occasionally join those of the men. The kava makers, however, are almost invariably women, and during at least one period in every Tongan woman's life, the circles are very exciting things. Romance, like everything else in this country, is a gregarious affair. The well-brought-up young Tongan girl does not go off alone as our young girls do, on "dates" with her admirer. There are no nights at the

pictures, no walks in the country, much less any
drives in high-powered automobiles. For the lovelorn
young things here there are nights when the boy,
accompanied by three or four of his friends, brings
a root of kava to the girl's house and asks her parents
to let her pound it for them. To our eyes there may
seem to be nothing remotely romantic about sitting
in a room making an insipid drink for one's love
and his friends, but a Tongan girl finds it exciting.
And why shouldn't she?

She is wearing her best dress and over it a gay
kiekia, the grass overskirt, which rustles alluringly
whenever she moves. Her hair and her body shine
from the sweet-smelling oil with which she has
rubbed herself, and anyone who sits in the circle
can plainly see how beautiful she is. Anyone who
is at all observant can notice, too, how cleverly her
hands slide through the age-old motions of kava
making and anyone with ears can enjoy her witty
conversation and her soulful singing. Strict decorum
is observed and the friends never leave the young
couple alone, but parties last to hours that would
alarm the most liberal white parents—until three and
four and five in the morning—and sometime or other,
the most proper young people seem to manage a word
or two of love.

If a boy and a girl think of marriage, they confide
in their respective families, and the arrangements for
the wedding are decided on by their elders in a whole
series of kava circles. During the actual wedding
celebrations, much root is pounded, and a kava bowl
with a set of well-polished coconut-shell cups and kava

stones is the one essential item without which the young couple wouldn't dream of setting up house-keeping. From the girl's point of view the most important of all the circles is the one which follows the consummation of her marriage. Then, if she prove to have been a virgin, she presides as chief of a circle which is composed of members of both families, important people of the community, and friends. Before them all, she is officially recognized as a virtuous girl who is on the threshold of her new life as a married woman and a full-fledged member of the village.

Tu'ifua first explained to me these courtship procedures. When she had finished, I said, "I guess kava circle romances are all right for Tongans, but American boys would never put up with such a long round-about way of making love."

"Oh, but they would," she corrected me. "During the war, there were a lot of Americans in Nuku'alofa and they liked very much to drink kava with the girls."

"Yes?" I said doubtfully.

"Yes," she affirmed, "but the Tongan boys got jealous because, of course, the Americans had more money, and they could bring the girls better presents. The girls liked that and after a time they wouldn't make kava for the Tongans at all, but only for the Americans.

"The Tongan boys used to go to a girl's house, walking as Tongan boys do, quietly, barefooted. They would call out, 'Come, make kava for us.' But the girls would reply from behind darkened doors, 'Go away. We're sleeping,' or 'Go away. We're sick,' or 'Go away. We have no light for our lamps.'

"And the boys would turn and go away, but sometimes before they had gone out of the road, they would meet a group of Americans in their heavy battle boots tramping up to the girl's house. They would hear them yell out, 'Let us in. We want kava,' and they would see a light go on and the door open and they would hear the girl welcoming the Americans and telling them to come inside."

"So what did they do?" I asked. "Wait for the Americans and beat them up?"

"Naturally not," she replied scornfully. "Tongan boys are polite."

"So didn't they do anything?"

"They did," she said with a smile. "They learned to say 'Let us in' in English and they bought themselves heavy boots to wear."

Tourists often complain that although these islands are beautiful, there is really nothing to see in them. What they are looking for, of course, are the old buildings and ancient monuments of Europe and Asia, and it is perfectly true that they never find anything like them here. That is not to say that Tonga has nothing old; for she has. However, her old things are buried, not in the ground, but in the memories of her people. There you may discover the long-remembered tales which explain the beginnings of all the things in this world. From out of that ancient memory, Tu'ifua told me one day the story of the beginning of kava.

"Long, long ago," she began, "there lived a man

and his wife and they had no children. They were
very sad, indeed, and every day they wished for a
child. After a long time, when they were getting so
old that they were afraid they'd die with no one
to shut their eyes for them, a little daughter was
born. Then they were very happy and happier still
when they saw how beautiful she was.

"When she grew to be a child, she was as good and
kind as she was beautiful, and her mother and father
and all her family and everyone else in the whole
village loved her very much, indeed. Her parents
never let her out of their sight, and they spent all
their time thinking about her and making plans
for her future."

For a moment Tu'ifua paused, letting me make
for myself a mental picture of that little girl so
beauteous and so beloved. Then she shattered my
vision by the sudden announcement, "But the little
girl died."

"Died!" I exclaimed. "But why?"

"Why?" repeated Tu'ifua. "Why does anyone die?
I don't know. She got sick and her mother and father
sent to all the villages near and far asking the men
who were clever at healing diseases to come and
cure her. They came, and they tried everything they
knew, but nothing was any help. She died.

"And when her funeral was over, and she had been
buried, her mother and father could not stop thinking
about her. Every day they went to her grave and they
weeded it, weeping all the while as they worked.
They brought white stones and little round black
stones for her burial mound and hung over it beauti-

ful grass skirts with flowers and sweet-smelling leaves woven into them.

"Years passed and the neighbors forgot the little girl and in the memory of some of the family her image grew dim, but her parents never forgot. They still went each day to her grave and wept over it and weeded it and rearranged the stones on top of it.

"One day they were very surprised to see growing there right out of the center of the grave two plants. One of them had a long thin leaf and the leaves of the other were a bright green and heart-shaped. They looked at them carefully, for they had never seen plants like them before. Then they called their family and their neighbors and they came and looked, too, but none of them had ever seen any plants like them.

" 'We could dig them up,' one man suggested, but the little girl's mother and father would not agree to that. 'Leave them there to grow,' they said. 'They are a present to us from our daughter. We do not want you to move them.'

"So the people went away and left the two new plants there on the grave. One year, two years, three years, they grew until they were fine big plants—both of them—the one with the narrow leaf and the other with the bright green heart-shaped leaf.

"At the end of three years a most unusual thing happened in the little village where the girl's mother and father lived. The great chief, Lo'au, came for a visit. He had not announced his coming and no one was expecting him so there had been none of the usual preparations. No big pigs had been put into the earth ovens to bake and no collection of yams had been made. There were neither fine mats nor new tapas to present to him. There was nothing at all and the villagers were in despair, for, if they gave nothing to their chief, they would be forever shamed before the men of all the other villages of Tonga.

"And then the mother and father came forward. 'Pull up our two plants,' they said. 'Let them be the gift of this village to the chief. It will be a good gift, for these plants are new to this world.'

"So the villagers pulled up the two plants from the grave of the little girl and they carried them to Lo'au and laid them at his feet.

"Lo'au had never heard of any of the chiefs who had come before him being given a new plant, so he was very pleased; but when his speakers had thanked the people, he began to wonder what use the new plants would be.

" 'Try them,' he commanded a servant, 'and see what they are like.'

"Obediently, the man took the plants. First, the thin-leafed one. Cautiously, he chewed a bit of the stalk and a delightful sweetness trickled into his mouth.

" 'It is good,' he said, and a second servant chewed a piece.

" 'Very good,' agreed the second man.

"Then Lo'au chewed a piece and he was greatly pleased. 'We shall call this "to," sugar cane,' he said. 'It will be very useful to our people.'

"The servant next took up the other plant. He

nibbled at the heart-shaped leaf, but it did not taste very good; so he tried the branches, but they were no better. At last he broke off a bit of the thick root and chewed it.

" 'Is it also good?' demanded Lo'au.

" 'It is strange,' faltered the servant and then, in a burst of inspiration, added, 'I think that if water were added to it, it would make a fine drink.'

"And soon after that," finished Tu'ifua, "Lo'au and his men sat down in the first of all kava circles." Her words had scarcely died away when we heard coming down from the village above us the noise of the kava maker's stone: pound, pound, pound. Tu'ifua smiled. "Listen," she said, "they're drinking with Lo'au now."

17 Sela and Her Children

There are some people beside whom you can live and work for years without ever coming to feel that you really know them at all. With others, whom you may meet but rarely, you feel an instantaneous rapport. For me, Sela belonged to this latter class of delightful people. It was always easy for us to find words to say to each other, but we never had to rush into speech. The occasional silences that rose between us were comfortable silences full of understanding.

Our first talk, as well as a good many of the ones that followed it, was about flowers. Sela was an indefatigable gardener who never wearied of planting cuttings and sowing seeds, and she was a generous person who liked to share whatever good things she had. I can see her now as she used to come down the beach carrying in her hand a green branch or a bunch of bulbs.

"These are for you," she would say, holding them out to me. "Plant them and care for them and they will be beautiful."

I would take the things from her and thank her and we would stand for a few minutes talking together in the warm sun.

228

Very often she carried, also, an empty bottle which she would ask me to have Farquhar fill with medicine; for Sela was grandmother and great-grandmother to half the children in the village, and there was always one of them who had some little ailment which needed her attention. I asked her one day how she ever managed to remember all the young things who called her grandmother.

She laughed gently and replied, "Why, I love them all. You can't forget people you love."

Certain it is that Sela never forgot the people she loved. She was always busy doing something for the young ones of her family. Whenever I walked through the village, I would find her under the big mango tree that spread its cool shade beside her house. Sometimes she would be sousing a naked brown baby in a tub full of suds, sometimes she taught a group of little girls to weave, guiding their chubby, awkward fingers with infinite patience. I like most to remember the times when she sat on a gnarled root of the tree with her church hat beside her, reading from her tattered Bible and explaining its lessons to the group of Sunday-scrubbed and sobered boys and girls who sat in a circle around her; and the long summer nights when, letting her thoughts drift back into the past, she spoke of her own youth and beyond that, of the youth of Tonga itself, and far beyond that, to the very beginnings of all the islands of this Polynesian world.

Sela might easily have filled all her days sitting there under her mango tree with her family gathered about her, but she was an active old woman, and her heart was big enough to include many other people. There was a place in it for everyone in the village and for us, too, when we became a part of the village. In the months before my daughter was born, she used often to come down to see me.

"How are you today?" she would inquire as she came up onto the verandah, "and how is the baby?" and she would hold her long, frail hand against my body until she felt the child within me move.

"Your baby lives!" she would exclaim then, her voice vibrating with excitement. " 'Utulei will have a papalangi baby all its own."

One day I noticed a look of sadness come over her usually cheerful face. When I asked if anything were wrong, she smiled.

"No," she said, but a moment later she added wistfully, "I hope I'll see your baby."

"Of course, you'll see the baby," I said cheerfully.

Happily enough, I was right. Many times in the first few months of little Tu'ifua's life, Sela saw her. She would hold her in her arms and the sober-faced baby and the smiling old woman would stare long and intently into each other's eyes as if, between them, they shared all the mystery of life.

Then, when Tu'ifua was about four months old, I noticed that Sela stopped visiting us. She walked along the beach as she had always done and waved and called out a greeting, but she no longer came into the garden to talk.

"Come in," I called out one day as she was passing, but she shook her head.

"Thank you, but I can't," she replied.

"Why not?" I persisted. "It's so long since you've seen the baby."

She walked up then and stood on the other side of the fence. "I must not come to see the baby any more. You know I love her and love you, too. That is why I must stay away. I—" But her words were broken off by a spasm of coughing. When it had passed, she seemed exhausted and leaned against the fence for support, but she managed a faint smile. "There, that's why," she said. "I don't want to make the baby sick, and now I have this cough I must stay away."

Suddenly alarmed, I ran around to her side. "You should go home to bed," I said.

She nodded her head in agreement. "Perhaps you are right," she said as if the idea had not occurred to her before, and without speaking again, she let me lead her up the hill to her house.

Later that day, Farquhar went up to examine her and ordered her to the hospital at once.

"I'm afraid it's pneumonia," he said to me when he came back.

"Is it serious?" I asked anxiously. "Will she be all right again?" He replied patiently, "I think we can get her over the pneumonia, but I doubt if she'll ever again be very active. She has worked too hard and lived too long and there's no cure for that."

As it turned out, he was perfectly correct. The pneumonia cleared up and, in a couple of weeks, Sela came home from the hospital. She smiled and said she felt very well, but when one of her grandsons came to lift her out of the boat, he felt no more weight than if she had been a bundle of light reeds for making a small mat.

At the far end of the garden, in a high place overlooking the beach, Sela's family had built a cool woven-reed resthouse, and it was to it that her grandson carried her. He laid her down on a bed of new mats and a fresh tapa which her daughters had prepared, and she was quite content to stay there. Through the open door, she could see the children running and playing on the sand below, and far beyond them, the ever-changing face of the sea washing over the reef.

She did not get up again. Her legs could no longer support her and the strength had gone out from all her body, but she did not have any pain and was always, as she said herself, "Very well."

Whenever I stopped by to see her, I would find her lying there smiling, with a daughter or a granddaughter sitting close by. Sometimes the children ran in for a minute's rest from their play, or the men on their way home from the bush would stop to tell her how their crops were coming on. The women took their sewing or their weaving and sat on the floor beside the bed, and she talked to them as they worked or, if she was tired, listened to their chatter, watching them all the while with her kind brown eyes.

In a very short time, Sela's little house became the true center of the village. Everyone looked forward to stopping in to see her, and young and old alike treasured the feeling of peace and quiet happiness that they carried away from their visits to the old woman. It must have been her smile and her spark-

ling eyes that kept us from noticing that she grew
more thin and more frail all the time. None of us
were prepared for the day when her great-granddaughter, Seini, came running to tell us that Sela was
about to die.

"She wants to see you," Seini told me. "She wants
to say good-by because she's going to die very soon."

"How do you know she's going to die?" I demanded.

The child tossed her head angrily and rubbed away
the tear that stood in her eye. "I don't know," she
said, "but it's true, because Sela knows."

I took the baby and walked up to Sela's house. As
I stooped to go through the low door, it seemed that
everything there was the same as it had always been,
but when I looked into the face of the daughter who
sat beside the bed, I saw that she had been crying, and
when I looked at Sela I saw that her eyes were closed
as if she were sleeping.

"Thank you for coming to say good-by," her
daughter said and added, smiling, "Thank you for
bringing the baby. Sela loves her so much.

"I'll try to wake her," she said then and began to
call, "Sela, Sela, here's someone to see you." I shook
my head. "Don't disturb her. It's best to let her
sleep."

"Perhaps you are right," the daughter agreed with
a sigh.

The baby, whom I had set down on the floor,
crawled close to me. I picked her up and held her
so she could see Sela, but she did not recognize her
old friend now that her eyes were closed and, un-

comprehending, she turned away. I put her down
again, and she crawled over to the door and sat
there watching the sea and cooing to herself.

Perhaps Sela heard the small sound of the baby's
voice. She turned on her bed and the faintest trace
of a smile curved her lips. I leaned over then and
kissed her on the cheek. "Dear Sela," I said. "Good-
by."

Early the next morning she was dead, but before
she died, she regained consciousness for a short time
and called her daughters to come close to her. Her
last thoughts were, as all her thoughts had always
been, for others.

"I want to send my love to my family and friends,"
she said, and then in a firm voice she named them
all, one by one, saying as she pronounced each name,
"To you, my love." Her daughter Anna told me
about it later, and I felt a throb of proud joy when
she said that, amongst all the others, Sela had remembered Farquhar and little Tu'ifua and me.

Grief to the average white man is a close and
personal thing, and he feels a sense of guilty shame
if anyone finds him in it. Quite the opposite, Tongans
are as gregarious in their sorrow as they are in their
joy. Sela's death was a matter, not for her family
alone, but for the whole village. As soon as the
church bells tolled her passing, all the men and women
fastened their mourning mats about their waists and
busied themselves with funeral preparations.

A group of the girls ran down to ask for the white
flowers from the garden with which to make Sela a
wreath and a crown. As they gathered the blossoms,

one of them said to me, "We wear mats for anyone who dies and we weep, too, but this is different. We are sad in our hearts now."

"I know," I replied, "I am sad, too," and I found, as the girls did, a certain comfort in speaking of my sorrow.

When we had talked together for a while, a great-granddaughter of Sela's asked, "Will you come today and take a picture of Sela for us?"

I remembered having seen in the houses of many of my Tongan friends pictures of members of their family as they lay shrouded, waiting for the grave. I quickly pushed aside my personal dislike for such photography and asked, "Are you very sure your family wants me to come?"

"Oh, yes," replied the girl, and naming all the daughters of Sela, she added, "They told me to be sure to ask you."

Later that day, as I walked toward Sela's house, I passed little groups of villagers standing together talking. They all wore funeral mats, and the women, in accordance with Tongan custom, had, as a further mark of mourning, let down their long hair and tossed it until it looked as if they might have torn it in grief. When they noticed my camera (which is the only one in the village), they stopped talking and followed along behind me.

As we approached the house, the sunny atmosphere was pierced by the unworldly cries of the mourners who sat with the body. "Oiaue, oiaue, oiaue," they cried, their shrieks rising ever higher. The wailing had started as soon as the church bell had tolled, and it would continue all that day and all that night and on into the next morning until the burial took place, and before it was over, every man and woman in the village would have taken his turn.

"Oiaue, oiaue, oi—" The wailing stopped with a theatrical abruptness as the word went around that I was coming with my camera. Sela's oldest daughter, brushing her tears aside, came to greet me.

She drew me after her into the house, where I found all the closest members of the family grouped around the body of the old woman. They had dressed her in her best clothes and laid her on fresh tapa and over her body they had drawn a long piece of heavy white satin. On her carefully arranged hair, she wore the crown woven from my white garden flowers which, with the satin, gave her the incongruous look of a bride. It was obvious that a great deal of care had been taken preparing her and that her family were very proud of the result, so I exclaimed over how fine she looked as I set about taking the pictures. I was a long time over the job, too, for everyone was anxious to have a last picture taken with the beloved Sela. When at last I had finished and had been thanked again by everyone, I went away. As I left the house, the wailing began again and all the way home the piercing cries followed me: "Oiaue, oiaue, oiaue."

In the morning the men dug the grave and the boys came down to the beach for sand, for Tongans do not use gravestones or monuments, but mark their graves only by terraced mounds of sand. They shoveled it into sacks, loaded the sacks across the backs of their horses and galloped up to the cemetery, and as they worked they laughed and whistled and shouted, but they meant no disrespect to Sela and later that morning when she was buried there was not one of them with dry eyes.

Winter rains and summer winds have come and gone and come again and still on Sela's grave the sand is piled high. Gay marigolds planted by the children grow around the mound, and all the cemetery is filled with the music of the wind in the tea trees. Down in the village there is rejoicing over the birth of the newest great-granddaughter, to whom the family, in love and remembrance, have given the name Sela.

18 The Girl and the Tattooed Men

If one can believe the alarmists, the old arts are dying. Literature, they say, has succumbed to the comic strip and both painting and drama are being shoved aside by television. It is happier, of course, not to believe them; but it is impossible to escape from the depressing fear that they just might be right. And they might be, too, because arts do die. The past century, for instance, has witnessed the death of one of the most widespread and highly cultivated of all the Polynesian arts, that of tattooing.

If your whole experience of tattooing has been gained from circus side shows or from watching hula girls or mermaids writhing over the biceps of burly sailors, you will scoff at the idea of calling tattooing an art; but never doubt that it is, or—to be more exact—was one. What you have seen is merely a degenerate form of something which no longer exists, a garish sort of death mask.

Tattooing, the genuine kind, was a very old art, indeed, much older than the memory of these island men. Certain it is that the Polynesians brought with them when they first came to live in these islands of the South Seas the skill of applying to the human body designs of great beauty. In some places and at some times, tattooing has had a definite connection with religious beliefs. Here in Tonga, however, it seems to have been associated only with that strongest of human feelings, vanity. A tattooed man—in Tonga it was purely a masculine prerogative—had the same prestige among his fellows as has a woman of our society who wears an original Paris gown. Like Paris gowns, tattooing was something that couldn't be found at home. Strangely enough the Tongans, although they had a great appreciation of the art, were not skilled in it. When a man longed to wear a masterpiece he went off to Samoa to get it.

Getting it was not easy. Being tattooed was a very painful process, and only the knowledge that he would forever after be greatly admired made a man able to bear the agonies it caused. The one who was to be tattooed lay on a mat on the ground with his head supported by a low wooden rest of the sort known nowadays as a Tongan pillow. The tattooer came to him and with charcoal mixed with water drew on his skin the pattern of the tattoo. Then he took up his instrument which looked like a cross between a needle and a chisel and drove it along the line of the design. It cut deep, the blood oozing out along its path. The blood brought flies, and often terrible infections, which sometimes resulted in death, followed. Even if there were no infection, the pain was almost unbearable and the flies buzzing about and biting were a maddening irritation. The strongest man could stand only a little of it at a time. A complete job would take several months and it was not uncommon for a man to acquire his tattoo in instalments, returning to Samoa year after year to have a bit more added each time.

Many of my older Tongan friends remember a grandfather whose body was a veritable art gallery. One of them reports the embarrassment endured by the whole family because Grandfather would not obey the missionary's command that he wear a shirt. Worse than that, because he could see no sense in a religion which found anything of shame in something as beautiful as his carefully tattooed back, he refused to become a Christian and, much to his family's chagrin, died a happy old heathen.

I myself have seen only a single example of tattooing since I have been in Tonga. One day when I went with Farquhar to the hospital in Neiafu, a ward attendant came and asked me if I would like to see a tattooed man. I replied that I would like to very much if the man wouldn't mind.

"Mind!" the attendant exclaimed. "Why, of course not. He'll be pleased." And he led me to the bedside of a very, very old man who was suffering from nothing but the incurable disease of too many years. He was a cheerful fellow, though, and, gregarious as all Tongans are, was delighted to have a visitor.

When he was told that I had come to see his tattoo, his faded eyes brightened with pride. With one hand he beckoned me to come closer while with the other he pulled aside his sheet to give me a better view. His tattoo fitted him like an old-fashioned pair of winter drawers, for it reached from his waist to just below his knees. The intricate design of the rectilineal pattern was so beautifully executed that it was difficult to believe it had been done by hand with crude instruments. It was easier to think the old man was wearing knee breeches of some fine printed blue textile. As a matter of fact, his tattooed clothes had decided advantages over textile ones. After fifty years, their pattern was still as bright and fresh as the day they were put on, and they were still a perfect fit. It is sad to reflect that by now the beautiful design and the cheery old man who owned it and wore it have forever passed away.

The art of tattooing itself has had no such natural death. Here in Tonga, it was killed by the missionaries who, if they have been responsible for destruction of some evil, have also been to blame for the loss of much beauty. Obviously a long trip to Samoa was out of the reach of common men who could not leave their families and their gardens for the four or five months required for a tattooing jaunt. Only a rich and powerful chief who could count on the loyalty of his people during his absence could afford to make the trip. Consequently, tattooing became not merely a mark of vanity, but also a sign of rank and riches. Rank, riches, vanity—to the early missionaries those were enemies to be fought against quite as much as Maui, the gay young Polynesian god who, in one day's fishing, caught all these Tongan islands on his line and pulled them up one by one from the bottom of the sea. So they frowned on tattooing, and they got the doctors to say it was dangerous and unhealthy, and they talked the rulers of the land into passing laws against it, and in time it began to disappear.

Perhaps, on the whole, its passing has been a good thing, but there must be a loss whenever a people is suddenly cut off from one whole field of creative expression. And if the value of art lies in the intimacy with which men are associated with it, how can tattooing ever be surpassed?

The art dies, but it is still talked of, and many are the tales the people of Vava'u tell of the old-time trips to Samoa. Of them all, I like best the one of Akasito and the tattooed men which I shall set down here just as it was told to me.

It happened long ago in the days when the oldest of the old people was young or not yet born that ten of the chiefs of Vava'u decided to go up to Samoa to be tattooed. There were no steamers then nor any launches or cutters, so the trip had to be made in outrigger canoes. Today there are plenty of outriggers in Vava'u harbor, but they are hastily made affairs fit only for carrying three or four men on short fishing trips. The old-time canoes were very different. For one thing, they were bigger—so much so that an average-sized one held twenty-five people while the larger ones could easily accommodate fifty. Then, they were better made, for a canoe that must go out into the stormy waters of the open sea must be a masterpiece of balance. They were decked over, too, so that the water wouldn't come in, and they carried sails made of woven mats.

The ten chiefs of our story ordered their people to make for them two strong new canoes. When they were finished and had been tested in the calm harbor waters and in the wilder seas that surround the outer islands, the chiefs were well pleased. They set their men to collect food and kava and fishhooks and white shell necklaces and all sorts of other things to give as presents to their hosts along the way. It took a long time to gather everything together, but at last it was done. Then all that remained was to choose the people who were to go along on the trip. They selected twenty young and handsome youths to make up a dance party, and they took the strongest men from each village to paddle the boats. There were others, too. Those old-time chiefs liked to be waited on.

At last the canoes were loaded and all the people who were to go were assembled on the beach and all their families were standing about saying good-by to them and kissing them on the cheeks again, as Polynesians do. They were all ready to set out when one of the chiefs saw the maiden Akasito walking through the village.

Akasito was beautiful, so beautiful that when the young men saw her they forgot all the other girls. As for the old men, even those who had wives they loved dearly, they couldn't keep their eyes off her and, in their kava circles, they could talk of nothing but her charms. She was a chiefly girl, too, and she had been well brought up so that she knew all the old Tongan customs. She could dance and sing better than anyone else in all Vava'u, and she was kind and gentle in all her ways.

All of those things came to the mind of the chief

when he saw her walking in the village, and they made him think what a fine thing it would be to take her along with them to Samoa. When the tattooing started and the blood began to pour from them, Akasito could sit by and fan the flies away, and if she sang to them the magic of her song would take all the pain out of the tattooer's needle.

It didn't take that chief long to convince the others that Akasito should go. When he proposed it, each of the others wondered why he hadn't thought of it himself. Akasito, whose young heart leapt at the thought of an adventure, was more than willing. It must be admitted, however, that the joy over her going was not quite unanimous. The wives of the chiefs did not think much of the idea. They said it was most unsuitable for a young girl to go off alone with all those men. They spoke of the danger and the inconveniences of the trip and of Akasito's youth and inexperience, but when their husbands pointed out that they were only jealous, which was true, they held their peace. When the canoes set off, Akasito, smiling her brightest smile, sat proudly in the first one.

The canoes did not go directly from Vava'u to Samoa, but sailed first to Fiji. That was partly because there were favorable ocean currents to carry them that way and partly because all the chiefs had friends and relatives there, and they all wanted a time of celebration, feasting and dancing and singing, before they settled down to the ordeal of being tattooed.

It is over four hundred miles from Vava'u to Fiji— four hundred miles of gray Pacific swells which would have been monotonous for the travelers in the two canoes if it hadn't been for Akasito. As it was, she laughed and sang and talked so gaily that every one of the chiefs would have been happy if the trip had lasted forever. But good trips, like bad ones, are over at last. Toward sunset one day, they came in sight of the green hills of Fiji.

"Now, Akasito," said one of the chiefs in his most paternal voice, "this is your first time away from home, and you must remember to be careful. The young men of Fiji sing beautiful songs and their voices are soft and gentle and—"

Akasito tossed her head proudly. "I don't care for the men of Fiji," she said. "They are black as the mud in the mangrove swamps. It is only the men of Tonga that I love."

It seemed to the chief that, as she uttered her last words, she was talking directly to him. The fatherly feeling within him melted and his fears for her—and everything else he should have remembered—were forgotten. "Of course, my dear," he said, "I know you'll be all right," and he gave her a foolish, fatuous smile.

Soon after that, the canoes ran aground on the beach of Fiji, and before long Akasito and the chiefs and all their men and supplies had been moved to the pleasant thatched guest houses which the Fijian chiefs provided for their Tongan visitors. Courtesies were exchanged in the kava circle and then a great feast was set out.

Akasito, modestly dressed in a simple white tapa gown, with no decoration save her long black hair which hung down her back in shiny tresses, sat demurely in the midst of the Tongan chiefs. Near them sat the high chief of Fiji with his son, a tall young warrior who was to be married in two days' time. Once Akasito raised her eyes to the young man, but she lowered them in such proper quick confusion that the chief who sat beside her smiled approval.

For three hours the feast went on. The Fijians were fine hosts who held nothing back when it came to entertaining guests from over the seas. When at last it was over, the ceremonial dances began. After their long days at sea in the cramped confines of the canoes, the Tongan chiefs were not content merely to sit by and watch the dancers. Nothing would do but that they get up and join them. The Fijians, not to be outdone by their guests, set themselves to dancing, too. Even the high chief called to his son to come and dance, but the young man did not come forward. Then the chief sent his attendants to search for his son, but he could not be found anywhere. It was then that the Tongan chiefs called for Akasito to come and sing, but they discovered that from their very midst, from under their very eyes, she was gone.

It was only later that the people from an outlying village reported that the chief's son and Akasito had passed by together. For four days the Fijians berated the Tongans for bringing to their land temptation to lure their high chief's son from the path of duty. For four days the Tongans stormed back at the Fijians, condemning the wayward manners of their young men. At the end of four days, the couple were found in a hut on the distant side of the island. Torn from their private paradise by the high chief's warriors, they returned, the chief's son to his father and Akasito to the old Tongan chiefs.

What the high chief said to his son, and whether he ever married the girl he was supposed to marry, no one knows, for the Fijians were feeling so hostile that the Tongans took to their canoes at once and sailed away as fast as they could. When they were well on the way to Samoa, they began to scold Akasito for running away.

Girls who rebel or girls who cry can be scolded successfully, but Akasito could not be. She only agreed with everything the chiefs said. Bowing her beautiful head, she admitted she had done a very wrong thing. They were right to be angry with her. She was very sorry. When she added that she would never again love any but a Tongan man, the chiefs could say no more cross words to her, and the rest of the trip proceeded merrily with the past forgotten and Akasito singing as gaily as innocence itself.

Only when they were nearing the shores of Samoa, did one of the chiefs voice his fears. "Akasito," he said, "I am much worried. If you ran off with a Fijian after saying that Fijians are black as the mud of the mangrove swamp, what will you do in Samoa which is full of the most handsome of men?"

The chief spoke sternly, but his heart warmed within him when Akasito, lowering her eyes and sighing prettily, said, "I am sorry about Fiji, but I have learned my lesson. I will love only Tongans as long as I live."

If anyone had doubted her then, his doubts

would have vanished in the days that followed. For a whole month before the tattooing began, the Samoan chiefs and the Tongan chiefs celebrated together in days that were an endless round of kava circles, feasts, and dances. Amidst the general merriment, the usual restrictions that bound the young were relaxed. There was much gaiety and several of the young men of the Tongan dance party found Samoan sweethearts. Through all those days, Akasito, with lowered eyes and quiet voice, sat with her chiefs, a perfect picture of a repentant maiden. Sometimes she smiled a bit, but she seemed to have no heart for the festivities. True, when they asked her, she would sing, but although the tune and the words were as clear as ever, there was no spirit in her voice. Only gentleness and obedience remained, and the chief who had spoken to her before they reached Samoa reproached himself and was reproached by his fellows for having killed within her the innocent gaiety of her young heart.

At last the celebrations were over and the tattooing was about to begin. The chiefs would have shuddered at the ordeal that faced them had it not been that they had Akasito to sit with them. They explained to her in great detail what they wanted her to do. They told her about the flies to be fanned away and hinted that cold water to bathe their faces would be welcome. They spoke of their favorite songs, and she listened with bowed head and said she understood very well and would do everything as they wished.

So the next day the tattooing began. Brave in battle though they were and leaders of their people, the chiefs, when the tattooer drove his pointed instrument into them, writhed in pain, as helpless as babies and as sorry for themselves.

"Akasito," they called. "Akasito, water. Akasito, fan the flies away. Akasito, come and sing to us. Akasito. Akasito. Akasito."

But they called in vain. Akasito did not come. Four long and painful months they lay there while the flies buzzed mercilessly about their bloodstained bodies. Sometimes in delirium and sometimes in rage, they called to Akasito, but they all knew it was useless; for, on the second day of the tattooing, it had been reported to them that she was living in a distant village with a broad-shouldered, curly-headed Samoan fisherman.

When at last the chiefs rose up again, their Samoan friends gave them another feast to celebrate the end of their tattooing. It was a great affair, inasmuch as each of them felt he was very fine to see, and very proud he was of the intricate purple designs on his body. Although four months had passed since any of them had seen Akasito, they each secretly hoped she would come back. Now that the pain of the tattooing was over, their anger against her had gone because anger is not so strong as vanity and they longed to be admired. No one they knew could utter such words of praise as she could, and no one knew so well how to crown a triumph. But all the feasts passed, and she did not come. Even when the canoes were ready for the trip back to Tonga, there was no sign of her.

Although each one of those ten chiefs—and all their followers, too—longed to see Akasito, none of them spoke of her. Why? Had she not twice run off and deserted them? They were all ashamed to admit to one another that they still thought of her. So, when they had said their last good-bys to the Samoans and could find no excuse for lingering longer, they pushed off the canoes.

High over the white surf the canoes leapt, rising to meet the oncoming waves, when, above the roar of the sea, came a cry from shore. Turning in the direction of the cry, the chiefs saw Akasito waving to them to come back. With difficulty, they turned in the churning water, but they came so slowly that Akasito, impatient with waiting, ran splashing through the water to meet them. When the first boat came up to her, she climbed into it and took her usual seat amongst the chiefs.

"You were going away without me," she reproached them.

And those weak men! They began to make excuses for sailing without her. Some of them said they thought she had decided to stay, and some said they supposed she had forgotten them. Some said one thing and some said another, but never a word did any of them say about her deserting her post while they were being tattooed, and not one of them mentioned the curly-headed Samoan fisherman.

When she had heard them all, she gathered her pretty lips into a pout. "How could you possibly think I'd want to stay there?" she demanded, and when none of them found any answer, she explained with a smile, "Fijian men are rather nice and Samoan men are even nicer, but it's only Tongan men that I love. I'll never love anyone, really, but a Tongan."

The chiefs listened to her and they forgave her— all ten of them forgave her, and their followers did, too. You who hear her story, if your heart has never leapt to the tune of a young girl's song, or your eyes feasted on the beauty of her face, may call those chiefs foolish men, but if youth and laughter and gaiety can melt your reason away, be content, as the Tongans are, to say, "But Akasito was very beautiful and the chiefs were only men and everyone knows about men when they see a beautiful girl."

Perhaps the story should end there, and if it were only a made-up thing it would, but Akasito's life, like most other people's, went on even after its great adventure was over. The canoes came safely back to Vava'u, and the ten chiefs were much admired by everyone who saw their tattoos. As for Akasito, it was not very long before a young chief saw her. He had heard the tales about the son of the Fijian high chief, and he was not unaware of the episode of the Samoan fisherman, but her charm was stronger than the stories and so he married her. Although Akasito grew to be a very old grandmother, she never outlived her beauty and today, in many a Vava'u village, a great-great-granddaughter of hers who has inherited her smile, or her shining hair, or her gentle manners, or her gay spirit, is turning the hearts of the young men—yes, and of the old ones, too!

19 Suicide

The Tongans, like the other Polynesians, did not have a written language when they were first visited by Europeans. It was only after the earliest missionaries, fired by the desire to give the newly discovered people the Bible in their own tongue, laboriously set down on paper the speech of the natives and reduced it to systematic spelling, that it became possible to read and write in the Tongan language. Since then the Bible has remained virtually the only Tongan book. Besides it, there are a few religious works sponsored by the various churches which have missions in the islands and some miscellaneous government bulletins, but there are no Tongan novelists or dramatists rushing into print. There are no writers of history to interpret the past and no popular-science men to predict the future. There are not even any daily newspapers.

In spite of these lacks, Tonga is known as the most literary of all Polynesian places. The reputation is well deserved; the people make poetry as naturally as they speak. My neighbors here in 'Utulei compose their own New Year's songs every season and, like the troubadors of old, go visiting about the distant villages singing their productions. Even the college girls, when I set them the task of writing a poem, made some excellent verses. Like most Tongan poetry, it was descriptive nature-poetry whose beautiful imagery was held together by the intense love which these people have for their land. The instinct for making poetry runs through all levels of Tongan society and Queen Salote shares her people's ability. When I was at the college, she wrote for my girls a delightful verse play based on the thirteen months of the ancient Tongan calendar. They acted it in old-style costumes at their annual concert and no number was better received. The Queen is famous, too, for her songs, especially for the hauntingly nostalgic love song which was written for her consort, Prince Tungi, just after his death.

The Tongan literary reputation does not rest on the single achievement of poetry. There is also their skill at storytelling. I often think its continuance is due largely to the very absence of a daily newspaper. Many a little event, which would be only a back-page item to be skimmed over one day and forgotten the next, becomes, in our slower life, the nucleus around which a whole story is built up. Stories here are not made to meet deadlines; they grow slowly. First, there is the fact, and then there are all the reports; reports not merely from eyewitnesses, but from everyone who knows anyone connected with it and from a great many people who only know people who know people who heard someone say. . . . And following the reports, there are discussions and interpretations

—hurried ones exchanged by men as they pass each other on their way to the bush, more leisurely ones murmured by women as they sit weaving, and the most profound of all given out at the kava circles in the long black nights. After the story has been reported and discussed and interpreted, it needs time to ripen. Then, if it is a good story, it can be told so that it will seem to the one who hears it as if the teller were there when it happened—more than that, as if he were privy to the thoughts and feelings of all the men and women concerned in it. Finally, if it is a good story, it will be true, not necessarily in the narrow newspaper sense of containing verifiable facts, but in the wider sense of chronicling human hearts and describing the lives of men and women.

Take, for example, the story of Lisi and Vaka. Anywhere besides Tonga it would have been forgotten long ago, but here it lives on. Farquhar told me the fact about three years ago. He came home from the hospital one day, looking upset as he always does when they have lost a patient they tried hard to save. When I asked him what had happened, he said briefly, "A suicide. A woman stabbed herself with one of those long knives they use for cutting grass. We couldn't save her. She'd lost too much blood and," he added, "she didn't seem to want to live."

"Why did she do it?" I asked.

He shrugged his shoulders, exhibiting his usual reluctance to discuss patients. "I don't know," he said. "There was something about a jealous husband, I think."

Farquhar is a medical man with little sense of

news value or else he would have made more of a suicide. They are common enough, I know, in our white world, so common that you can read of two or three in your morning paper without giving them any more thought than you give to the weather report, but here in Tonga they are rare. In the five years I have been in Vava'u, I have heard of only three. There was a man out at Leimatua who played poker for three nights and three days and lost all his money and his clothes. He shot himself, but it wasn't because of the money he had lost. Even the stupidest Tongan knows money doesn't matter that much. It was simply because he had heard his wife was very angry with him for staying away from home for so long and he didn't feel equal to facing her wrath. And there was a married man at Makave who was having an affair with a young girl. He was rather famous as a lay preacher and when the church authorities discovered his private life and forbade him to make any more sermons, he flung himself from a mango tree out of sheer chagrin at having his ministerial career terminated so ignominiously.

And the third was Lisi. Her story, which I heard last week again from one of my neighbors, goes back long before the suicide to the time when everyone was happy. Lisi herself was completely happy. She had everything any Tongan girl could possibly want. Youth and beauty and health she had, and a fine big house above the white sand beach and a handsome husband who loved her with a fierceness that would have frightened her had she not loved him as fiercely in return. She had, moreover, that greatest of all aids to happiness, a clear conscience. No shade of wrong-doing or even of wrong thinking was cast over her life. Nor had the years brought her any duty which she had not done thoroughly and cheerfully. She had been a good daughter and a good sister and now she was a good wife, faithful to her husband and attentive to all his wishes.

That Vaka, her husband, was happy goes without saying. How could he have been otherwise with such a wife? As to the man himself, he was a strong young fellow with all the pride and all the arrogance of his sex, so that he found joy not simply in the possession of Lisi, but also in the knowledge that so many of his friends envied him.

Lisi and Vaka, the happy ones, lived in their house above the white sand beach, and the sunny island days passed like time in a dream. Then, one fateful day, Lupeti wandered into the dream. He came quite naturally on one of the endless visits that Tongans are always making, to stay with Ofatoa, his aunt, who lived next door to the young couple. Also, quite naturally, he strolled out of his aunt's garden and into Lisi's. She was alone when he came. Vaka and some of the other village men had gone off to the bush to plant yams. Sitting under the breadfruit tree, she was plucking a chicken for the evening meal which she would have ready for Vaka when, tired and hungry, he got home that night.

"Thank you for plucking the chicken," Lupeti remarked, opening the conversation in the conventional Tongan manner.

"Yes. Thank you," Lisi replied, and she looked up

at the stranger, smiling and waiting for him to tell her who he was and what he wanted.

Now, whatever you may think of Lupeti by the end of this story, it is only fair to remember here that his motives for straying into Lisi's garden were purely innocent and social and any young man on a visit to his aunt would, likewise, have gone off to investigate the neighbors; since aunts in Tonga are sometimes as wearying as aunts anywhere else in the world and neighbors provide a brief escape, if nothing else.

"Thank you for plucking the chicken," Lupeti said, and those were the last casual words he ever spoke to Lisi. When she replied, she looked up and smiled. The smile was by no means extraordinary. It was merely Lisi's usual smile. Indeed, had Lupeti's aunt happened by in his place, she would have had the very same one. Still, Lupeti could not be expected to know that, and if it dazzled his eyes and his mind, it was not his fault.

"I'm Lupeti. Ofatoa is my aunt," he said, the words gushing out of him because of his great eagerness to identify himself for her.

"And I am Lisi," she replied, and added proudly, "the wife of Vaka."

A frown clouded Lupeti's face. "Vaka," he repeated. "Vaka. Who's he?"

Lisi was plucking her chicken, and she did not see the frown, nor did she notice the anger in his voice. She only heard the question and it pleased her, for it gave her an opportunity to speak of the one who was always in her thoughts.

"Vaka's father belongs to this village. He is the

minister here, and Ofatoa can tell you what a fine
man he is. And Vaka's mother's family comes from
Ha'apai—from 'Uiha—and all the men of the family
are noted for being very clever at fishing. Vaka, too,
is a very good fisher. He can always get something
with his spear, even when it is windy and stormy and
the fish hide in the dark holes in the reef."

Lupeti did not want to hear about Vaka, or his
family, either. The very words maddened him. Ever
since Lisi had smiled he had wanted only one thing—
and that was Lisi. The knowledge that she already
had a husband whom she obviously loved very much,
drove his heart into a frenzy. The words were maddening, but the voice which spoke them was low and
musical and soothing. From it, he gained strength
enough to whisper good-by and walk back to his
aunt's house.

That night, when Vaka came home, he was tired.
A whole day of planting yams in the airless bush is
enough to tire any man. He was cross, too, for he
hadn't finished his work and he would have to go
back the next day.

He had no greeting for Lisi as he came into the
kitchen. Only, "Where's my dinner?" he grunted.

Lisi was a good wife. She understood her husband's
mood. Instead of getting cross in turn, she merely
gave the chicken, which was stewing away in a big
black pot, a poke and said calmly, "It's here. It will be
ready for you as soon as you've had your bath." And
she went off to draw him a bucket of water from the
tank and lay out his clean clothes. When he had
bathed and dressed himself, he came into the dining

room and she served him, silently, as any wise wife would have done, waiting for food and rest to restore his good spirits.

At any other time, Vaka would have eaten his dinner, rested awhile on his mat, and forgotten all about the weariness of the day, but on that night things were fated to happen otherwise. He had finished only one leg of chicken when he heard footsteps on the path outside and looked up to see a strange young man lurching toward the house.

It was Lupeti, and he was as drunk as a man can be and still walk. Usually, he was a fairly temperate fellow, but when he had returned to his aunt's house with Lisi's smile fresh in his heart and desire for her aching through all his body, it had seemed to him, as it has to many another man before and since, that, if the object of his desire was unobtainable, he had best drown the desire in drink. It was easy for him to do so. He had in his box an almost full bottle of gin which he had brought along, thinking it might lessen the tedium of visiting his aunt. This he had taken out and then sat down and drank until it was an almost empty bottle of gin. The raw spirits worked on him, but the effect they produced was not the one for which he had been looking. Far from being drowned, his desire was increased until it crowded out every bit of the reason which usually controlled his life. It seemed to him then that he must go back next door and get Lisi. Whether or not she wanted to come with him did not matter in the least, and if her husband objected—well, let him!

Alcoholically, he mumbled a greeting as he came

bumping through the dining-room door to where Vaka sat, and Vaka replied automatically, but there was none of the traditional Tongan hospitality in his tone. He was tired and cross and even if he hadn't been, he never felt anything but disdain for wasters who befuddled themselves with kava papalangi.

Lupeti swayed against the wall, waiting for Vaka to tell him to sit down or to invite him to share his meal, but Vaka only stared up at him and asked roughly, "Who are you? Where do you come from? What do you want here?"

"I'm Lupeti from Kapa, and I want Lisi."

The words sounded like thunder in the little room, but Vaka went on calmly eating his chicken. Only when he had finished did he look up again.

"Lisi's outside in the kitchen," he said. "What do you want with her?"

"What do I want with her?" Lupeti repeated, and his voice rose into a wild laugh. "Why, what would I want with her? To make love with her, of course. To run off with her."

As desire had been kindled in Lupeti by Lisi's smile, so were jealousy and fury ignited in Vaka by Lupeti's words. Without waiting to hear more, without seeking an explanation, he sprang up and grasped the drunken intruder about the neck, searching with strong, furious fingers for the soft place that was his windpipe. He found it and pushed in until the blood-shot eyes began to bulge and the alcoholic breath came and went in irregular gasps. But Lupeti was not the man to let himself be choked to death—not while he had two fists with which to pound blows into

Vaka's head and two feet to kick into his body. Kicking and striking blows, pounding and choking, the two men struggled together, now trampling in the overturned remains of Vaka's dinner, now stumbling heavily against the walls until at last they fell together still fighting and still cursing one another.

Lisi, hearing the noise they made, came running in from the kitchen. When she found the two men rolling madly on the floor, she gasped in surprise, but when she noticed a stream of bright red blood trickling down Vaka's face, she screamed in terror. Next door, Ofatoa, Lupeti's old aunt, heard the scream and hurried over to see what the trouble was.

The two women, who understood nothing of the cause of the fight, pleaded with the men to stop and tried vainly to tear them apart, but they were flung aside, and the struggle continued in spite of all their entreaties and all their tears. Neither Lupeti nor Vaka could stop, for neither would give in, so they battled on until at last Lupeti reeled, blinded, into his aunt's arms and Vaka fell fainting to the floor.

Like most fights, Vaka's and Lupeti's proved nothing and settled nothing. All that happened was all that usually happens in a fight—everyone got hurt, including the innocent bystanders. From the blows they had given each other, Vaka and Lupeti recovered in a day or so and physically they were as good as ever; but there were other and deeper wounds which festered within them. In Lupeti, the desire for revenge flared, dimming even his desire for Lisi, while in Vaka the unreasoning poison of jealousy spread like a rotting infection. Lisi, whose thoughts had never strayed from Vaka, was hurt and puzzled when he turned away from her. When he accused her of encouraging Lupeti, she burst into tears and turned away. As to Ofatoa, poor old woman, she was angry as she had every right to be at being drawn into other people's quarrels.

The fight was between Lupeti and Vaka, but of course it was no time at all before the quarrel belonged to everyone in the village and everyone was discussing it. Ofatoa said Vaka was mad to be jealous of Lupeti and added as proof of her statement that he was her own nephew and he had always been a goodhearted boy.

"That may be true," replied an old man, "but he is grown now and Lisi is a beautiful woman and the world is the world."

"Vaka's always been jealous of everyone," said Sione Tuki, and his words were full of bitterness because he had once hoped that he would be Lisi's husband.

"Well," said another reasonably, "everything was all right until Lupeti came to town. It must be his fault."

And Heilala who was thirty years old and still unmarried shrugged her shoulders. "What's all the fuss over anyway?" she asked. "Lisi's nothing to fight about."

To which Lupe, who was thirty-four and likewise unmarried, added, "Lisi can't be so good as she pretends. There must be some reason for Vaka's jealousy, for the flower of every story has a seed of truth."

So the people spoke, and as time went on they began to remember things about Lisi and Vaka and Lupeti, little inconsequential things which suddenly took on a new importance. Some of them recalled that Lisi had always been a perfect model of propriety and others knew equally well that she had never found it hard to smile at any man. Some had stories of Vaka's uncontrollable temper and others praised his capacity for hard work. Rumors came from Kapa, Lupeti's home village, describing him as a dissolute scoundrel and counterrumors praised his frank, open nature.

In the end, when the true stories and the false ones had been hopelessly confused and the fight had been retold at every kava circle for miles around and all the people had ranged themselves on one side or another, Lupeti and Lisi and Vaka were bound tight in as vicious a triangle as ever existed.

Then, in the fine big house above the white sand beach, there was no longer any peace and there was no more happiness. Vaka's unplanted yams rotted in the bush while he stayed home to spy on Lisi, thinking, in the cunning of his jealous mind, to catch her in some fresh infidelity. Lisi, finding that Vaka refused to listen to her explanation of her meeting with Lupeti and indeed that he seemed to love her no longer, tried still to be a good wife. She kept the house clean and wove mats and made tapa and cooked the meals, but she no longer smiled. Her beautiful, gentle eyes were often blurred with tears and her heart was always clouded with a great despair.

Of the three, only Lupeti seemed happy. True, he

had not gained Lisi, but when he saw the young couple living in unhappy misunderstanding, he felt he was gaining revenge on her for making him desire her and on Vaka for beating him up. It is very sad to tell, but whatever had been good in Lupeti turned to evil and the never-ending desire for revenge changed his whole being from light to darkness. He went about to the kava circles in the village and, prodded by the men's curiosity, began first to hint at intimacies he said he had enjoyed with Lisi and then to boast openly of them. That they existed only in his own imagination did not at all hinder him from describing them in a manner so realistic that the men could scarcely wait to run home and tell their wives and their wives confided the tales to the neighbors and soon everyone in the village was talking about how often Lisi had slept with Lupeti and what she had said to him and . . .

And, of course, Vaka heard the stories and because his mind was already dimmed by jealousy, believed them and turned on Lisi and beat her until her body was blue with bruises and he himself was exhausted by his fury. The beatings poor Lisi might have borne, but the loss of Vaka's trust and love was a burden too great to carry; so one day she rolled an extra dress and a piece of tapa in her bed mat and, leaving the house above the white sand beach, traveled to the distant village where her family lived.

Naturally, her family took her in, but they could not, though they tried, understand her endless sorrow. None of them had ever known a love like the one she and Vaka had had for each other, and none of

them could measure her loss now that he had turned
against her. She told them her story and they believed
it as she told it, but it did not seem so tragic to them.
After all, husbands have been jealous since the first
morning the sun shone on this earth.

"Wait awhile," they counseled her, "and Vaka will
be lonely. Then he'll come for you and everything
will be all right again. Wait, and in the meantime,
be happy here."

Had it turned out as they said, Lisi might have
found her happiness once more, but Vaka was proud
and when, in the loneliness of his empty house, he
began to think that he might, after all, have wronged
his wife, he could not make himself go to her and
tell her so. "If she really loves me, she'll come back,"
he said stubbornly, and he sat in the house waiting
for her. In the end, it was not Vaka, but Lupeti who
went to her family's house to see her.

He came upon her in the garden as he had done
in the earlier time in the other house, but she turned
no smile on him and offered him no greeting. "Go
away! Go away!" she cried. "You have done enough
harm already. Go away!"

Had he come to ask forgiveness or was he still
seeking revenge? No one knows, but when he saw
Lisi's tears and heard the sighs that escaped her, the
old desire that had first risen at her smile swept over
him again, and he reached out and crushed her to
him. Wordlessly, wildly, she was struggling to free
herself when her uncle and her cousin, happening to
come out of the house, saw them together.

There are those who will call Lupeti a coward for

what he did next and perhaps he was, but Lisi's uncle and cousin were big, stern-looking men and he had no wish to get into a fight with them, so he simply turned and fled, leaving her to explain the matter however she could.

Her uncle came toward her with questions, but she, too shocked and heartsick to talk, pushed past him. "Leave me alone," she murmured and went into the house and lay down on her bed with her face turned toward the wall where no one could see her tears. To the despair that already filled her soul was added fresh despair. As she lay there, she heard her uncle and her cousin whispering together. They spoke of what they had seen in the garden and of the stories they had heard from the people who lived in the village where Lisi and Vaka had lived, and after a time, they whispered that she and Lupeti must, indeed, have been lovers.

Who can tell what last drop fills the cup of sorrow? For Lisi it may have been her family's disbelief or Lupeti's mad persistence or Vaka's continuous neglect. Who knows? Certain it is that that very night, the cup was filled for Lisi. When at last the whisperings of her family were muted into the heavy breathing of sleep, she got up and, taking her older brother's knife from its place beside the door, plunged it again and again into her body. If the pain was great, it was not so great as her sorrow, and she did not cry out. No one knew what she had done until the morning came, and they found her lying in a pool of blood on the floor. She was still alive, so they carried her to the hospital. To her family, it seemed that her attempted suicide confirmed her guilt, so they up-braided her as they went along for her sin and spoke of the shame she had brought on them, but when they arrived at the hospital the TMPs, who deal not in right and wrong, but in life and death, took one look at her and bade them be quiet.

Did she want anything? the TMPs asked. Was there anyone she wanted to see?

She shook her head. "No," she said clearly. "Nothing. No one." But as the morning ebbed away and her life with it, she gasped out the name that had meant all the happiness of life to her. "Vaka."

He was waiting outside. A message had been sent to him when she had been taken to the hospital. When she spoke his name, he came and knelt beside her bed. He took her hand in his, but he said nothing; there were no words he could say. Perhaps she saw, before she died, that all his love for her was as strong as it had been in the old happy days. Perhaps she knew that his jealousy had been killed by his horror at the thing she had done to herself. Perhaps she was too busy dying to know or care what he felt.

At any rate, he was with her when she died. When she had gone and with her all question of happiness for either one of them, he saw his jealousy for the madness it was and he knew that nothing Lisi had done had given rise to it. And bitter knowledge it was, as he sat beside the already cold body.

To Lupeti, also, Lisi's death brought a shock of enlightenment so that he saw his desire for revenge as the hateful thing it really was. While Lisi lived, he had desired her; now she was dead—and dead because of that desire—it seemed to him only fair that he should restore her to Vaka. With a spirit bowed down by contrition, he sought him and tearfully confessed that Lisi had been innocent in all things. He told of the smile that had inflamed him, of the fury that possessed him after the fight, and of the mad desire for revenge that flooded through him. Every despicable trick he told, sparing himself nothing. Vaka, who no longer needed Lupeti to tell him of Lisi's innocence, heard him without making any comment, saying quietly when he had finished, "Thank you for telling me."

20 Happy Birthday

Here in Tonga, there is no celebration that is happier or more important than the one held on the occasion of the first birthday of the first-born. That it should be important is only natural, considering that the family, which is the supreme unit in Polynesian life, owes its renewal and continuity to children. That it should be happy is inevitable, for Tongans are always so when they are with their young ones.

Were life a more certain thing, the celebration might occur at the time of the infant's birth, but Tongans are realists who know all too well that many children are born who never live to grow up. In the old days, the infant mortality rate was shockingly high. Even now it is alarming enough to make a young couple feel they would be tempting fate were they to indulge in any great ceremony at the time their child was born. If, however, the babe is strong enough to survive all the dangers of its first year, they feel safe in assuming that they have, indeed, produced an heir. Then, with hearts full of thanksgiving and joy, they prepare a great feast and call to all their family and friends to come to celebrate with them and to see the child of whom they are so proud.

As our little Tu'ifua neared the end of her first year, Farquhar and I began to think about her birthday feast. There had not been the slightest doubt in our minds about following that particular Tongan custom, because it seemed such a very pleasant one. Moreover, it would give us an opportunity to welcome to 'Utulei all the members of Big Tu'ifua's family who, from the beginning of her life, had accepted our daughter as one of their own. There were other friends, too, the hospital staff and some of my old tutors from the college, whom we wanted to invite to share our happiness. When I added up all the names, I found there were about fifty people whom we really must ask if the day were to be complete.

"That's all very well," Farquhar remarked practically, "but how are you going to feed fifty people?" He pointed out that, as I well knew, the year had been one of drought and consequently it was very difficult to obtain yams, taro, kumalas, or any of the other vegetables which appear at every proper feast.

"It is true," Big Tu'ifua said when we discussed the matter with her. "It is very hard to get yams this year, but this is the first birthday, and it is important, so we'll get them somehow. I'll talk to Lotu and everything will be all right."

Lotu was our yard boy, but titles are always misleading. He was much more than that. Among his most useful functions was that of supply sergeant. If we wanted reeds for a door, he knew where they grew. If we needed mangrove bark to stain the floors,

he could find it and prepare it. He knew which
women were the best weavers and which made the
finest tapa and, of course, like every sensible Tongan,
he knew where to find every conceivable sort of
food. When Tu'ifua talked to him, he readily agreed
with her that, between them, they could certainly find
everything we would need for a feast for fifty people.

Their assurances quickly dispelled my worries.
Lotu and Tu'ifua had arranged feasts for us before
and done it so efficiently that it had always seemed as
if food appeared from nowhere and was miraculously
ready just at the moment we wanted to eat it. There
had never been anything for us to concern ourselves
about except getting dressed in time to greet our
guests. I had not even had to worry about a clatter in
the kitchen because Tongan feasts are cooked entirely
in a pit dug in the earth and ours have always been
made down at the beach on the far end of the cape.

Still, our daughter's first birthday feast was something special and, once the invitations had been sent
out and the day was almost at hand, there were many
details which demanded attention. Farquhar and
Lotu put the garden in order and cleaned up the
beach while Tu'ifua, our little house girl, and I
scrubbed the house. When everything inside and out
was bright and shining, Tu'ifua and I were ready for
our baking days.

I have just said that a proper feast is cooked entirely
in an earth oven and that is quite true, but nowadays
Tongans have a well-developed sweet tooth which
makes them delight in cakes and puddings as well as
their traditional food. Their longing for sweet things

is traceably an effect of white influence. From the English they have taken over afternoon tea and from the New Zealanders, the multiple dessert. They have, of course, made modifications which bring the innovations into line with their own ideas. Tea, for instance, is usually replaced by syrupy, bright-colored soft drinks. Whereas the English put on their tables a supply of cakes which bears a definite relation to the number of people they are to serve, Tongans scorn such an allotment as niggardly in the utmost. As far as food is concerned, they feel that there is never enough until there is more than enough. They are really delighted by nothing short of a pile of cakes, and as for the multiple dessert plate, the more different kinds of sweets that are stacked onto it, the better they like it. At gala occasions, the multiple dessert is served immediately after the feast proper and tea follows without the slightest lapse of time. Needless to say, such amounts of food present serious problems to papalangi digestions, but Tongan stomachs manage them with ease. Since most of our guests were to be Tongans, I thought we should do our best to give them the sort of feast they liked; so Tu'ifua and I baked and cooked for the entire two days preceding the feast. Our labors were considerably lightened by my trusty village friend, 'Ugatea, who came down and stirred everything that needed stirring and washed the constant stream of dirty dishes we made. Lavinia, relieved of such arduous duties, devoted her energies to the more artistic pursuit of mixing up varicolored frostings for the cakes and squeezing out flowers, writing, curlicues, and other wondrous decorations.

When we had finished and stopped to take count of our productions, we found we had the meat safe and an enormous barrel both chock-full of assorted cakes, shortbreads, and cookies. For the multiple dessert there was white pudding, red jelly, yellow custard, fruit salad and ice cream, and the refrigerator held gallons of syrupy-sweet raspberry cordial.

"Well"—I sighed wearily—"I guess they'll have enough dessert anyway," and giving voice to the worries that had begun to stir in me, I added, "I'm afraid that's all they will have."

My fears were not entirely unfounded. Although Farquhar had brought home a big basket of yams a few days earlier and Lotu had cut the wood for the earth oven and his family had gathered coconuts and greens, it still seemed that we had nothing but the trimmings of our feast. Two people had promised to sell us a pig apiece, and we had ordered a dozen chickens, but on the afternoon before the birthday neither pigs nor chickens had appeared and a persistent wind which ruffled the harbor waters cut down all my hopes of getting any fish.

Farquhar, who refuses to be disturbed over domestic woes, was his usual calm self. "I doubt if they'll starve," he said, and he reminded me of the twenty-four pounds of canned corned beef we had got for making "lu," the dish composed of beef, coconut cream and the spinachlike "lu," which has become indispensable in the Tongan diet.

Tu'ifua, equally cheerful, pointed out that there was plenty of time left for things to arrive. The optimism they shared was, as it turned out, justified.

While we were having dinner the pigs and chickens arrived and, greatly relieved, I went out to see that they were all safely tied up. That night, I went to bed soothed by the reassuring grunts and cackles of the morrow's feast.

On the birthday morning, we all woke early. It was well we did for what we had to cope with was nothing short of a miracle—a miracle which was enacted in our own front garden. On the verandah long before breakfast time, the half-dozen young girls from the village whom I had asked to come down to help serve and greet our guests, were chattering away. I had just finished dressing when Fie'ilo, the youngest of them, came running to my bedroom door.

"Come to the verandah," she cried excitedly. "There's a present for little Tu'ifua."

I stopped just long enough to pick up the baby from her crib and then followed Fie'ilo to the verandah. Down below us on the grass was a beaming Lotu who, as soon as he saw us appear, hid his smiles and, lowering his eyes to the correct degree of abject politeness, said, "Forgive me, little Tu'ifua, please. I know today is a very important day. It is your first birthday. I would like to bring you a fine present, but I have nothing. I am a poor man." His eyes fell a bit more as he added, "There is only this small present for you from me and my family." With that, he ran over to the fence and spoke a few words to some men who sat outside. I could see them getting up with what seemed to be a great effort and soon I understood the reason. When they came over the fence, they bore on their shoulders a heavy pole to which was lashed one of the fattest, most protesting pigs I have ever seen. They put him down on the grass below us and he lay there kicking and squealing while I did my best to thank Lotu for his fine present. Little Tu'ifua, whose vocabulary on her first birthday was largely limited to her pet names for the people of our household, helped me thank him by cooing delightedly and crying out, " 'Otu, 'Otu, 'Otu."

We had no sooner gone back inside the house than Fie'ilo burst in exclaiming, "Come out, come out. Here's another present." We returned to the verandah to find another of our neighbors standing on the grass, hiding his pleasure beneath the humility which polite Tongans always assume when they present a gift.

All during breakfast and for an hour or so after it, the smiling Fie'ilo kept erupting into the house to summon us to the verandah. There are thirty families in 'Utulei and every one of them came that morning with a gift of food for the birthday. By the time they had all finished coming, the foot of our garden where the presents were put for safekeeping looked like nothing so much as a county fair. Tied up along the fence were seventeen pigs grunting and squealing the last grunts and squeals of their fat porcine lives while from every tree dozens of chickens cackled and crowed. There were high piles of vegetables and mounds of coconuts and greens. There was even a basket of fish which 'Usiah, a grandfather who can outfish the young men any day, had managed to catch in spite of the rough waters. There were people enough for a fair, too. All the men and women had stayed behind to help prepare the food. The children and dogs, shouting and barking, joined the excitement.

Giving a Tongan feast is, as I have said, a delightfully easy way for a papalangi to entertain. It must not be assumed, however, that I am unmindful of the vast amounts of labor which go into producing it. On the birthday morning, I saw the whole village hard at work to make little Tu'ifua's feast a memorable one. While the men and boys killed and cleaned the pigs and chickens, the women, working under a temporary shelter they had erected down on the beach, scraped coconuts and squeezed out the thick white cream that was to be used in the preparation of the chickens, the fish, and the beef, and also in the making of "Made to Eat," the delicious caramel breadfruit pudding which, wrapped in individual banana-leaf packages, is a deservedly popular dish. In addition to getting the food itself ready, some of the women were weaving the polas, the stretchers made of coconut fronds on which the feast is carried and served, and cleaning the banana leaves which are both plates and covers.

After all the foodstuff was ready, the men seized spades and hoes and began to dig out the pit for the oven. The advantages of such an elastic stove cannot be overemphasized—not when it is suddenly called on to accommodate a dozen pigs instead of two! Once the pit was large enough, it was lined with rocks and then a roaring fire was built on top of it. When the fire had burned down, all the food to be cooked was put into the oven on top of the embers. This work is

always done by the men for it requires both strength
and skill. Strong arms are needed to lift the pigs and
the heavy Tongan vegetables into position, and there
is an art in placing everything—pigs, vegetables and
leaf-wrapped packages of chicken, fish, corned-beef
"lu" and pudding—so that the whole meal will come
out evenly cooked. When everything was in, the top
was covered with clean leaves, sand was shoveled
over them, and it was left to bake—or, to be more
exact, to steam, until it was ready to be taken out and
eaten. Five of the pigs were left out and these the
men roasted over spits which they improvised on the
beach.

In the midst of all that activity, there was nothing
for Farquhar and me to do but walk about and talk
to the workers. Had we tried to help, our awkward
papalangi hands would only have slowed their task.
Our main job that morning was keeping track of our
daughter, who had just recently discovered what fun
it was to run about and explore the world and was
using her new knowledge to investigate all the excitement which she had, all unwittingly, caused.

Our provisions had multiplied miraculously, and
the oven had obligingly stretched to accommodate
them. One other thing had stretched too—our guest
list. As groups of people had come that morning with
food gifts, we had asked them to return in the afternoon to share the feast. When their work on the
beach was finished, the women and children went
home to bathe and dress, and about noon they began
to reappear. Once again they came with full hands,
bringing presents of mats, tapa, fans, and baskets

which they presented shyly before they drifted off to form brightly colored groups about the garden.

Soon after one o'clock, two launches came down from Neiafu bringing all our other guests and laughing Pita 'Uli and his string band whose music is an indispensable part of every Vava'u celebration. Our little party for fifty had swelled to over two hundred. We were still a bit breathless over the expansion as we stood at the foot of the stairs to greet all the people, and I, for one, was secretly relieved to find that they would all fit on the verandah.

After everyone had talked for a while, Big Tu'ifua came to tell me that the living room was ready for the brief religious service which is a standard part of every Tongan birthday feast. I looked in and saw that the L-shaped sofa was draped with fine mats and tapas and the walls were festooned with frangipani leis and flowered capes which the girls had made for the guests of honor.

On the thronelike sofa sat Big Tu'ifua's father, Fevale'aki, whom we had asked to conduct the service, our birthday baby, and Farquhar and myself. Our guests, all of whom managed to crowd into the room, sat facing us in rows on the floor and the men left the earth oven and the roasting pigs and came up onto the verandah to watch through the open French doors.

That day we were all of one spirit. Looking down at our fair-haired daughter who smiled gravely out at the friends who had come to celebrate her birthday, I understood why the people of these islands feel children are the greatest of life's gifts. I knew, too, the pride of sharing my joy with my friends and the quietening, intensifying experience of pausing with them to give thanks. My heart was full as I bowed my head and listened to Fevale'aki's grave old voice speaking once again the familiar words of the Bible.

When the service was over, we all returned to the verandah which the girls had decorated with the dark, shiny fronds of the little starch palm and hung with tapas. There was a round or two of kava and much chattering and laughing and then, from Pita, a loud twanging chord on the guitar and a great shout of "Kai, food!" We all turned and looked down to the beach where we saw that the oven had already been opened and the men were lifting up the steaming food and putting it onto the coconut-frond polas. In another minute the first pola was carried up onto the verandah. A great, green stretcher piled high with food, it took four men to bear it. The others followed quickly and soon there were two long lines of food laid out the length of the verandah.

Quickly we found our places on the mats in front of the polas and, sitting with our legs folded beneath us in polite Tongan style, were soon eating heartily. A feast is best described in its preparation. Once the eating has begun everyone is too busy for words. True, there are speeches, but there is none of the incidental conversation of European dinners. Indeed, idle chatter at meals is frowned on. As my neighbor, Sione, once explained it, "There is the eating mouth and there is the talking mouth and they are not the same."

While our eating mouths were busy, we listened to the soft strumming of the guitars or the friendly words of the speechmakers. The day was a bright, sunny one with just enough breeze to stir the harbor into sparkling wavelets and as it went on, the warmth, the good food, the music, and the feeling of being surrounded by well-loved friends combined to produce in us all that state of euphoria which is the result of all good feasts.

When no one, not even the greediest little boy, could eat another bite, the polas were cleared away and the girls passed basins of water and towels. By the time everyone's hands (which are the only implements used in eating a feast) had been washed, the dessert and the cakes and the raspberry drinks appeared and, getting a second appetite, everyone began to eat again.

After all had finished the second time over, we sat on, listening to Pita's music and talking together until Vaed, the youngest and prettiest of the nurses, and Kalala, our village beauty, got up and danced a ta'olunga, the more graceful Tongan version of the hula. No sooner had they stopped than another couple took their place and before long the verandah was full of dancers. And so the afternoon passed in dancing and singing and talking, and all too soon the launches came to take our Neiafu guests away. All of us who belong to 'Utulei went down to the beach to see them off. When the last good-by had been shouted back across the darkening water, the villagers, too, made their farewells and wandered up the hill to their homes. Farquhar and I turned and walked across the garden back to the house and at our side was Big Tu'ifua, who carried in her arms a limp little Tu'ifua who had fallen sound asleep just as the last departing guest had called a final "Happy Birthday."

21 A Hospital, a Church, and a School

One day not long after we came to 'Utulei, Lutui, the head TMP in Vava'u, and Farquhar were discussing the case of a child who had died in hospital a few days before of complications resulting from septic sores. The conversation had been proceeding on the usual scientific lines, when suddenly Lutui sighed deeply and said, "Doctor, I feel very sad about that child because she should not have died."

Farquhar, who knows well that Lutui is the conscientious sort of doctor who never stops worrying about his cases, replied, "I thought when I first examined her in the hospital that she had a very poor chance."

"Yes," agreed Lutui quickly. "She had no chance when she was brought in, but only two weeks ago I saw her in her village. I dressed the sores and told her parents what to do for her and she should have been all right in a day or two. She would have been, too," he added bitterly, "if they hadn't grown impatient and taken her to a bush doctor. He rubbed her sores with ground-up coral and bound them with grass—and look what happened."

He was silent for a minute and then he burst out, "The government educates us so we'll be able to help the people when they are sick and what do the people do? They go to some ignorant bush doctor and when he's made them worse, they come to us to die."

"But they don't all die," Farquhar reminded him. "We save a lot of them."

"That's true," Lutui conceded, "but bush doctors do nothing but make trouble for us. They should all be put in jail and anyone who goes to them should be put in jail, too. It's stupid and ignorant to go to them when the government provides a perfectly good medical service."

"It is that," Farquhar agreed, "but you won't change it by putting people in jail. The only way to drive out stupidity and ignorance is by education. As people begin to see that our way is better, they will give up the bush doctors and—"

"But they're so slow to see," wailed Lutui, and Farquhar could only reply, "All real education is slow."

It is easy to sympathize with Lutui's bitterness about bush doctors. They are responsible each year for many deaths and for uncounted hours of needless suffering. The country is full of them, too. Had Farquhar gone to live in Harley Street, he could scarcely have been surrounded by more medical practitioners than he is in 'Utulei which, small though it is, has its full complement of specialists. Every adult woman is, ex officio, a midwife. In addition, Ane massages sprained and broken limbs, Litia, with a brew made from a tiny green weed that grows in our garden, treats sore eyes and upset stomachs, Alisi deals in strange interior pains, and Siaki specializes in boils. There are also many Tongan faith healers. Some of them—in a direct line from their pre-Christian ancestors—commune with the spirits of the dead in order to effect their cures, while others, more modern if equally unenlightened, say Christian prayers over water which, according to their claims, then becomes more effective than a whole hospital full of doctors and TMPs.

Bush doctors might be even more formidable competitors were it not that the Tongan government so wholeheartedly endorses Western medicine. Each year it sends some of the country's brightest young men to Suva to study at the Central Medical School which trains people from all the Pacific islands. When they return to Tonga after their four-year course, they are qualified TMPs; which is to say, they have a good practical knowledge of medicine and simple surgery plus an ability to deal with dental emergencies. TMPs who show themselves particularly gifted in some one aspect of medicine often have the opportunity to do postgraduate work in Fiji or New Zealand. A European matron stationed at the hospital in Nuku'alofa trains nurses who, like the TMPs, get a sound working knowledge of their job.

"They're all so eager to learn," Farquhar says whenever he talks of his Tongan colleagues, and everyone who meets, even casually, any of the young men or women of the Medical Department notices at once the enthusiasm they have for their work. It is due to their zest that the department has grown so much in recent years—for, in spite of Lutui's occasional pessimism, it has grown. Tongans, when they are sick, tend more and more to come into hospital or to consult a TMP rather than a native. Here in 'Utulei, we have noticed that although the bush doctors still practice on their patients with as much fervor as ever, they themselves, when anything is wrong with them, run down to Farquhar as fast as they can.

"But, Doctor, you can't really work here! There's no X-ray and no lab and this theater is impossible."

The speaker was a recent graduate of Otago University's Medical School who was on his way to Samoa to take a job in the hospital there. Over in 'Utulei, where he had morning tea with us, he had discoursed learnedly of all the latest drugs and the newest surgical techniques. Yet, for all his knowledge, he had seemed a polite young man. Whenever Farquhar spoke, he listened deferentially as he might have done to one of his professors, but in the hospital in Neiafu his politeness vanished and the respect he had given Farquhar as an older member of his profession gave way to an ill-concealed condescension. It was obvious from his manner that the ancient frame building that was the Vava'u hospital seemed to him as primitive as a witch doctor's tent and obvious, too, that he considered that no one but a witch doctor could possibly work there.

"Impossible," he repeated. "Quite impossible."

"Still," Farquhar replied calmly, "we've done a lot of work here and had very good results, too."

The young man took no notice of his words, but strode across the room to the instrument cabinet. For a minute he peered in through the cracked glass window, muttering to himself as he did so, "No proper retractors, insufficient clamps, old-fashioned forceps. . . ." Then he turned and faced Farquhar. "I'm sorry, Doctor," he said, in the tone of a judge passing sentence, "but you can't practice medicine here. It's—why it's like trying to drive a car with flat tires."

Farquhar smiled tolerantly. "You're quite correct," he said, "but the best drivers can always fix a flat if they have to."

The young man, however, was not to be placated. When, a few hours later, we took him down to the steamer, he was still talking about the frightful conditions in Vava'u.

"Poor fellow," Farquhar said to me as we waved good-by to him. "He thinks he knows so much and he has everything to learn. Practicing medicine in a big city hospital where you've got all the latest equipment and staffs of technicians at your command is one thing, but practicing in the islands is quite another. Here it's a question of do the best you can with what you've got and do without what you can't get."

The young man, to give him his due, was only one of many who, having visited the hospital in Vava'u, went away feeling that, medically speaking, Tonga was very much in the dark ages. To tell the truth, although we couldn't agree with them, we could sympathize with them. A quarter of a century ago when Farquhar came as a tourist on his never-to-be-forgotten trip to Tonga, he visited the Neiafu hospital. He wasn't long out of medical school then, himself, and, if he was less critical than our young man from Otago, still he found many inadequacies in the little hospital.

"And when I came back to live and work here," he says, "the place was still just as I had remembered it —except that it was older and shabbier."

To describe it truly, as it was when we were first married, the Vava'u hospital with its sagging verandah and its board sides which were so sadly in need of a coat of paint looked like nothing so much as a slum. The resemblance was heightened by the fact that the place was always overrun by the patients' relatives and friends who, as the hospital had neither nurses, nor kitchen, nor laundry, were there to feed and to care for their sick. The wards themselves were dark, rather airless, and completely unfurnished. If a patient owned a bed, he usually brought it with him. If he didn't, his sleeping mats were spread out on the floor. There, too, his accompanying family slept and cooked and ate and washed, and through that mass of human activity, Farquhar and Lutui went to make their daily rounds and the dressers and attendants came to perform their services for the sick. In spite of its decrepit condition and the many necessities it lacked, the old hospital maintained a fine record and its patients, cured and convinced, went back to their villages to tell the people there that the papalangi's medicine was really a very good thing, after all.

One day when we had not been married very long,

a launch came down the harbor to our beach. It had no sooner touched the shore than Suli, one of the hospital attendants, jumped off and ran up to the house with a note for Farquhar.

"It's from Lutui," he said, turning to me when he had read it. "I'll have to go over at once. There's a bad appendix case he wants me to do."

"Let me go with you," I begged and, rather to my surprise, he agreed at once. "Come if you like. You can watch if you want to."

I had seen an operation or two at home in California, sitting far from the operating table behind a sterile glass window, watching an unknown surgeon working over an unknown patient; and a remote, unreal sort of experience it had been. But I looked forward that day with a definite sense of excitement to seeing Farquhar operate, for I had not yet seen my husband at his most important work.

When we reached the hospital, we went into the little cubbyhole that served as both consulting room and office while Farquhar looked at the patient's chart and heard Lutui's analysis of the case. Then he went off to see her for himself and I waited alone, listening to the distant roar of the Primus stove heating up the sterilizer and the closer murmur of voices from the neighboring ward. Before long the office door opened and Lutui stuck his head in. "Come along to the theater," he said. "We're getting ready." I followed him through the door into the dark cupboardlike pharmacy and out again down a narrow back hall.

The theater itself was light and airy—the more so

as some of the windows which had long ago been broken had never been repaired. From outside, through the holes, peeked little boys, eager for the show to begin. In one corner of the room Farquhar and Lutui, who was to assist him, were getting into their gowns and washing up while in another Semisi, the anesthetist, was measuring out chloroform and ether. From time to time the door banged open and Suli came in carrying a tray of sterile instruments or Isaleli came to adjust the rusty operating table which creaked ominously whenever he touched it.

At last everything was in readiness. The door was flung open, and the patient, a pretty young girl of eighteen who wore a sheet wrapped valalike around her body, was brought in by Peni, the dispenser, and Suli. Peni helped her up onto the table, where she lay quietly while he and Isaleli adjusted the leg straps. Meanwhile, through the still-open door, surged a whole crowd of men and women who pushed their way into the room and spread themselves out against the four walls. One worried-looking woman came again and again to lean over the table and speak to the patient who, though her eyes were bright with pain, looked up reassuringly.

"That's her mother," Suli whispered in my ear.

"And all those other people?" I asked. "Who are they and what are they doing here?"

Suli shrugged. "They're friends and relatives."

I watched them, waiting for Farquhar to order them out so he could begin work, but he seemed not to notice them at all. In fact, ever since he had put on his gown, he had become a different, remote person who seemed to have no thoughts for anything except the operation he was about to perform. With Lutui at the far end of the room, he stood talking in a low voice; but he had not, as he seemed to have done, forgotten the theater and everyone in it. When the patient was adjusted, he spoke to Semisi. "If you're ready," he said.

Semisi nodded and took his place in the chair at the patient's head. Just behind him a high stool was placed and Farquhar, pointing to it, said to me, "Sit up there. You'll be able to see everything from there."

I scrambled up just in time to hear Semisi lean over the patient and say in a low voice, "Breathe deeply and count." He poured some of the sweet-smelling anesthetic onto a gauze cone which he pressed over the girl's face. She breathed deeply, the shadow of a smile traced itself across her face, and she shut her eyes, but Semisi roused her. "Count," he ordered.

Sleepily she obeyed. "Taha, ua, tolu . . . one, two, three."

He poured out some more liquid and she counted on haltingly, repeating herself, halting again and then stopping altogether.

"She counted thirty-four," I heard one of the relatives behind me whisper to the man next to him. I smiled. Even here the Tongan love of detail manifested itself!

"Count," Semisi urged, "count." He leaned close and spoke into the girl's ear, but he had no response save her heavy, regular breathing which for a few minutes was the only sound in all the theater. Semisi straightened, turned back the girl's closed eyelid, examined her eye, felt her skin, and nodded to Farquhar. "She's ready, Doctor."

"Ready then," Farquhar repeated, and he and Lutui came up to the table where they stood silently waiting while Suli pushed back the sheet and painted the girl's abdomen with bright yellow antiseptic.

"Yellow," one of the relatives whispered and I knew that when, at a kava circle, he described the operation, he would not fail to mention that fact.

Knife in hand, Farquhar stood for a second contemplating the yellow patch before him and then, with a sure motion, cut into the skin.

"Blood," whispered a relative. I looked up to see if the talking bothered Farquhar, but when I saw his face calm and concentrated, I realized that he had not even heard it. For him at that moment nothing in the world existed except that bit of flesh before him which somewhere in its interior contained an appendix he had to remove.

Perched up on my stool behind Semisi, I stared down into the gaping red wound. A wave of dizziness swept over me. I swayed, but caught myself in time. "If I faint now," I told myself, "Farquhar will never let me come here again." Then, quite as if I had been a Tongan, I thought, "I'd be ashamed to faint," and papalangilike, finding excuses, reflected that it had been nothing but the sweet sickly smell of the chloroform that had made me giddy.

I turned and looked at the relatives and was surprised that none of them—not even the patient's mother who had been so disturbed before the operation began—seemed to display the slightest emotion. If they were worried, no one could have guessed it from looking at them. They all stared stolidly at the table, showing not the least trace of the Tongan's usual volatile nature. The truth of the matter was that they were fascinated by what was going on, every detail of which they continued to whisper about among themselves.

Oblivious to everything, Farquhar and Lutui worked on, their fingers moving skillfully and gently. Once there was a burst of laughter from the inquisitive little boys who still stared in at the window. Everyone in the room stirred and Lutui muttered without turning, "Go away," but Farquhar went on, unhearing. Suli filled a syringe with cold water and, creeping to the open window, shot it into the boys' faces. Shouting and screaming in surprise, they ran off, leaving the place in peace.

After a time, through the silence, Farquhar spoke. With a start, I heard him addressing me. "Here's the appendix," he said, pointing to a twisted red tube embedded deep in the scarlet flesh. "Watch now."

I stared while he cut it away and, lifting it out, threw it into the tray on a little table behind him. "That's done now," he said, and it seemed that, with the appendix safely out, he returned from the solitary place of fierce concentration to the ordinary world about him. Suli lifted the tray with the severed appendix in it and, as if he were exhibiting some great treasure, passed it about for all the relatives to see.

"Oh, good, thank you very much," they exclaimed,

obviously pleased. Later, Farquhar told me that the Tongans were always delighted when, at an operation, something was removed. It gave visible proof that the doctor had done his work and made it easy for them to believe in the patient's recovery.

Back in the little hospital office after the operation had been completed, Farquhar and Lutui lit cigarettes and discussed their case.

"It went very well," Lutui said and added, "But it will be so much easier when we have our new hospital."

"Yes," agreed Farquhar, and for a few minutes they talked animatedly of the wonderful new hospital that would be built someday in Vava'u.

"You're dreaming," I said to them at last.

"No, not just dreaming," maintained Lutui. "Look on the estimates and you can see there's a big allotment for building the new Vava'u hospital."

That time, I was the pessimistic one. "I know," I said. "It's been on the estimates for years and that is where it stays."

Unfortunately, I was right. Long ago the rumor that there was to be a new hospital built in Vava'u came drifting up from Nuku'alofa. For years it was only a rumor. Later, the rumor was backed up by the government estimates, but still there was no sign of building. Then Farquhar was asked to submit plans for a theater wing and for an outpatients' clinic, and there was more talk of the hospital and the workers in the shabby old frame building had in their minds a vision of a fine new structure that would be light and airy and big enough for all their patients. Sometimes they believed the vision and imagined that the hospital would soon be a reality. More often they told themselves that the government would never spend that much money on Vava'u. But even in their moments of deepest pessimism, there was an unextinguishable ray of hope. Someday, somehow, they would have the new place. In the meantime, they would do their best in the old one.

Time moves slowly here where one sunny day flows almost imperceptibly into the next one, but it does move. After enough of it had rolled away into the past, there came a morning when a gang of Public Works men appeared at the hospital and told Farquhar and Lutui that they had come to work on the new building. They could scarcely believe it was really so, but soon a large area which had never been anything except a tangle of bush was leveled off by roaring bulldozers. The ground was really broken, the new hospital began to rise on its foundations, but still it remained a vision rather than a reality. Sometimes the work went slowly and sometimes, while the Minister of Finance in Nuku'alofa haggled over the price of timber or concrete, it stopped entirely and the men went off. Then the workers in the old frame building would shrug their shoulders, and if it had been a good day, they would say, "Never mind, it will be done someday," and if it had been a bad day, they would say, "It will never be finished."

One year, two years, three and four passed by bringing good days and bad and then, in spite of all delays, in spite of pessimism and optimism, there, towering over the dingy old hospital, rose the com-

pleted new building. There was a theater that little
boys couldn't peek into and wards with real beds.
There was a big private office and an X-ray room,
a dental clinic and a spacious outpatients' clinic.
There was a lab and a dispensary—there, in fact, was
a modern seventy-bed hospital.

The pessimists of the frame building were almost
conquered, but still they found one thing to grumble
about. "It's fine," they agreed with their more opti-
mistic colleagues, "but there it is and here we are and
when we'll ever get into it no one knows."

And no one did know. For when Tonga spends
£30,000 to build the most modern, most ambitious
structure in the whole country; when, furthermore,
she spends it in Vava'u, which is usually the forgotten
spot, it is a great event and great events call for
ceremonies.

The Medical Department had a way of referring to
"our new hospital," but as a matter of fact, it is far
too big and important a thing to belong to any one
group of people. It belongs to everyone and everyone
felt that there was no one in all Tonga important
enough to open it except one—and that one was
Queen Salote. The Queen shared with her people
their pride in the fine new building, and great was
the rejoicing here when she agreed to come up and
open it—especially as she had not been in Vava'u
since the day two years ago in 1953 when she set off
on her long journey to England for Queen Elizabeth's
coronation.

Yet, even after she had agreed to come, there were
delays. First there was an extra session of Parliament

which dragged on interminably, and neither the Queen nor the nobles who were to come with her could leave Nuku'alofa until it was over. Then, someone discovered that the electric plant for the new hospital was not yet ready and suggested the opening be delayed until the lights were installed. First there was one reason for postponing the opening and then there was another, and all the while an endless stream of cables, letters, and rumors came up from Nuku'alofa, and all the time the fine new hospital with its spacious wards lay empty and beside it the old hospital bulged with sick people. Seeing the crowded conditions there, some of the white men asked Farquhar why he didn't move the patients in before the formal opening, but none of the Tongans asked that question. They all knew that to have used the hospital before it was formally opened would have been much against their custom. Indeed, although there was nothing to prevent men from entering the place to look about, had any woman so much as set foot inside the finished building, the Queen would have refused to open it and all the celebrations would have been ruined.

Years ago, when the interisland boat, the *'Aoniu,* was being brought to Tonga for the first time, the people had proudly planned elaborate christening ceremonies for her. Since she was coming from Fiji where there were many Tongans longing for passage home, the captain wired the Tongan government for permission to bring passengers. It was granted and the *'Aoniu* sailed with a load of homesick Tongans. All would have been well had she brought only men, but alas! there was on board one Tongan woman. Poor woman! Because she had broken the tapu and set foot on the unchristened boat, the ceremonies dwindled to a shameful, hasty business and the Queen, who was to have officiated, stayed in the palace, taking no part whatsoever in them. Such behavior, it must be pointed out, is no sign of a sulky royal nature, but is merely evidence that for queens, as for other people, tapus are powerful forces which must be respected.

There was never the slightest danger that such a disaster might befall the hospital opening, for Lutui kept the keys safely hidden and the big building stood alone and inviolate.

At last the opening date was set. A full week before it, the *Tofua* arrived and in it came Queen Salote with an official party of eighty from Nuku'alofa. To have read their names would have been to read a Tongan *Who's Who*. In addition to Prince Tu'ipele-hake and his wife, Melenaite, and young son 'Uluvalu, there was Tungi's son Taufa, and nobles and chiefs and matabules (the "talking men" for the Queen and nobles) and all sorts of other important people, and all of them were in holiday mood.

Some of the visitors went off to stay with their friends and relatives, but those who were closest to the Queen went with her to Veitatalo, the house of Vava'u's hereditary noble, 'Ulukalala, where she always stays when she comes here. A big place with spacious grounds, it stands in the center of Neiafu, just across the street from the post office. There, for all the week before the opening, she stayed, a royal prisoner, bound by a seemingly endless stream of people who came with presents of food and mats and tapa, with dance parties and song and conversation, to see her.

Even here in 'Utulei, a mile across the harbor, we were constantly aware of the demonstrations that were going on in Veitatalo. At any time of the day or night, we could hear the distant sound of music, the stirring military boom of the band or the older primitive measures of laka-laka dance music. And going up the harbor we saw launches and rowboats and little canoes carrying the happy people to their ruler. Our own house, like those of most of our neighbors, was full of company who had come for the celebrations; so, giving way to the sense of excitement that filled the land, we made holiday.

Then, at last, after all the waiting, the great day came. Farquhar and I with our little Tu'ifua trotting beside us on her sturdy two-year-old legs, walked up the curving driveway to the wonderful new building. Once Lutui, who had come out to meet us, and Farquhar turned back to look at the dingy old hospital.

"There was lots of good work done there," Farquhar said and Lutui replied, "Yes, and we've been happy working there together." But their moment of sentimental farewell was brief; their eyes, like those of everyone else, were on the new building.

Under the portico at the entrance a platform had been built for the Queen. Beside it, all of us who belonged to the official party sat on chairs and benches while the rest of the crowd fanned out over the grass. Nature herself was in a festive mood. She had made a perfect day—bright and sunny and warm with a welcome cool breeze sweeping up from the sea far below. While we waited for the ceremony to commence, we looked sometimes at the fine view of the distant blue stretch of Vava'u harbor and sometimes scanned the crowd for faces of seldom-seen friends from the outer islands.

Beat of drum! Blare of trumpet! And the band playing a triumphant march came up the hill followed by the children. When they came to the hospital driveway, they spread out, lining the road on either side to form a guard of honor for the Queen. At our side the white-dressed girls and women of the Neiafu choir were assembling and little Tu'ifua, spotting Big Tu'ifua among them, forsook us and ran over to her.

At the appointed hour, exactly at ten o'clock, Queen Salote, who seems to be a firm believer in the old saying that punctuality is the politeness of kings, arrived in the town's one taxi. As she got out, the band struck up the first notes of the national anthem and once again the people with their Queen sang tribute to their beloved country.

God and Tonga are mine inheritance is the motto which appears on the Tongan coat of arms. It is graven, too, on the hearts of the people of these islands—on that of the Queen as well as on those of her subjects. In accordance with her wishes, the opening ceremony was predominately a religious one. There was a prayer and there were hymns in which everyone joined and the choir sang several anthems. Then Prince Tu'ipelehake, who is the pre-

sent Minister of Health, rose and gave the key of
the new building to his queen and mother. It was
particularly fitting that he do so; for she has given
the hospital his own first name, Sione Ngu. Smilingly
she thanked him, letting her eyes linger for a minute
on her treasured younger son. Then, stepping forward,
she spoke to her people.

"Let us always remember," she said, "that this
fine building which we open today is not only a
hospital. It is also a church and a school."

And she explained that whoever entered there
should remember to give thanks to God for the gift
of life and to ask His blessing on the men and women
who worked there. She spoke, too, of her hope that
the Sione Ngu hospital would be not only a place
where the sick were healed, but also one to which all
the people could come to learn how to improve their
daily living standards.

As she spoke her simple, heartfelt words, I looked
about me at the shining faces of her people. Then
I turned and watched her and as I did so the beginning of a Tongan hymn sang itself into my mind.
"Ko Tonga monu'ia"—"lucky Tonga"—and I
thought, For reasons without count, Tonga is a
lucky little country and not the least of them is the
happy fact that Salote Tupou, with her great understanding and her great love for her people, is their
queen.

When she had finished speaking, there was nothing
left but to open the door and walk in, and soon
she had done that. After her went Tu'ipelehake and
Melenaite with their son 'Uluvalu and Taufa, the

son of Tungi. Then came the Governor Ahome'e and his wife and their daughters and all the most important nobles, and with them all of us of the medical department. The Queen went into the office where she sat at the big new desk and wrote her name on the first page of the visitors' book. Then, ward by ward, she examined the new hospital. It was no cursory trip she made; for every nook and corner was of interest to her and some proud member of the medical department stepped forward to answer every question she asked. By the time her inspection was over, the morning was over, too, and it was time for us all to go down to the mala'e, the big green field in the center of town where the villagers of Vava'u, working all together, had prepared a tremendous feast to mark the occasion.

All around the edges of the vast field, eating shelters had been erected. As members of the official party, Farquhar and I ate in the eating house which had been especially prepared for the Queen. It was a pleasant, breezy place spread with fine mats and decorated with the miniature fronds of the little starch palm.

The Queen, who, according to custom, eats alone, had her own individual pola, filled with feast foods, placed in the center of the house and there she sat, banked by sky-blue satin pillows which some thoughtful subject had provided for her royal comfort. The rest of us sat on mats ranged against the walls with our polas before us.

Great occasions become more memorable when they are shared with those we love. So it was that I felt a sense of well-being at seeing between Farquhar and myself our fair-haired little daughter, who was soon exploring all the good things that were placed before us. Indeed, our "family" was complete; for our Big Tu'ifua was there, too. Here in Tonga there is no "servant class." Everyone, at some time or other in his life, is served and everyone at some time serves. To be chosen to serve the Queen is the greatest honor of all, and Farquhar and I were proud that it fell that day to Tu'ifua. Little Tu'ifua was proud, too; for she has already a very real sense of the Queen's importance—not, it must be confessed, because she is the ruler of all these Tongan islands, but because, among other distinctions, she has that of being "Grandma" to Pilolevu, Tungi's young daughter, whom little Tu'ifua considers as her "special" playmate.

Serving us was Losimani, the beautiful chiefly girl from the village of Makave, whom I knew during my year at the college as a mischievous fifth-former.

The meal was eaten, as Tongan meals are, in silence, but when it was over and the polas had been cleared away, the Queen came and talked to us, speaking of her pleasure in the day. There was little time for conversation, however, for soon the dances, the traditional laka-lakas which had been prepared by all the different villages of this group, commenced and we took our places to watch them.

To a white man, Tongan dances are an aesthetic delight. To see twenty or more women executing the graceful motions of the laka-laka as if they were one woman and, opposite them, twenty or more men performing as one man their more vigorous staccato motions in a sort of counterpoint of movement, is an unforgettable experience. Added to it is the haunting Polynesian music which is sometimes sung by the dancers themselves and sometimes by a choir standing behind them. To a Tongan, there is the further interest of the words of the song—an interest from which all of us papalangis are cut off. Though we may have mastered enough of the language to see us through the ordinary affairs of daily life, laka-laka words are beyond us. They are written in poetry and Tongan poetry is, I think, the most allusive, allegorical, symbolical poetry in the world.

Words or no words, there was poetry enough for us all in the dances we saw that day—in the beautiful costumes and the fragrant oils which scented the air everywhere and in the rhythms which filled our minds until we were hypnotized by them and moved in spite of ourselves in unison with the dancers.

Hour after hour we sat on, ourselves a part of the dances we watched, until, at last, the afternoon grew heavy with sunset. Then the Queen called to her side her handsome young nephew, Vaea, who acts as her aide, and told him that, if there were yet more dances to come, they must be done at Veitatalo because the day had been long and there were many people who had far to travel before they reached their homes.

Vaea communicated the royal wishes. The dances stopped, the band played, and the Queen's car came and took her off to Veitatalo. When she had gone, the rest of us went off to our homes, too.

And the next day, Lutui said to Farquhar, "Well, it's over. Now we can get back to the practice of medicine."

And they went into the new hospital, the mighty concrete fortress from which they wage their war against bush doctors and ignorance.

22 Steamer Day

An hour ago, the *Tofua* left the wharf at Neiafu and sailed down the harbor bound for Niue island, its next port of call. As it turned around 'Utulei cape, the passengers lining its decks could see the Stars and Stripes flying—as it always does on Steamer Days—from our verandah. A welcome to whatever Americans may be wandering in this part of the world, it did not fly in vain today; for there was a couple from California on board. I found them—as fellow countrymen have a way of finding one another—when Farquhar and I went over to Neiafu this morning, and we brought them across to 'Utulei for lunch. We had with us also a doctor who, like Farquhar, had been educated at the University of Glasgow's Medical School; so, while I learned of the changes that had taken place in downtown San Francisco since last I saw it, Farquhar and his Scotsman reminisced about their old professors. To both of us it was good to hear again the voices of our old homes and good, too, to have the knowledge that the three people to whom we waved good-by just a while ago had come to Vava'u this morning as strangers to us and left this afternoon as friends.

Now the sky is streaked with sunset, the *Tofua* is far out on the open sea, and Farquhar and I are sitting on the verandah. Down on the beach, Lotu pulls up the boat for the night, talking as he does so to the two Tu'ifuas—the big one, our friend, who sits on an upturned canoe and the little one, our daughter, who runs shouting and laughing between her and the sea. Their voices drift up to us and now and then we catch, also, scraps of conversation from homeward-bound people passing in their boats. Closer, from the kitchen at the back of the house, comes the rattle of dishes and silver and the endless murmur of light-hearted chatter from Lavinia and Tama'a who are preparing dinner.

With these evening sounds as background, Farquhar and I watch the sunset and review the day. Here in these "Down Under" islands where Christmas comes in the hottest part of summer and Thanksgiving and Halloween never come at all, holidays have little meaning. Even the Fourth of July which, by virtue of being the birthday of Crown Prince Tungi, is a day of celebration in Tonga also, never conveys the same feeling as the picnic and firecracker day of my childhood. But there is one holiday which makes up for the loss of all the others—or, perhaps I should say, twelve holidays, since, barring waterside strikes in Auckland and similar disasters, Steamer Day comes once a month. For all of us here, whatever the country of our origin, and for the islanders too, it is the great festive day. Like all the best holidays everywhere, Steamer Day has offerings for both our stomachs and our spirits. Then we get our monthly supply of butter and meat and the only taste of fresh apples and pears we ever have. Steamer night our table, which for all the thin week before the boat arrived has been meagerly furnished with the monotonous contents of cans, groans beneath a freshly roasted joint and all sorts of delicacies from the grocers in New Zealand and Australia.

The fare for our minds and spirits is even more exciting than that for our stomachs. There is contact with all the world and interesting new people to meet. Tomorrow, when the package mail is opened, there will be new surprises, but today we have the books and magazines and the letters. There is a new French novel by a man whose Rabelaisian humor delights us, and a little package of Pelicans from my New Zealand friend, Laurene, who always manages to choose the very books for which I've been longing, and a volume or two from Heffer's in Cambridge in whose wonderful catalogues we do all our book browsing. And the magazines and papers—what a pile of them there is! . . . Gray-covered medical journals, *France Illustration* and *Scottish Field, Time* and the *New Yorker* and *Punch,* a New Zealand agricultural paper and the Polynesian *Journal, Discovery* and a stray San Francisco *Chronicle.*

"Did you get a good mail?" Farquhar asks. I pat the fat stack of opened letters which lies on my lap and say happily, "Very good." And I tell him about it all:

About Mother's long letter telling me of her new patio furniture and describing, as she always does, the flowers in the living room so that, as I read, I can almost smell the faint fresh fragrance of the azaleas on the drum table and the spicy tang of the red roses she keeps beside my picture.

And about the note from Father in his concise, characteristic printing which told me he had caught ten trout on the first day of the season.

And the one from Farquhar's brother sending his love and "something" for little Tu'ifua's bank account.

I show him the pictures that Mary and Alec, who are missionaries, sent of their new post in the back country of Columbia and read bits that my University friend Marian, who still lives in Seattle close to our old campus, wrote of books and writers and plans and ideas and all the things we used to discuss in the endless bull sessions of our junior year.

I tell him of Fran, whom I knew in WAC days, who writes of the bustle of New York and Sue who, with a Rockefeller grant to study folk customs around the world, dashed off a note from Singapore.

When I have finished, Farquhar shares his mail with me, telling me of the family and friends in distant places. From America and Scotland comes the family mail and from the four corners of the earth letters from friends and acquaintances with whom, on Steamer Day, we share for a little while their daily lives and live again in memory the old days we knew together.

On our first few Steamer Days, when the visitors had gone and the mail had been opened and read and reread, Farquhar used to say, "Perhaps this makes you homesick," and when the *Tofua* sailed past he would inquire apprehensively, "Do you wish you were on her?" Nowadays he never asks. There is no need; for, although he is bound to Scotland and I to America in the indissoluble way that a child is forever bound to its parents, we both belong now in our little island world of Tonga.

Steamer Day is a wonderful day, bringing visitors and books and magazines and news of those we love, but when it is over and the *Tofua* is safely on her northward way, we breathe a little sigh of relief and turn back to the busy routine of daily life.

And now, while we have been talking, the sky has grown dark and a cool breeze has risen from the sea. I call to the Tu'ifuas. They come up from the beach and cross the shadowy garden. "It's getting late," Farquhar says, and he stoops and takes our tiny daughter in his arms. For a minute, we pause there on the verandah, watching through the glass door the soft yellow light of the lamp lighting up our familiar room. Then we go in—Farquhar and little Tu'ifua and Big Tu'ifua and I—and I shut the door and close out the night behind us. We are at home.

(2)